SPSS

VERSION
18.0 for Windows

Analysis **without Anguish**

Sheridan J Coakes • Clara Ong

WILEY

John Wiley & Sons Australia, Ltd

First published 2011 by
John Wiley & Sons Australia, Ltd
42 McDougall Street, Milton, Qld 4064

Typeset in 11/13 pt Times LT

National Library of Australia
Cataloguing-in-publication data

Author:	Coakes, Sheridan J.
Title:	SPSS: analysis without anguish: version 18 for Windows / Sheridan Coakes, Clara Ong.
Edition:	Version 18.0
ISBN:	978 1 74246 727 6 (pbk.)
Notes:	Includes index.
Subjects:	SPSS for Windows — Handbooks, manuals, etc. Social sciences — Statistical methods — Computer programs.
Other Authors/Contributors:	Ong, Clara.
Dewey Number:	300.285555

Typeset in India by diacriTech

Printed in China by
Printplus Limited

10 9 8 7 6 5 4 3

Contents

Preface

IBM SPSS, formerly known as SPSS, is a sophisticated piece of software used by social scientists and related professionals for statistical analysis. This workbook is based on version 18 of the software, which is compatible with the Windows environment.

IBM SPSS version 18 is segmented into modules, each with enhanced data management and reporting capabilities. The base module, IBM SPSS Base, has traditionally been the basis of many deployments and could be expanded by purchasing a number of add-on modules. However, an important change with the release of version 18 is that each add-on module can now be installed and run separately, or used in conjunction with other modules with or without the Base. The Base module is no longer a requirement. This change offers greater flexibility and versatility in the use of the software.

The Student version (IBM SPSS GradPack 18) includes the full version of the Base as well as two add-on modules (IBM SPSS Regression and IBM SPSS Advanced Statistics). For Windows users, a separate module for structural equation modelling (SEM) is also included. Students are therefore afforded access to a wide range of basic and advanced statistics and analytical techniques that are not available in most other student software packages. Using the Gradpack version, students can now perform a range of analyses from the basic crosstabs and frequency analyses, to the more advanced procedures that include regression and structural equation modelling, as well as general linear models.

While the Base facilitates most of the analyses outlined in this book, you will require the SPSS Advanced Statistics and IBM SPSS Categories modules to undertake the analyses specified below:

- Two-way repeated measures analysis of variance ANOVA — chapter 11
- Mixed/split plot design — chapter 13
- Multiple analysis of variance or MANOVA — chapter 18
- Multidimensional scaling — chapter 21.

The IBM SPSS website (www.spss.com/statistics) caters for a range of frequently asked questions about installation and running of the software, as well as the different types of modules available for purchase. In addition, the IBM SPSS website also offers a number of data files for users to download for practice using the software package.

What is new in IBM SPSS version 18 for Windows?

IBM SPSS version 18 offers a number of new features and some changes in the functionality of features from earlier versions. The user interface for version 18 is now more user-intuitive, enabling more seamless navigation across the different analytical tools. Building on SPSS version 17.0, the current version also offers highly interactive chart editing features as well as an easy-to-use syntax editor for both beginners and experienced users.

IBM SPSS version 18 offers a suite of new modules which improves the efficiency and accessibility of some analytical techniques. For instance, the Automated Data Preparation (ADP) module helps you detect errors or anomalies in your data, as well as correct and impute missing values in one easy step. Another add-on, IBM SPSS Custom Tables, has also been enhanced in this current version to allow computation of new categories in a table after it has been created, eliminating the need to export outputs into a separate spreadsheet program (such as Excel) for further analyses. Significance test results are also now presented in the main outputs table as part of the Custom Tables add-on enhancement, allowing users to seamlessly import the main table into a separate Word document or other reporting platforms for presentation purposes.

Also new to IBM SPSS version 18, in particular the Base module, is the new non-parametric statistics tests. For instance, the current version now offers capabilities to help you choose the most appropriate nonparametric test based on your data characteristics. The new features also allow you to make multiple comparisons about your data and to choose the most accurate and robust outcomes. How these new features work is outlined in detail in chapter 19.

The IBM SPSS website (www.spss.com/statistics) provides further information on what is new in the latest release in comparison to earlier versions. Also, support and online tutorials on the use of the latest features are available through the program's Help menu.

This edition
••

This edition of *SPSS: Analysis without Anguish* continues the trend of previous editions in providing a practical text intended as an introduction to SPSS and a guide for users who wish to conduct analytical procedures. We've also tried to improve the text from the feedback we have obtained from our readers.

Section 1 introduces the user to many of the features and techniques available within the IBM SPSS package. In this section, the user will learn how to prepare data files, screen and transform data, and conduct various statistical analyses ranging from descriptive statistics, correlation to inferential and multivariate statistics, reliability and factor analysis.

Building on knowledge obtained in section 1, section 2 enables the user to examine 'real-life' data obtained from actual research projects. This provides students with a valuable opportunity to conduct a range of analyses on data which has been obtained through applied research practice. 'Chapter 23: Introduction and research questions' contains links to research questions, and adapted datasets that can be used with the Student version on the John Wiley website accompanying this title. The homework exercises and research scenarios in 'Chapter 24: Practising analytical techniques' have varying degrees of complexity to facilitate:

• students to undertake analysis at home

• lecturers to set take-home assignments based on the homework exercises.

The opportunity to examine data sets in this way, we believe more closely reflects actual research practice. A range of research questions are posed and different techniques employed. Additionally, we have included actual questionnaire items and data sets as part of the homework exercises, enabling users to visualise and experience hands-on analysis of applied social science research methodology.

In line with previous editions, practice examples are included in section 3 to provide the user with some extra practice!

Users will be able to obtain a quick and easy access to all the relevant data files on the Wiley website (www.johnwiley.com.au/highered/spssv18/student-res/index.html).

As requested, we have included reporting at the end of each relevant chapter to illustrate how significant results from each of the particular tests should be presented. We have also introduced, where relevant, a 'handy hints' section at the end of most chapters, highlighting the significant points to remember when applying the particular techniques.

Although the workbook outlines each statistical procedure, this is not a statistical text and a degree of statistical knowledge is assumed. At the beginning of each chapter, general assumption testing for each procedure is discussed and the procedure is approached simply and systematically.

Again, we've tried to keep the text clear and simple. No one text will satisfy all our readers; however, we hope that, as with past editions, the text is a useful and practical guide to statistical analysis.

The concept of the workbook arose from our collective experience of teaching and using research methods in an applied context. It has evolved from a recognised need to make research methodology more accessible and understandable to students who are undertaking research methods courses and to professionals who are taking part in social research within and across a range of disciplinary settings.

We still receive very positive feedback from you, the users of the book, who tell us that we have helped alleviate some of the 'anguish' associated with the analysis of research data. We trust that this edition continues to help in this regard.

Having worked through the book, you will be well on your way to effective research from coding, entering and exploring data, and undertaking appropriate analysis to creating meaningful data output.

We wish you well in your research endeavours. A very big thank-you goes out to you, our readers, for your continued support.

Dr Sheridan Coakes, Director,
Coakes Consulting — Social Impact and Community Consultants
PO Box 1027, Kalamunda WA 6926

Dr Clara Ong, Director,
S3 Global — Software Design and Usability Consultants, Perth WA 6009

September 2010

SECTION 1

How to use **SPSS**

Introduction to SPSS

This chapter provides an introduction to using SPSS version 18.0 (now also known as IBM® SPSS® Statistics 18) for Windows. It discusses aspects of the SPSS environment, describes the menu options and toolbars, and provides instructions on how to begin and end an SPSS session.

Getting started

If this is one of your first experiences with the SPSS package, do not be put off. Before long, you will be able to manoeuvre around the package with ease and carry out all kinds of analytical procedures. Now, it's time to familiarise ourselves with the SPSS program and its attributes.

When SPSS is initially installed, the SPSS program group is created in the **Programs** menu. To start an SPSS session, click on the PASW Statistics 18 icon.

The SPSS environment

SPSS for Windows provides a powerful statistical analysis and data management system in a graphical environment, using descriptive menus and simple dialogue boxes to do most of the work for you. Most tasks can be accomplished simply by pointing and clicking the mouse.

In addition to the simple point-and-click interface for statistical analysis, SPSS has eight different types of windows:

- Data Editor
- Viewer
- Draft Viewer
- Pivot Table Editor
- Chart Editor and Graphboard Editor
- Text Output Editor
- Syntax Editor
- Script Editor.

Data Editor

The Data Editor is a versatile spreadsheet-like system for defining, entering, editing and displaying data. This window opens when you start an SPSS session and displays the contents of a data file. In this window, you can create new data files or modify existing ones. As outlined, the data editor is like a spreadsheet in which cases are represented in rows and variables are represented in columns.

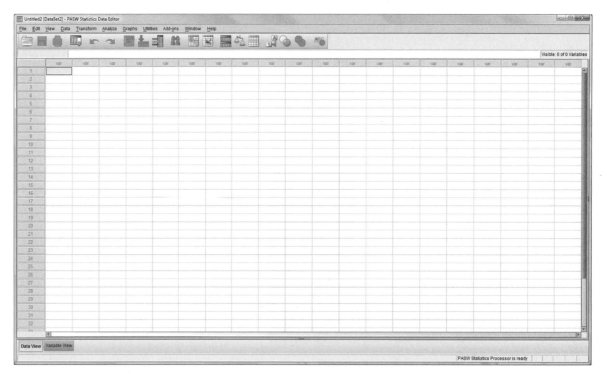

Viewer and Draft Viewer

••

The Viewer makes it easy to browse your results, selectively show and hide output, change the display, order results and move presentation-quality tables and charts between SPSS and other applications. This window opens automatically the first time you run a procedure that generates some output. The window displays all statistical results, tables and charts, and allows you to edit the output and save it in an output file for later use. This window also allows you to access the Pivot Table Editor, Text Output Editor and Chart Editor, and to move between SPSS and other applications, for example Word.

The window is divided into two panes. The left pane, referred to as the outline pane, contains an outline view of the output contents, and can be used to navigate through your output and control the output display — very handy if you have a lot of output. The right pane of the window is the contents pane, which contains statistical tables, charts and text output. If you select an item in the outline pane, the corresponding item in the contents pane is highlighted. Moving an item in the outline pane moves the corresponding item in the contents pane. The width of the outline pane can also be changed by clicking on the right-hand border and dragging it to the desired width.

You can also display output as simple text (instead of in interactive pivot tables) in the Draft Viewer.

Pivot Table Editor

Output displayed in pivot tables can be modified in different ways. Using this editor, it is possible to edit text, rearrange rows, columns and layers, add colour, create multi-dimensional tables and selectively hide and display results. You move into the Pivot Table Editor from the Viewer by selecting the table you want to edit, and clicking the right mouse button to select Edit Content In Viewer. You may also predefine the number of rows you would like your table to display by selecting the Set Rows to Display feature.

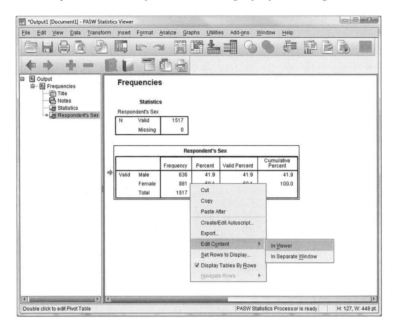

Double-click at any point inside the table you want to edit, and then click the right mouse button to select Pivoting Trays and Toolbar. This will reveal the Pivot Table, formatting toolbar and pivot trays, and allow editing of tables to begin.

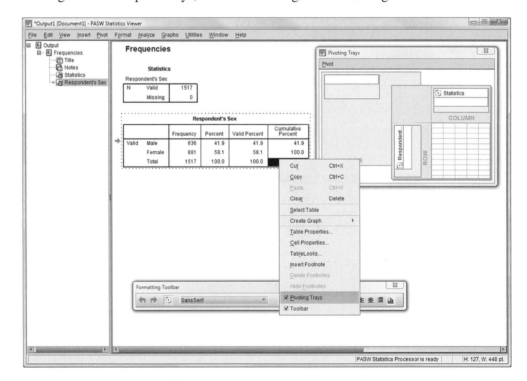

Chart and Graphboard Editors

High-resolution, full-colour pie charts, bar charts, histograms, scatterplots, 3-D graphics and more are included as standard features in SPSS. These can be edited in either the Chart Editor or the Graphboard Editor, allowing changes in colour, font, axes, rotations and chart types.

If you have used the Chart Builder to create your chart, double-clicking on the chart will open the Chart Editor from the Viewer and allow the editing of charts to begin.

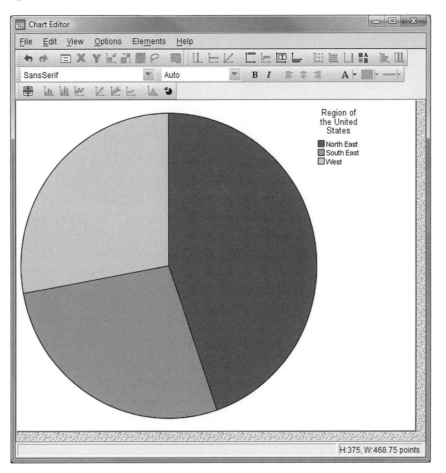

If you have used the Graphboard Template Chooser to create your chart, double-clicking on the chart will open the Graphboard Editor from the Viewer. Like the Chart Editor, the Graphboard Editor allows you to perform a range of different edits to your charts, including changing the size of the chart's elements as well as sorting and excluding categories on the categorical axis.

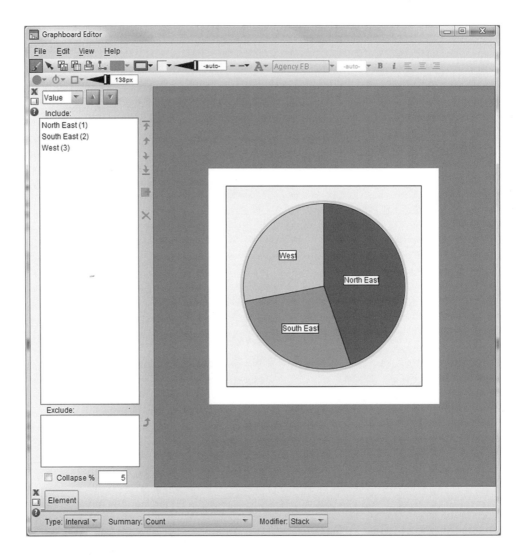

Text Output Editor

Text in the Viewer that is not displayed in pivot tables or charts can also be modified using the Text Output Editor. Possible modifications include changes to font characteristics such as colour, type, style and size.

Syntax Editor

Although most tasks can be accomplished by simply pointing and clicking, SPSS also provides a powerful command language, which allows you to save and automate many common tasks. The command language also provides some functionality not found in the menus and dialogue boxes.

As you undertake particular procedures in SPSS, you can paste your dialogue box choices into a syntax window. This window contains the command syntax that reflects the choices you have made in selecting menu options. These commands can then be edited to include special features not available through the pull-down menus and dialogue boxes, and they can be saved in a file for further use.

The Syntax Editor is accessible for both beginners and more experienced statistical programmers. The Syntax Editor colour codes and highlights commands, subcommands and keywords. In addition, the editor undertakes auto-completion of syntax strings, and has a gutter adjacent to the editor pane that displays information such as line numbers and breakpoint positions. There is also an error pane beneath the editor pane that displays further information on runtime errors.

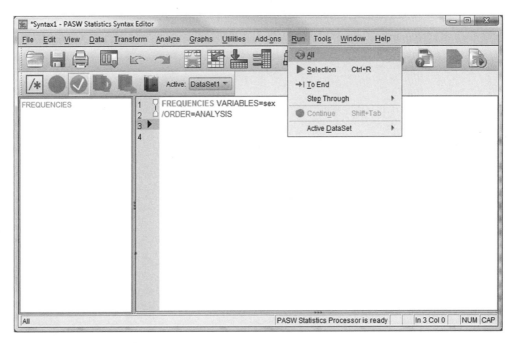

On the toolbar at the top of the syntax window, click on the **Run** menu and select **All**. This will allow you to process the commands in the Syntax Editor. If you have multiple commands in the Syntax Editor and would only like to run specific commands, simply highlight the specific commands which you would like to process, then click on the ▶ tool to run.

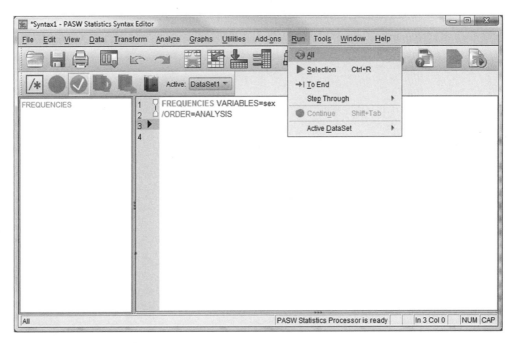

Script Editor

••

Scripting and object linking and embedding (OLE) automation allow you to customise and automate many tasks in SPSS. With the Script Editor, you are able to create and modify basic scripts within the program.

At the top of each window you will have noticed a menu and an icon bar (referred to as the toolbar). We will now look at these particular features, which provide quick and easy access to the special features available in each of the SPSS windows.

Menus

SPSS is menu driven and has a variety of pull-down menus available for the user. The main menu bar in the Data Editor contains ten menus:

- File
- Edit
- View
- Data
- Transform
- Analyze
- Graphs
- Utilities
- Window
- Help.

The **Analyze** and **Graphs** menus are available in all windows, making it much easier to generate new output without having to switch between windows.

File

The **File** menu allows you to create new files, open existing files, read in files from other software programs, save files and print.

![Screenshot of SPSS Data Editor showing the File menu open with options including New, Open, Open Database, Read Text Data, Close, Save, Save As, Save All Data, Export to Database, Mark File Read Only, Rename Dataset, Display Data File Information, Cache Data, Stop Processor, Switch Server, Print Preview, Print, Recently Used Data, Recently Used Files, Exit. Data columns shown: happy, life, sibs, childs, age, educ, paeduc, maeduc.]

Edit

The **Edit** menu allows you to modify or copy text from the output or syntax windows, search for and replace text or data, and set personal preference options. You may also use the Edit menu to identify data imputations for missing values (applicable only to the IBM SPSS Missing Values add-on module).

View

The **View** menu allows you to make the status bar and toolbar active, and to change particular characteristics of the window (e.g. by removing grid lines, displaying value labels and changing font style and size). In addition, the View menu enables you to mark imputed data used to replace missing values in your data set (applicable only to the IBM SPSS Missing Values add-on module).

Data

The **Data** menu allows you to define variables and create variable templates. In addition, more global changes to SPSS data files are available, such as merging files, inserting, sorting and transposing variables and cases, and selecting and weighting cases. If you have the IBM SPSS Data Preparation add-on module, the Data menu will also allow you to perform data checks and validation by identifying unusual cases and anomalies within your data sets.

Transform

The **Transform** menu allows you to change certain variables in the data file using commands such as **Recode** and **Rank Cases**, as well as create new variables using the **Compute** command.

SPSS: Analysis without Anguish

Analyze

••

The **Analyze** menu allows you to select the analysis you require. A variety of statistical procedures are available, ranging from summarising data through to more complex designs.

The **Codebook** procedure is a handy procedure located within the **Analyze** menu. It allows users to automatically create a codebook describing their dataset. This codebook contains dictionary information such as variable names and labels, missing values and frequencies, thereby eliminating the need for creating one manually from at the start of each data set analysis.

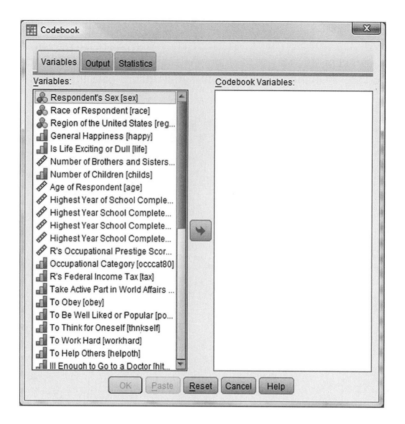

sex

		Value	Count	Percent
Standard Attributes	Position	1		
	Label	Respondent's Sex		
	Type	Numeric		
	Format	F1		
	Measurement	Nominal		
	Role	Input		
Valid Values	1	Male	636	41.9%
	2	Female	881	58.1%

Graphs

The **Graphs** menu allows you to create bar, line, area and pie charts, as well as histograms and scatterplots.

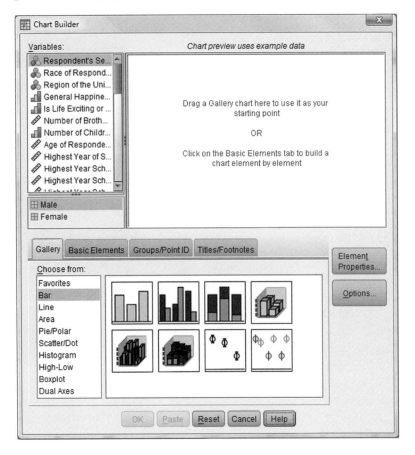

The **Chart Builder** allows you to build your own charts from a predefined gallery of charts or from a chart's individual elements such as its scales and axes. You build a chart by dragging and dropping the gallery charts or basic elements onto the canvas, which provides a rough preview of what the chart would look like.

Similar to SPSS version 17.0, the **Graphboard Template Chooser** allows you to visualise the type of graph that would best represent your data. The template chooser consists of two main methods for creating a visualisation from a template. The Basic method (located within the Basic tab) requires you to first select the data that you are analysing, followed by the graph which you think is appropriate for the data. The Detailed method (located within the Detailed tab) requires you to first select a graph type prior to specifying the data. You may also predefine chart titles and footnotes within the template chooser, as well as specify other options such as output labels and styling.

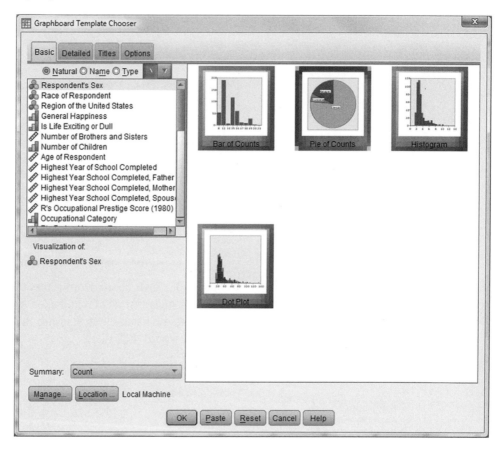

Utilities

The **Utilities** menu allows you to display file and variable information. In addition, it allows you to define and use different variable sets, as well as create and manage custom dialogues for generating command syntax.

Window

The **Window** menu allows you to arrange, select and control the attributes of the various windows. Using this menu, you can move efficiently among data, syntax, output and chart windows.

Help

The **Help** menu allows you to access information on how to use the many features of SPSS. The SPSS tutorial can be accessed through the **Help** menu.

Toolbar

The toolbar, located just below the menu bar, provides quick, easy access to many frequently used features. The toolbar contains tools that are available when a particular type of window is active. Each window has its own toolbar. When you put the mouse cursor on a tool in an active window, a brief description of that tool is displayed.

Tools in the Data Editor include:

- **File Open** allows particular data files to be opened for analysis.
- **File Save** saves the file in the active window.
- **File Print** prints the file in the active window.
- **Dialogue Recall** displays a list of recently opened dialogue boxes, any of which can be selected by clicking on their name.
- **Go to Case** allows the typing in of the number of the case you want to go to and it will be found in the data file.
- **Go to Variable** allows the typing in of the variable name you want to go to and it will be found in the data file.
- **Variables** provides data definition information for all variables in the working data file.
- **Find** allows data to be found easily within the data editor.
- **Insert Cases** inserts a case above the case containing the active cell.

- **Insert Variable** inserts a variable to the left of the variable containing the active cell.
- **Split File** splits the data file into separate groups for analysis based on the values of one or more grouping variables.
- **Weight Cases** gives cases different weights for statistical analysis.
- **Select Cases** provides several methods for selecting a subgroup of cases based on criteria that include variables and complex expressions.
- **Value Labels** allows toggling between actual values and value labels in the Data Editor.
- **Use Sets** allows the selection of sets of variables to be displayed in the dialogue boxes.
- **Spell-check** allows a spelling check for text-string variables.

Some of the tools in the Viewer include:

- **Print Preview** allows what will be printed to be viewed.
- **Export Output** saves pivot tables and text output in HTML, text, Word/RTF and Excel format, and it saves charts in a variety of common formats used by other applications.
- **Go to Data** moves directly into the data file and makes the Data Editor window active.
- **Insert Heading**, **Title**, **Text** allows headings, titles and text to be added into your output.
- **Select Last Output** allows you to select the previous output within the Viewer.
- **Show/Hide** allows output to be shown or hidden.

The Chart Editor has a range of tools that can be used to make your charts more interpretable and attractive, including:

- **Show Properties Window** shows the properties of the chart.
- **Insert a Text Box** allows the insertion of a text box.
- **Show/Hide Legend** allows the legend on a chart to be shown or hidden.
- **Show Data Labels** allows the data labels to be shown on the chart.

In the Syntax Editor Window, the tools are similar to those in the Data Editor, with a few additions:

- The ▶ tool allows you to process the commands in the Syntax Editor.
- **Syntax Help** helps you with the syntax for the analysis you are doing.

Dialogue boxes for statistical procedures

When you choose a statistical procedure, a dialogue box appears on the screen. Each main dialogue box has four basic components: the source variable list, the target variable list, command pushbuttons and the option to choose subdialogue boxes.

Source variable list

••

The source variable list is a list of all the variables in the data file.

 To select a single variable

Highlight the variable and click on the ⊡ button next to the selected variable list box.

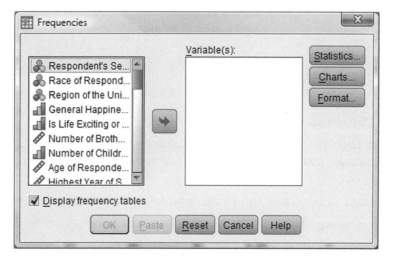

To select multiple variables that are grouped together in the variable list

Click on the first variable you wish to select, then hold the Shift key and click on the last variable in the group. Then click on the ⊡ button.

► To select multiple variables that are *not* grouped together

Click on the first variable, then hold the Ctrl key and click on the next variable, and so on. Then click on the ⮊ button.

Selected variable list

• •

The selected variable list is a list or lists of variables you have chosen for certain analyses. For certain statistical procedures, both dependent and independent variable lists are created.

If you wish to remove variables from this list, highlight the variable and click on the ⮌ button, which you will notice is now reversed. This process is called deselection of variables.

Command pushbuttons

• •

The five standard command pushbuttons in most dialogue boxes are:

• **OK**   Runs the procedure.

• **Paste**   Pastes the syntax associated with a procedure into the Syntax Editor window. This command syntax can then be modified if necessary or new syntax can be added.

• **Reset**   Deselects the variables in the selected variable list or lists and resets all specifications in the dialogue and subdialogue boxes.

- **Cancel** Cancels any changes in the dialogue box settings since it was last opened, then closes it.

- **Help** Allows access to a Help window relevant to the current procedure.

Accessing subdialogue boxes

When selecting a statistical procedure, you can make additional specifications that are available in the subdialogue boxes. These are accessed by selecting the buttons at the bottom or on the side of the main dialogue box. These buttons may include **Statistics...**, **Charts...**, **Format...**, **Options...**, **Save...**, **Plots...** and **Cells...**

The three command pushbuttons within subdialogue boxes are:

- **Continue** Saves any changes to the settings and returns to the main dialogue box.

- **Cancel** Ignores any changes, restores the previous settings and returns to the main dialogue box.

- **Help** Allows access to a Help window relevant to the current procedure.

<table>
<tr><td colspan="2">⊞ Frequencies: Statistics   ✕</td></tr>
</table>

Percentile Values
- ☐ Quartiles
- ☐ Cut points for: 10   equal groups
- ☐ Percentile(s):
  - Add
  - Change
  - Remove

Central Tendency
- ☐ Mean
- ☐ Median
- ☐ Mode
- ☐ Sum

☐ Values are group midpoints

Dispersion
- ☐ Std. deviation ☐ Minimum
- ☐ Variance ☐ Maximum
- ☐ Range ☐ S.E. mean

Distribution
- ☐ Skewness
- ☐ Kurtosis

[Continue] [Cancel] [Help]

Check boxes, radio buttons and drop-down lists

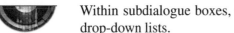

Within subdialogue boxes, choices can be made using check boxes, radio buttons and drop-down lists.

Check boxes

Check boxes (☐) allow you to select certain options within subdialogue boxes. When you click on the box, a ✓ is displayed in the check box ☑. To deselect this option, click the box again. Multiple check boxes can be selected if required.

Radio buttons

Radio buttons (○) allow you to make single selections within subdialogue boxes. When you click on the radio button, a solid circle appears in the centre of the button ⦿.

Drop-down lists

Drop-down menus or lists allow you to make single selections from a list of alternatives.

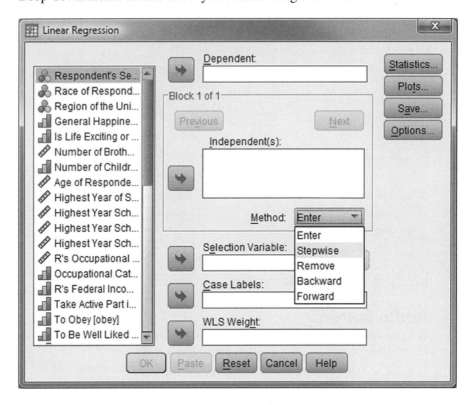

Saving files and ending a session

To save files in SPSS, the **Save As...** command is selected from the **File** menu. If you are working in the Data Editor window, then the file extension .sav will be displayed in the **Save as type:** box and you will be prompted to type in a file name in the **File name:** box. If you are in the Viewer window, then the extension .spo will be displayed. If you are in the Syntax Editor window, then the extension .sps will appear.

To end a session, select the **File** menu and the Exit option. If you exit a session without first saving your files, then SPSS will prompt you to save the contents of each window.

1991 General Social Survey.sav [DataSet1] – PASW Statistics Data Editor

File   Edit   View   Data   Transform   Analyze   Graphs   Utilities   Add-ons   Window   Help

New
Open
Open Database
Read Text Data...
Close   Ctrl+F4
Save   Ctrl+S
Save As...
Save All Data
Export to Database...
Mark File Read Only
Rename Dataset...
Display Data File Information
Cache Data...
Stop Processor   Ctrl+Period
Switch Server...
Print Preview
Print...   Ctrl+P
Recently Used Data
Recently Used Files
Exit

Visible: 43 of 43 Variables

n	happy	life	sibs	childs	age	educ	paeduc	maeduc	speduc	prestg80	occcat80	tax	usintl	obey	popular	thnkself
1.00	1	1	1	2	61	12	97	12	97	22	3.00	1	1	0	0	0
1.00	2	1	2	1	32	20	20	18	20	75	1.00	1	0	5	4	1
1.00	1	0	2	1	35	20	16	14	17	59	1.00	0	1	5	4	1
1.00	9	2	2	0	26	20	20	20	97	48	1.00	1	0	4	5	1
1.00	2	1	4	0	25	12	98	98	97	42	3.00	1	1	0	0	0
1.00	2	0	7	5	59	10	8	6	97	0		0	2	5	2	4
1.00	1	1	7	3	46	10	8	98	97	0		8	0	5	2	1
1.00	2	0	7	4	99	16	5	6	97	60	2.00	0	8	5	3	4
1.00	2	2	7	3	57	10	6	5	97	0		8	0	4	5	1
1.00	2	1	1	2	64	14	8	12	20	38	6.00	1	1	0	0	0
1.00	2	1	6	0	72	9	12	98	97	36	6.00	1	1	0	0	0
1.00	1	0	2	5	67	12	8	8	13	28	6.00	0	1	4	5	2
1.00	2	0	1	0	33	15	11	12	14	65	1.00	0	1	5	4	2
1.00	2	2	2	1	23	14	12	12	97	49	2.00	1	2	0	0	0
1.00	2	2	7	1	33	12	12	12	97	50	2.00	1	0	3	5	1
1.00	1	2	6	2	59	12	8	98	12	0		1	1	0	0	0
1.00	2	0	4	1	60	14	6	6	97	32	2.00	0	1	4	5	1
1.00	1	2	6	2	77	9	0	0	8	36	6.00	2	2	0	0	0
1.00	2	0	12	2	52	14	8	12	8	51	2.00	0	1	4	5	1

			n	happy	life	sibs	childs	age	educ	paeduc	maeduc	speduc	prestg80	occcat80	tax	usintl	obey	popular	thnkself
20	1	2	1.00	1	3	5	1	55	7	98	98	16	42	3.00	1	0	1	5	4
21	2	2	1.00	1	2	2	1	37	14	12	12	97	42	3.00	1	1	0	0	0
22	2	3	1.00	2	0	7	0	45	9	8	99	97	0		0	8	1	4	2
23	2	2	1.00	3	2	4	0	34	12	98	98	98	42	3.00	8	0	2	4	1
24	2	2	1.00	3	1	7	3	35	9	98	98	9	0		8	2	0	0	0
25	2	2	1.00	2	2	6	1	35	13	8	98	97	0		2	0	5	4	2
26	1	2	1.00	3	1	7	0	47	12	97	9	97	41	2.00	1	1	0	0	0
27	2	2	1.00	3	0	4	3	24	11	99	99	97	55	1.00	0	2	4	5	1
28	2	2	1.00	2	2	5	0	28	12	12	14	11	42	3.00	1	0	1	5	3
29	1	1	1.00	1	0	1	2	57	19	16	12	12	75	1.00	0	1	5	3	2
30	1	3	1.00	1	1	1	2	44	18	15	12	12	65	1.00	2	0	5	3	2
31	2	1	1.00	2	0	7	1	75	14	98	8	97	66	1.00	0	1	1	5	3
32	2	1	1.00	2	0	0	3	58	16	12	98	97	60	1.00	0	1	4	5	1
33	1	1	1.00	2	2	1	1	49	13	8	8	12	36	5.00	0	1	1	5	2
34	1	1	1.00	1	0	2	0	22	14	12	99	97	49	2.00	0	1	5	4	1
35	2	1	1.00	1	2	0	3	44	17	18	12	20	52	1.00	1	0	5	4	1
36	1	1	1.00	2	0	1	2	48	19	15	99	16	75	1.00	0	1	5	4	1
37	2	1	1.00	3	2	4	2	23	12	12	98	12	41	2.00	1	0	4	5	1
38	1	1	1.00	1	1	1	0	56	15	97	98	97	51	1.00	2	0	4	5	3

Data View   Variable View

Exit   PASW Statistics Processor is ready

Preparation of data files

This chapter describes the process involved to move from data source to data file; that is, the conversion of raw source material to a usable data file. It focuses on defining variables, assigning appropriate numeric codes to alphanumeric data and dealing with missing data. These preparatory steps are desirable before data entry can begin. Other procedures such as applying variable definition attributes to other variables, entering data, inserting and deleting cases and variables, saving data and opening existing data files are also addressed.

Working example

You have developed a questionnaire that asks questions relating to an individual's shopping behaviour. The variables you have measured include: gender, age, desire for 24-hour shopping, choice of shopping area and amount spent on groceries per week. You have assigned a participant identification number to each case.

Defining variables

The process of defining variables has seven optional steps. The primary step is naming your variable and the other steps cover variable type, variable labels, variable values, missing values, column format, measurement level and roles.

Naming a variable

Variable names must comply with certain rules:

- Must begin with a letter. The remaining characters can be a letter, any digit, a full stop or the symbols @, #, _ or $.
- Cannot end with a full stop or underscore.
- Blanks and special characters (e.g. !, ?, ', and *) cannot be used.
- Must be unique; duplication is not allowed.
- The length of the name cannot exceed 64 bytes (typically 64 characters in single-byte languages, e.g. English, German, French and Spanish).
- Reserved keywords cannot be used as variable names (e.g. ALL, AND, BY, EQ, GE, GT, LE, LT, NE, NOT, OR, TO, WITH).
- Names are not case sensitive, that is, they can be written in upper or lower case.
- Long variable names need to wrap to multiple lines in the output, so SPSS attempts to break lines at underscores, periods, and a change from lower to upper case.

In the case of the variable *age*, the variable name can be age because this name complies with all of the rules listed. The variable *choice of shopping area* can be labelled *area*, and the other variables on the questionnaire could be *id*, *gender*, *allday* and *cost*.

Variable type

By default, SPSS assumes that all new variables are numeric with two decimal places.

However, it is possible to select other variable types (such as date, currency, string) and vary the number of decimal places.

▶ Variable width

If you have a string variable type (i.e. your data is entered in text instead of numerical value), you may adjust the number of text characters by changing the width value. By default, SPSS sets the length of string variables to 8 characters.

▶ Decimals

By default, SPSS predetermines two decimal places for all numeric variables. However, it is possible to adjust the decimal places according to your preference.

Variable labels

The variable label is the full description of the variable name, and is an optional means of improving the interpretability of the output. For example, the first variable you will name in the data file is *id*, and the label for this variable is 'participant identification number'. Suggested variable labels for the other variables appear in the following table.

Variable name	Label
gender	optional
age	optional
allday	desire for 24-hour shopping facilities
area	choice of shopping area
cost	amount spent on groceries per week

You will notice that the gender and age variables do not require variable labels because the variable names are self-explanatory.

Variable values

It is possible to use alphanumeric codes for the variables; however, you may also wish to use a numeric code. For example, for gender you could assign a code of 1 for female and 2 for male. This type of variable is categorical because it has discrete categories. The variables *allday* and *area* are also categorical. When variables are measured using interval or ratio scales, coding is not relevant unless categorisation is required.

Value codes and labels for the above variables are illustrated in the following table.

Variable name	Label
id	not applicable
gender	1 = female 2 = male
age	not applicable
allday	1 = would use 24-hour shopping 2 = would not use 24-hour shopping
area	1 = shop in suburb where living 2 = travel to next suburb 3 = travel further to shop
cost	not applicable

Missing values

It is rare to obtain complete data sets for all cases. When dealing with missing data, you may leave the cell blank or assign missing value codes. If you choose the latter, then some rules apply:

• Missing value codes must be of the same data type as the data they represent. For example, for missing numeric data, missing value codes must also be numeric.

• Missing value codes cannot occur as data in the data set.

• By convention, the choice of digit is usually 9.

Column format

It is possible to adjust the width of the Data Editor columns or change the alignment of data in the column (left, centre or right).

Measurement level

You can specify the level of measurement as scale (interval or ratio), ordinal or nominal.

Role

You can specify the role type of your variable. By default, all variables are assigned the Input role. The following table provides a description of the various roles which you can assign to your variables.

Role	Description
Input	The variable will be used as an input (e.g. predictor, independent variable).
Target	The variable will be used as an output or target (e.g. dependet variable).
Both	The variable will be used as both input and output.
None	The variable has no role assignment.

▶ **To define a variable**

1   Working in the **Untitled — Data Editor** window, double-click a variable name at the top of the column in the Data View or click the **Variable View** tab.

2   In the first blank cell of the **Name** column, type the first variable name (i.e. *id*) and press **Enter**.

3   In the first blank cell of the **Label** column, type the label for the variable, i.e. *Identification Number*.

For the variable *id*, there are no value labels or missing values, and the other properties are appropriate, so you can move on to the second variable.

If you return to the Data View, by clicking the **Data View** tab, you will notice that the variable name *id* has appeared in the first column as a heading.

▶ **To repeat this process for the second variable,** *gender*

1   Working in the Variable View, in the second blank cell of the **Name** column, type
        the second variable name (i.e. *gender*) and press **Enter**.

Again, SPSS automatically supplies other properties such as type, width and values.
Because *gender* requires no further explanation, a label will not be typed in. However,
values are assigned.

2   Click on the second cell of the **Values** column and then on the button on the
        right to open the **Value Labels** box. In the **Value:** box, type the first value code
        for the variable (i.e. *1*) then tab. In the **Label:** box, type the label for this value
        (i.e. *female*).

3   Click on **Add**. You will notice that the value and its label have moved into the box
        below.

4   Repeat this process for the second value.

Value Labels
Value Labels
Value: [   ]   Spelling...
Label: [   ]
1.00 = "female"
Add   2.00 = "male"
Change
Remove
OK   Cancel   Help

5   Click on **OK**. You will notice that there is now information in the cell.

▶ **To create a missing value**

1   Click on the second cell of the **Missing** column and then on the button on the
        right to open the **Missing Values** dialogue box.

2   Select the **Discrete missing values** radio button.

3   In the first box, type the missing value code, i.e. *9*.

Missing Values
○ No missing values
◉ Discrete missing values
[9] [   ] [   ]
○ Range plus one optional discrete missing value
Low: [   ]   High: [   ]
Discrete value: [   ]
OK   Cancel   Help

4   Click on **OK**. You will notice that the missing value has been recorded.

The previous process is then repeated for each variable you wish to define in your data file. As highlighted earlier in this chapter, other options such as **Type**, **Column Width** and **Measurement Level** are also available if you are dealing with different types of variable that require special conditions. For the variable *gender*, you may wish to select the nominal scale of measurement.

Applying variable definition attributes to other variables

Once you have nominated variable definition attributes for a variable, you can copy one or more attributes and apply them to one or more variables. Basic copy and paste operations are used to apply variable definition attributes. For example, you may have several variables with a Likert scale response format. That is, you may have several variables that use the same response scale, in which 1 = strongly disagree, 2 = disagree, 3 = neutral, 4 = agree and 5 = strongly agree. Having defined these value labels for one variable, you can copy them to other variables.

To apply variable definition attributes to other variables

1   In the Variable View, select the attribute cell(s) you want to apply to other variables.

2   From the **Edit** menu, click on **Copy**.

3   Select the attribute cell(s) to which you want to apply the attribute(s). You can select multiple target variables.

4   From the **Edit** menu, click on **Paste**.

If you copy attributes to blank rows, then new variables are created with default attributes for all but the selected attributes.

Entering data

▶ To enter the following two cases

id	gender	age	allday	area	cost
1	male	27	1	1	4
2	female	34	2	3	7

1   In the Data View, click on the first cell in the **Untitled — Data Editor** window. You will notice that a heavy border appears around the cell and that it is highlighted, indicating that it is now active.

2   Type in the first value for *id* (i.e. *1*). This value is displayed in the cell editor at the top of the **Data Editor** window and also in the cell itself.

3   Press **Enter** or move to another cell by using the arrow keys or mouse. Data values are not recorded until you press Enter or select another cell. Remember that it is more efficient to code gender numerically.

4   To move around your data file quickly, you can hold down the Control key with an arrow key to take you to the limit of the file in that direction.

Having entered data for the first two cases, your **Data View** window will look like this:

id	gender	age	allday	area	cost	var	var	var	var	var	var	var
1.00	2.00	27.00	1.00	1.00	4.00							
2.00	1.00	34.00	2.00	3.00	7.00							

Inserting and deleting cases and variables

Often you may need to insert or delete extra cases (rows) and variables (columns) in the existing data file. You can achieve this by using the menus as described below or by using the appropriate tools from the toolbar.

 To insert a new case between existing cases

1 Select any cell in the case (row) below the position where you want to insert the new case.

2 Select the **Edit** menu and click on **Insert Cases** or click on the **Insert Cases** tool. A new case (row) will be inserted.

 To insert a new variable between existing variables

1 Select any cell in the variable (column) to the right of the position where you want to insert a new variable.

2 Select the **Edit** menu and click on **Insert Variable** or click on the **Insert Variable** tool. A new variable (column) will be inserted.

 To delete a case (row)

1 Click on the case number on the left side of the row if you wish to delete the entire case or select any cell in the row that you wish to delete.

2 Select the **Edit** menu and click on **Clear**. Alternatively, you can use the Delete button on the keyboard.

To delete a variable (column)

1 Click on the variable name at the top of the column if you wish to delete the entire variable, or select any cell within the column that you wish to remove.

2 Select the **Edit** menu and click on **Clear**. Again, you can use the Delete button if you wish.

Moving variables

You may wish to change the sequence of variables in the **Data View** window. If you want to position the variable between two existing variables, then insert a new variable in the position where you want to move the variable.

To move a variable

1 For the variable you want to move, click the variable name at the top of the column in the Data View or the row number in the Variable View. The entire variable is highlighted.

2 Select the **Edit** menu and click on **Cut**.

3 Click the variable name in the **Data View** or the row number in the **Variable View** where you want to move the variable to. The entire variable is highlighted.

4 Select the **Edit** menu and click on **Paste**.

Saving data files

To save a data file for the first time

1 First ensure that you are in the **Data View** window.

2 Click on the **File Save** tool.

3 You will be asked to give the file a name.

or

1 Select the **File** menu and click on **Save As...** to open the **Save Data As** dialogue box.

2 In the box for **File Name:** type in the file name of your choice. SPSS will append the extension .sav automatically. If you are saving data to a portable hard drive, then remember to change to the appropriate drive.

3 Click on **Save**.

To save an existing data file

1 First ensure that you are in the **Data Editor** window.

2 Click on the **File Save** tool.

or

1 Select the **File** menu and click on **Save Data**. Your changes will be saved to the existing file.

Opening an existing data file

Once a data file has been saved in SPSS, it can be accessed in subsequent sessions. Furthermore, files that have been created in other software packages can be imported into SPSS.

 To open an existing SPSS data file

1   Select the **File** menu.

2   Click on **Open** and **Data...** to open the **Open File** dialogue box.

3   Select the file from the file list.

4   Click on **Open**.

 To read a text data file

1   Select the **File** menu.

2   Click on **Read Text Data** to open the **Open File** dialogue box.

3   Select the file from the file list.

4   Click on **Open**.

Handy hints

• It is more efficient to code gender numerically.

• Remember, basic copy and paste operations can be applied to variable definition attributes.

CHAPTER 3

Data screening and transformation

Data screening and transformation techniques are useful in making sure that data have been correctly entered and that the distributions of variables that are to be used in analysis are normal. If variable distributions deviate dramatically, then this may affect the validity of the results that are produced. If distributions do vary from normal, then non-normal distributions may be transformed before further analysis. Furthermore, if distributions deviate dramatically, nonparametric techniques may also be used because they are less powerful than their parametric counterparts.

Data may also need to be transformed using **Recode** and **Compute** commands. In addition, if data files have missing values, mean substitution may be an alternative.

It is often useful to be able to conduct analyses on subsets of the data and to make conditional transformations of variables. These can be achieved using the **Select If** and **Compute If** commands.

These procedures are demonstrated in the context of the following research example.

Working example

Community residents were surveyed to determine their attitudes towards physical exercise. Participants were also asked their age, number of hours per week spent in physical activity and whether they participated in team sports.

Each individual (of the 99 students who participated) was given an identity number. Attitude towards exercise was measured using a seven-item scale comprising statements to which participants agreed or disagreed, using a five-point Likert response format such that: 1 = strongly agree, 2 = agree, 3 = neither agree nor disagree, 4 = disagree and 5 = strongly disagree.

The data can be found in Work3.sav on the website that accompanies this title and are shown in the following figure. Several items of this scale were negatively worded and therefore required recoding.

	id	att1	att2	att3	att4	att5	att6	att7	hoursex	teampart	age	var	var
1	1	2	4	4	4	4	4	4	5	2	39		
2	2	2	3	4	4	4	4	2	11	2	44		
3	3	2	4	4	4	4	4	4	30	2	32		
4	4	2	2	3	4	4	4	4	40	1	70		
5	5	3	5	4	5	5	5	5	23	2	47		
6	6	3	5	5	5	5	4	5	72	1	72		
7	7	3	5	2	4	4	4	4	27	2	57		
8	8	1	5	4	5	4	3	5	11	2	42		
9	9	1	5	4	5	4	4	4	35	2	52		
10	10	3	5	3	3	5	5	3	7	2	42		
11	11	1	5	3	4	5	3	4	7	1	57		
12	12	2	4	4	5	5	5	4	3	2	58		
13	13	3	3	4	5	5	2	5	2	2	38		
14	14	2	3	5	5	4	3	4	10	2	50		
15	15	3	5	4	4	5	3	3	4	2	27		
16	16	3	4	4	4	4	5	4	7	2	45		
17	17	1	5	5	5	5	5	5	51	1	40		
18	18	1	5	5	5	5	5	5	45	2	45		
19	19	3	3	3	3	4	3	3	6	2	56		
20	20	4	2	2	4	5	4	2	5	2	43		
21	21	2	4	3	5	4	3	3	20	2	49		
22	22	1	5	3	5	5	4	5	30	2	47		
23	23	2	2	2	4	5	2	2	1	2	24		
24	24	5	5	5	5	5	3	5	14	2	30		

You wish to determine whether the distributions of the continuous variables (i.e. age, hours spent doing exercise and attitude to exercise) are normal. This procedure is not necessary for team participation because this is a categorical variable.

Errors in data entry

Errors in data entry are common and, therefore, data files must be carefully screened. For example, while responses to the attitude items are being entered, out-of-range values can be detected easily using the **Frequencies** or **Descriptives** commands and replaced in the data file with the correct value.

> **Data Preparation and Missing Values Modules**
>
> In addition to the IBM SPSS Base, the IBM SPSS Data Preparation and Missing Values add-on modules can assist you in detecting data anomalies or unusual data cases. These add-on modules can also help you correct and impute missing values, optimising the overall accuracy of your analysis and allowing you to make more valid conclusions from your data.

To obtain frequencies

1   Select the **Analyze** menu.

2   Click on **Descriptive Statistics** and then **Frequencies...** to open the **Frequencies** dialogue box.

3   Select *att1* to *att7* and click on the ➡ button to move these variables into the **Variable(s):** box.

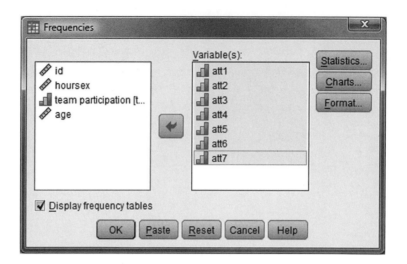

4   Click on **OK**.

You will observe that all cases for *att1* are within the expected range of 1–5. You must ensure the other items are also within the expected range.

att1

		Frequency	Percent	Valid Percent	Cumulative Percent
Valid	strongly agree	22	22.2	22.2	22.2
	agree	31	31.3	31.3	53.5
	neither agree nor disagree	38	38.4	38.4	91.9
	disagree	3	3.0	3.0	94.9
	strongly disagree	5	5.1	5.1	100.0
	Total	99	100.0	100.0	

Assessing normality

The assumption of normality is a prerequisite for many inferential statistical techniques. There are a number of different ways to explore this assumption graphically:

* histogram
* stem-and-leaf plot
* boxplot
* normal probability plot
* detrended normal plot.

Furthermore, a number of statistics are available to test normality:

* Kolmogorov–Smirnov statistic, with a Lilliefors significance level and the Shapiro–Wilk statistic
* skewness
* kurtosis.

There are several procedures available to obtain these graphs and statistics but the **Explore** procedure is the most convenient when both graphs and statistics are required.

    To obtain these graphs and statistics

1   Select the **Analyze** menu.

2   Click on **Descriptive Statistics** and then **Explore...** to open the **Explore** dialogue box.

3 Select the variable you require (i.e. *age*) and click on the ⬇ button to move this variable into the **Dependent List:** box.

4 In the **Display** box, ensure that **Both** is activated.

5 Click on the **Plots...** command pushbutton to obtain the **Explore: Plots** sub-dialogue box.

6 Click on the **Histogram** check box and the **Normality plots with tests** check box, and ensure that the **Factor levels together** radio button is selected in the **Boxplots** display.

7 Click on **Continue**.

8 Click on the **Options...** command pushbutton to open the **Explore: Options** sub-dialogue box.

9 In the **Missing Values** box, click on the **Exclude cases pairwise** radio button. If this option is not selected then, by default, any variable with missing data will be excluded from the analysis. That is, plots and statistics will be generated only for cases with complete data.

10 Click on **Continue** and then **OK**.

Histograms

●●●

Histogram

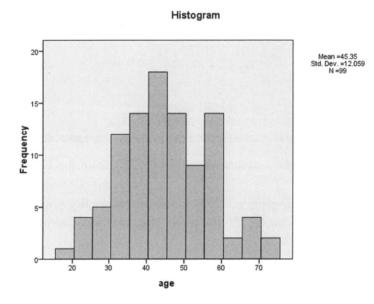

Above is a histogram of *age*. The values on the vertical axis indicate the frequency of cases. The values on the horizontal axis are midpoints of value ranges. For example, the midpoint of the first bar is 20 and the midpoint of the second bar is 25, indicating that each bar covers a range of 5. The shape of the distribution is considered normal.

Stem-and-leaf plots and boxplots

●●●

Closely related to the histogram are the stem-and-leaf plot and the boxplot. These plots provide more information about the actual values in the distribution than the histogram does.

```
age Stem-and-Leaf Plot

  Frequency    Stem &  Leaf

      1.00        1 .  8
      8.00        2 .  23347889
     23.00        3 .  01122233344456777788999
     29.00        4 .  00001222233445555555556777889
     27.00        5 .  000000022223455566677778888
      7.00        6 .  0005566
      4.00        7 .  0025

 Stem width:    10
 Each leaf:        1 case(s)
```

The stem-and-leaf plot is very similar to the histogram but is displayed on its side. The length of each row corresponds to the number of cases that fall into a particular interval. A stem-and-leaf plot represents each case with a numeric value that corresponds to the actual observed value. For example, the stem of the graph corresponds to the first digit of a score (2), while the leaf is the trailing digit (23347889).

The boxplot, illustrated below, also summarises information about the distribution of scores. Unlike the histogram and the stem-and-leaf plot, which plot actual values, it plots summary statistics such as the median, 25th and 75th percentiles, and extreme scores in the distribution. The lower boundary of the box is the 25th percentile and the upper boundary is the 75th percentile. The median is represented by a horizontal line through the centre of the box. The smallest and largest observed values within the distribution are represented by the horizontal lines at either end of the box, commonly referred to as whiskers.

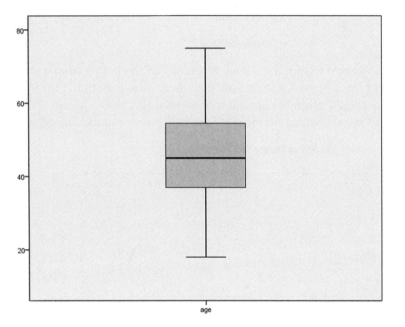

If the distribution has any extreme scores — that is, three or more box lengths from the upper or lower edge of the box — then these will be represented by an asterisk (*). Cases with values between one-and-a-half and three box lengths from the upper or lower edge of the box are called outliers, and these are designated by a circle.

To determine whether a distribution is normal, you look at the median, which should be positioned in the centre of the box. If the median is closer to the top of the box, then the distribution is negatively skewed, and if it is closer to the bottom of the box, then it is positively skewed. The spread or variability of the scores can be determined from the length of the box.

Normal probability plots and detrended normal plots
●●
In a normal probability plot, each observed value is paired with its expected value from the normal distribution. If the sample is from a normal distribution, then the cases fall more or less in a straight line.

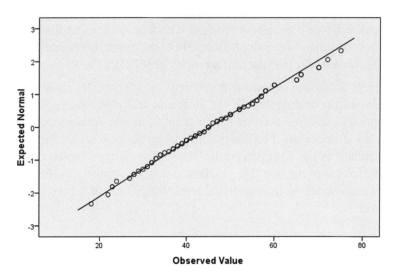

Normal Q-Q Plot of age

It is also possible to plot the actual deviations of the points from a straight line. If the sample is from a normal distribution, then there is no pattern to the clustering of points; the points should assemble around a horizontal line through zero. This type of plot is referred to as a detrended normal plot and is illustrated in the following figure.

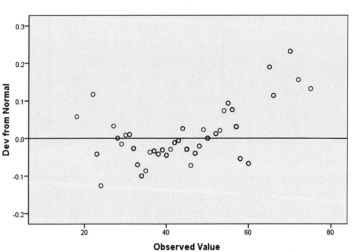

Detrended Normal Q-Q Plot of age

Kolmogorov–Smirnov and Shapiro–Wilk statistics

The Kolmogorov–Smirnov statistic with a Lilliefors significance level for testing normality is produced with the normal probability and detrended probability plots. If the significance level is greater than .05, then normality is assumed. The Shapiro–Wilk statistic is also calculated if the sample size is less than one hundred.

Tests of Normality

	Kolmogorov-Smirnov[a]			Shapiro-Wilk		
	Statistic	df	Sig.	Statistic	df	Sig.
age	.057	99	.200[*]	.992	99	.825

a. Lilliefors Significance Correction

*. This is a lower bound of the true significance.

Skewness and kurtosis

Skewness and kurtosis refer to the shape of the distribution, and are used with interval and ratio level data. Values for skewness and kurtosis are zero if the observed distribution is exactly normal. Positive values for skewness indicate a positive skew, while positive values for kurtosis indicate a distribution that is peaked (leptokurtic). Negative values for skewness indicate a negative skew, while negative values for kurtosis indicate a distribution that is flatter (platykurtic). Other descriptive statistics, such as measures of central tendency and variability, can also be used to determine the normality of the distribution.

Descriptives

			Statistic	Std. Error
age	Mean		45.35	1.212
	95% Confidence Interval for Mean	Lower Bound	42.95	
		Upper Bound	47.76	
	5% Trimmed Mean		45.25	
	Median		45.00	
	Variance		145.415	
	Std. Deviation		12.059	
	Minimum		18	
	Maximum		75	
	Range		57	
	Interquartile Range		18	
	Skewness		.126	.243
	Kurtosis		-.316	.481

You should be familiar with most of the preceding statistics. However, you may not have encountered the 5 per cent trim statistic, which is the mean of the distribution with the top 5 per cent and the bottom 5 per cent of scores removed. The purpose of this trimming is to obtain a measure of central tendency that is unaffected by extreme values.

Assessing normality by group

It is sometimes necessary to assess the normality of a variable across two or more levels of another variable. For example, you may wish to assess the normality of age for team participants and nonteam participants separately. This can be achieved using the above procedure with one addition. You will notice a **Factor List:** box in the **Explore** dialogue box. By transferring your group variable (i.e. *team participation*) into this box, the chosen statistics and plots will be generated for each group independently.

Variable transformation

Variables rarely conform to a classic normal distribution. More often, distributions are skewed and display varying degrees of kurtosis. When skewness and kurtosis are extreme, transformation is an option.

The decision to transform variables depends on the severity of the departure from normality. Having decided that transformation is desirable, the researcher must select the most appropriate transformation methods. The options available can be found in any good chapter on data screening.

To illustrate the process of transformation, the hours of exercise variable will be examined using the preceding steps. Plots and normality statistics were obtained.

Descriptives

			Statistic	Std. Error
hoursex	Mean		17.67	1.816
	95% Confidence Interval for Mean	Lower Bound	14.06	
		Upper Bound	21.27	
	5% Trimmed Mean		15.49	
	Median		11.00	
	Variance		326.367	
	Std. Deviation		18.066	
	Minimum		1	
	Maximum		87	
	Range		86	
	Interquartile Range		21	
	Skewness		1.770	.243
	Kurtosis		'3.475	.481

Tests of Normality

	Kolmogorov-Smirnov[a]			Shapiro-Wilk		
	Statistic	df	Sig.	Statistic	df	Sig.
hoursex	.178	99	.000	.810	99	.000

a. Lilliefors Significance Correction

Histogram

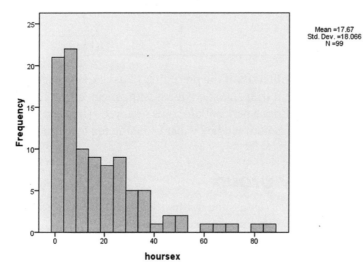

Mean =17.67
Std. Dev. =18.066
N =99

hoursex Stem-and-Leaf Plot

```
Frequency    Stem &  Leaf

   43.00        0 .   11111112222333333333344444555555566777777788
   19.00        1 .   0001111233444567778
   18.00        2 .   000012234455556779
    9.00        3 .   002245555
    3.00        4 .   057
    2.00        5 .   01
    5.00 Extremes     (>=60)

Stem width:       10
Each leaf:        1 case(s)
```

Normal Q-Q Plot of hoursex

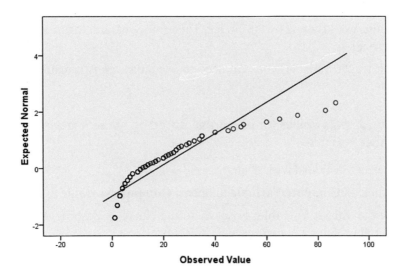

Detrended Normal Q-Q Plot of hoursex

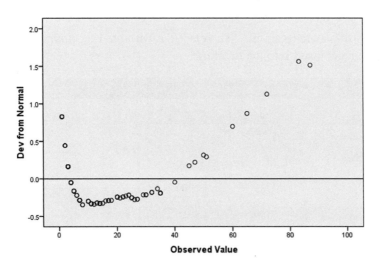

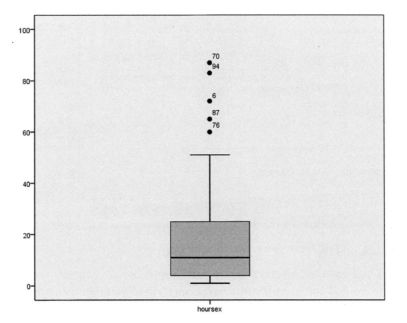

All the preceding charts and statistics suggest that the variable *hoursex* is not normally distributed but is significantly positively skewed. The boxplot indicates that there are five outliers, as illustrated by the circles. Therefore, a natural logarithmic transformation is appropriate.

To transform the variable, you will need to use a data transformation command called **Compute**.

▶ **To compute values for a variable based on numeric transformations of other variables**

1   Select the **Transform** menu.

2   Click on **Compute Variable** to open a **Compute Variable** dialogue box.

3   In the **Target Variable:** box, where the cursor is flashing, type an appropriate variable name (i.e. *Lnhours*).

4   From the **Function Group:** box select the appropriate transformation (i.e. *Arithmetic*).

5   From the **Functions and Special Variables:** box select LN and press the ▸ button.

6   From the source variable list, select the variable (i.e. *hoursex*) and press the ▸ button and insert into the function.

7   Click on **OK**.

Now that you have transformed the variable *hoursex* into *Lnhours*, you can obtain normality graphs and statistics for this new transformed variable using the procedures outlined at the beginning of the chapter. This output appears in the following.

Descriptives

			Statistic	Std. Error
Lnhours	Mean		2.3183	.11596
	95% Confidence Interval for Mean	Lower Bound	2.0881	
		Upper Bound	2.5484	
	5% Trimmed Mean		2.3376	
	Median		2.3979	
	Variance		1.331	
	Std. Deviation		1.15383	
	Minimum		.00	
	Maximum		4.47	
	Range		4.47	
	Interquartile Range		1.83	
	Skewness		-.312	.243
	Kurtosis		-.706	.481

Tests of Normality

	Kolmogorov-Smirnov[a]			Shapiro-Wilk		
	Statistic	df	Sig.	Statistic	df	Sig.
Lnhours	.095	99	.027	.965	99	.010

a. Lilliefors Significance Correction

Histogram

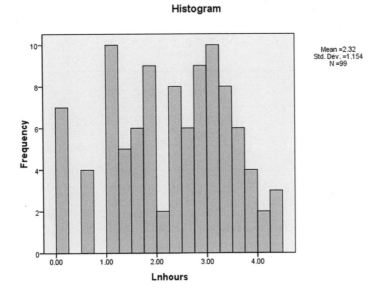

Mean =2.32
Std. Dev. =1.154
N =99

```
Lnhours Stem-and-Leaf Plot

 Frequency    Stem &  Leaf

     7.00        0 .  0000000
     4.00        0 .  6666
    15.00        1 .  000000000033333
    15.00        1 .  666666779999999
    10.00        2 .  0033333334
    15.00        2 .  556667788889999
    18.00        3 .  000111222222234444
    10.00        3 .  5555568899
     5.00        4 .  01244


 Stem width:      1.00
 Each leaf:       1 case(s)
```

Normal Q-Q Plot of Lnhours

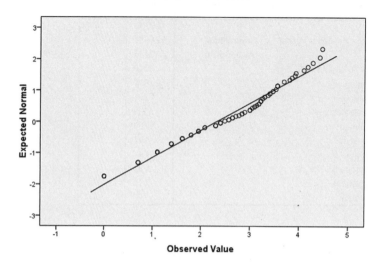

Detrended Normal Q-Q Plot of Lnhours

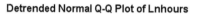

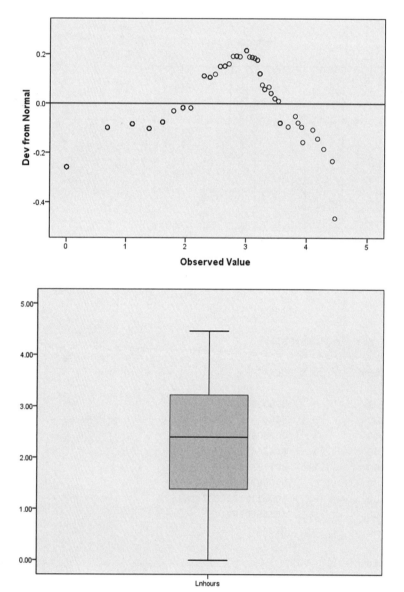

It is apparent from the preceding statistics and graphs that the natural logarithmic transformation was appropriate because the distribution of *hoursex* is now relatively normal. The Lilliefors statistic would suggest that there is still a slight problem but all the other diagnostic data are satisfactory. It is important to note that when reporting and interpreting results involving transformed variables, you must acknowledge that a transformation has been done on the data.

Data transformation

Recoding

••

You can modify data values by recoding. There are three instances where recoding variables is appropriate:

- collapsing continuous variables into categorical variables (e.g. median split)
- recoding negatively worded scale items
- replacing missing values and bringing outlying cases into the distribution.

To collapse a continuous variable

In relation to the research example, you wish to obtain a median split on the variable *age*.

1   Select the **Transform** menu.

2   Click on **Recode into Different Variables** to open the **Recode into Different Variables** dialogue box. By selecting **Into Different Variables**, you will retain the original data.

3   In the source variable list, select the variable you wish to recode (i.e. *age*) and click on the ⊡ button to move the variable into the **Numeric Variable -> Output Variable:** box.

4   In the **Name:** box of the **Output Variable** box, type the new variable name (i.e. *agecat*).

5   Click on the **Change** command pushbutton.

Recode into Different Variables

Numeric Variable -> Output Variable:

age --> ?

Output Variable

Name:
agecat

Label:
age categorical

Change

id
att1
att2
att3
att4
att5
att6
att7
hoursex
team participation [t...
Lnhours

Old and New Values...

If... (optional case selection condition)

OK   Paste   Reset   Cancel   Help

6   Click on the **Old and New Values...** command pushbutton to open the **Recode into Different Variables: Old and New Values** subdialogue box.

7   Click on the second **Range:** radio button and type the median in the box (i.e. *44*).

8   In the **New Value** box, type the new value (i.e. *1*).

9   Click on the **Add** command pushbutton.

10   Click on the third **Range:** radio button and type the median plus one (i.e. *45*).

11   In the **New Value** box, type the new value (i.e. *2*).

12   Click on the **Add** command pushbutton.

13   Click on **Continue** and then **OK**.

If you now go back into your data file, you will notice that the variable *agecat* now has two possible values: 1 = 0–44 years and 2 = 45+ years. This variable can now be used in analysis where categories are required.

To recode negatively worded scale items

Three of the items on the attitude scale required recoding because they were negatively worded. Remember that the response format for the items was 1 = strongly agree, 2 = agree, 3 = neutral, 4 = disagree and 5 = strongly disagree.

1   Select the **Transform** menu.

2   Click on **Recode into Same Variables** to open the **Recode into Same Variables** dialogue box. By selecting **Into Same Variables**, you will overwrite the original data.

3   In the source variable list, select the variable(s) you wish to recode (i.e. *att2*, *att4* and *att6*) and click on the ⬇ button to move the variable(s) into the **Variables:** box.

4   Click on the **Old and New Values...** command pushbutton to open the **Recode into Same Variables: Old and New Values** subdialogue box.

5   In the **Old Value** box, type the old value (i.e. *1*).

6   In the **New Value** box, type the new value (i.e. *5*).

7   Click on the **Add** command pushbutton.

8   In the **Old Value** box, type the second old value (i.e. *2*).

9   In the **New Value** box, type the new second value (i.e. *4*).

10   Click on the **Add** command pushbutton.

11   Repeat steps 8, 9 and 10 for the remaining two values.

```
┌─────────────────────────────────────────────────────────────────────────────┐
│ ▦ Recode into Same Variables: Old and New Values                        [×]  │
├─────────────────────────────────────────────────────────────────────────────┤
│ ┌─Old Value─────────────────────────┐  ┌─New Value──────────────────────┐    │
│ │ ◉ Value:                          │  │ ◉ Value: [                 ]   │    │
│ │ [                              ]  │  │ ○ System-missing               │    │
│ │ ○ System-missing                  │  │                                │    │
│ │ ○ System- or user-missing         │  │            Old --> New:        │    │
│ │ ○ Range:                          │  │          ┌──────────────────┐  │    │
│ │                                   │  │          │ 1 --> 5          │  │    │
│ │   [                  ]            │  │  ┌─────┐ │ 2 --> 4          │  │    │
│ │   through                         │  │  │ Add │ │ 4 --> 2          │  │    │
│ │   [                  ]            │  │  └─────┘ │ 5 --> 1          │  │    │
│ │                                   │  │  ┌────────┐                 │  │    │
│ │ ○ Range, LOWEST through value:    │  │  │ Change │                 │  │    │
│ │   [                  ]            │  │  └────────┘                 │  │    │
│ │                                   │  │  ┌────────┐                 │  │    │
│ │ ○ Range, value through HIGHEST:   │  │  │ Remove │                 │  │    │
│ │   [                  ]            │  │  └────────┘ └──────────────────┘  │    │
│ │ ○ All other values                │  │                                │    │
│ └───────────────────────────────────┘  └────────────────────────────────┘    │
│               ┌──────────┐  ┌────────┐  ┌──────┐                              │
│               │ Continue │  │ Cancel │  │ Help │                              │
│               └──────────┘  └────────┘  └──────┘                              │
└─────────────────────────────────────────────────────────────────────────────┘
```

12   Click on **Continue** and then **OK**.

The variables *att2*, *att4* and *att6* have now been recoded to allow computation of a composite variable.

 To replace missing values

Missing observations can be problematic. To avoid this problem, you can replace missing values with estimates computed with one of several methods. If you do not have access to the IBM SPSS Data Preparation or Missing Values add-on modules, a commonly used method to replace missing values is mean substitution.

1   Select the **Transform** menu.

2   Click on **Recode into Same Variables** to open the **Recode into Same Variables** dialogue box.

3   In the source variable list, select the variable(s) you wish to recode (i.e. *att1*) and click on the ▶ button to move the variable into the **Variables:** box.

4   Click on the **Old and New Values...** command pushbutton to open the **Recode into Same Variables: Old and New Values** subdialogue box.

5   In the **Old Value** box, select the **System- or user-missing** radio button.

6   In the **New Value** box, type the mean of the variable (i.e. *2.37*, as obtained by calculating the average score on the *att1* item).

7   Click on the **Add** command pushbutton.

Recode into Same Variables: Old and New Values

Old Value
- ○ Value:
- ○ System-missing
- ◉ System- or user-missing
- ○ Range:

  through

- ○ Range, LOWEST through value:
- ○ Range, value through HIGHEST:
- ○ All other values

New Value
- ◉ Value:
- ○ System-missing

Old --> New:

MISSING --> 2.37

[Add] [Change] [Remove]

[Continue] [Cancel] [Help]

8   Click on **Continue** and then **OK**.

Any missing data for the variable *att1* will be replaced with the mean of 2.37. Recoding missing values using mean substitution allows you to include all cases in your analysis. Alternatively, you may prefer to deal with missing cases in each analysis. Most procedures allow you to exclude missing cases either pairwise or listwise. Exclusion of missing cases pairwise involves the deletion of cases with missing values only on the relevant variables. Listwise deletion involves the elimination of cases with a missing value for any variable on the data list. More advanced procedures, such as factor analysis, give you the opportunity to replace missing data with the mean for particular variables during the procedure itself.

Computing

Transformation of variables is just one instance where the **Compute** command may be used. The **Compute** command is most commonly used to obtain composite scores for items on a scale. This can be achieved for the whole data set or only a subset if certain conditions apply. In the research example, a total attitude score would be appropriate. This can be obtained by adding the responses to the seven items comprising the scale for each individual case.

 To compute a new variable

1   Select the **Transform** menu.

2   Click on **Compute Variable** to open the **Compute Variable** dialogue box. If previous settings remain, these can be cleared with the **Reset** command pushbutton.

3   In the **Target Variable:** box, type an appropriate variable name (i.e. *total_att*).

4   Select the first scale item from the source variable list (i.e. *att1*) and click on the ⊡ button to move the variable into the **Numeric Expression:** box.

5   Click on the + button.

6   Select the second scale item from the source variable list (i.e. *att2*) and repeat steps 4 and 5.

Compute Variable

Target Variable:

total_att

Type & Label...

id
att1
att2
att3
att4
att5
att6
att7
hoursex
team participation [t...
age
Lnhours
age categorical [age...

= Numeric Expression:

att1+att2+att3+att4+att5+att6+att7

Function group:

All
Arithmetic
CDF & Noncentral CDF
Conversion
Current Date/Time
Date Arithmetic
Date Creation

Functions and Special Variables:

+	<	>	7	8	9
-	<=	>=	4	5	6
*	=	~=	1	2	3
/	&	|	0	.	
**	~	( )	Delete		

If... (optional case selection condition)

OK   Paste   Reset   Cancel   Help

7 Click on **OK**.

Again, if you move back into your data file (remember to use the SPSS Manager) you will notice that you have added items to obtain a new composite variable in your data file — *total_att*.

File Edit View Data Transform Analyze Graphs Utilities Add-ons Window Help

Visible: 14 of 14 Variables

	id	att1	att2	att3	att4	att5	att6	att7	hoursex	teampart	age	Lnhours	agecat	total_att	var
1	1	2	2	4	2	4	2	4	5	2	39	1.61	1.00	20.00	
2	2	2	3	4	2	4	2	2	11	2	44	2.40	1.00	19.00	
3	3	2	2	4	2	4	2	4	30	2	32	3.40	1.00	20.00	
4	4	2	4	3	2	4	2	4	40	1	70	3.69	2.00	21.00	
5	5	3	1	4	1	5	1	5	23	2	47	3.14	2.00	20.00	
6	6	3	1	5	1	5	2	5	72	1	72	4.28	2.00	22.00	
7	7	3	1	2	2	4	2	4	27	2	57	3.30	2.00	18.00	
8	8	1	1	4	1	4	3	5	11	2	42	2.40	1.00	19.00	
9	9	1	1	4	1	4	2	4	35	2	52	3.56	2.00	17.00	
10	10	3	1	3	3	5	1	3	7	2	42	1.95	1.00	19.00	
11	11	1	1	3	2	5	3	4	7	1	57	1.95	2.00	19.00	
12	12	2	2	4	1	5	1	4	3	2	58	1.10	2.00	19.00	
13	13	3	3	4	1	5	4	5	2	2	38	.69	1.00	25.00	
14	14	2	3	5	1	4	3	4	10	2	50	2.30	2.00	22.00	
15	15	3	1	4	2	5	3	3	4	2	27	1.39	1.00	21.00	
16	16	3	2	4	2	4	1	4	7	2	45	1.95	2.00	20.00	
17	17	1	1	5	1	5	1	5	51	1	40	3.93	1.00	19.00	
18	18	1	1	5	1	5	1	5	45	2	45	3.81	2.00	19.00	
19	19	3	3	3	3	4	3	3	6	2	56	1.79	2.00	22.00	
20	20	4	4	2	2	5	2	2	5	2	43	1.61	1.00	21.00	
21	21	2	2	3	1	4	3	3	20	2	49	3.00	2.00	18.00	
22	22	1	1	3	1	5	2	5	30	2	47	3.40	2.00	18.00	
23	23	2	4	2	2	5	4	2	1	2	24	.0	1.00	21.00	
24	24	5	1	5	1	5	3	5	14	2	30	2.64	1.00	25.00	
25	25	5	1	3	1	5	2	5	20	2	57	3.00	2.00	22.00	
26	26	5	1	5	1	5	1	3	3	2	58	1.10	2.00	21.00	
27	27	3	2	3	2	5	1	3	1	2	31	.0	1.00	19.00	
28	28	3	2	4	1	4	3	4	2	2	55	.69	2.00	21.00	
29	29	3	1	3	2	5	2	2	3	2	53	1.10	2.00	18.00	
30	30	2	2	3	1	5	2	5	4	2	75	1.39	2.00	20.00	
31	31	2	2	2	2	2	4	4	11	2	36	2.40	1.00	18.00	
32	32	3	1	5	1	5	1	5	5	2	50	1.61	2.00	21.00	

Data View Variable View

PASW Statistics Processor is ready

Other transformations are possible using the calculator pad and functions options in the **Compute Variable** dialogue box.

If you wish to compute a new variable based on certain conditions, then a slightly different procedure is required. For example, you may wish to compute a total attitude score for only those people who exercise for four hours per week or less.

 To compute new variables based on certain conditions

1   Select the **Transform** menu.

2   Click on **Compute Variable** to open the **Compute Variable** dialogue box.

3   In the **Target Variable:** box, type an appropriate variable name (i.e. *total_att*).

4   Select the first scale item from the source variable list (i.e. *att1*) and click on the button to move the variable into the **Numeric Expression:** box.

5   Click on the + button.

6   Select the second scale item from the source variable list (i.e. *att2*) and repeat steps 4 and 5 until all items are entered.

7   Click on the **If...** command pushbutton to open the **Compute Variable: If Cases** subdialogue box.

8   Select the **Include if case satisfies condition:** radio button.

9   Select the variable on which the condition is based (i.e. *hoursex*) and click on the ⬛ button to move the variable into the box.

10   Select the <= operator button, which moves the symbol into the box above, then click on the digit *4*.

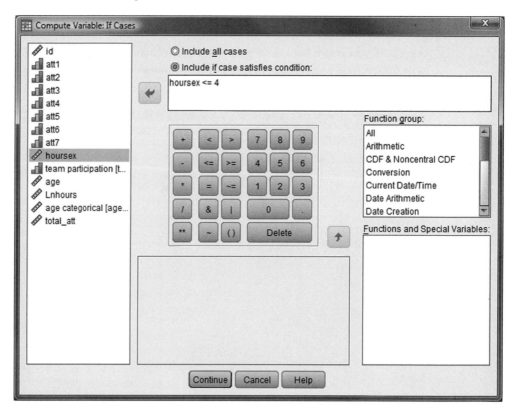

11   Click on **Continue** and then **OK**.

In this example, a new variable has been computed — *total_att* — based on certain conditions, that is, for those individuals who spent four hours or less (hoursex <= 4) in physical activity.

Data selection

In the **Select Cases** option in the **Data** menu, there are a number of procedures that can be chosen:

- selection of specified cases using the **If** option
- selection of a random sample of cases using the **Sample** option
- selection of cases based on time or case range using the **Range** option.

Selection of cases using the **If** option is most commonly used. For example, you may wish to examine the descriptive statistics of only males or females, or you may wish to analyse only half your data set.

 To select the first 50 cases in the data file for subsequent analysis

1   Select the **Data** menu.

2   Click on **Select Cases...** or click on the **Select Cases** tool to open the **Select Cases** dialogue box.

3   In the **Select** box, click on the **If condition is satisfied** radio button.

4   Click on the **If...** command pushbutton to open the **Select Cases: If** subdialogue box.

5   Select the variable you require (i.e. *id*) and click on the ⊡ button to move the variable into the box.

6   Click on the operator of your choice (i.e. <=), which will then be pasted into the box above.

7   Type in the value you require (i.e. *50*).

![Select Cases: If dialogue box]

8   Click on **Continue** and then **OK**.

You are now ready to do analysis on the 50 cases selected. If you go back into your data file (using the SPSS Manager) you will see that cases 51 to 99 have been crossed through.

Handy hints

- When working in the **Recode into Same variable: Old and new values** subdialogue box, make sure that any previous data transformation that you have performed is removed from the **Old → New** box.

- When assessing normality, remember while in the **Explore: Options** subdialogue box to click on the **Exclude cases pairwise** radio button. Otherwise, by default, any variable with missing data will be excluded from the analysis, and statistics generated only for cases with a complete data set.

- If you have extreme values, you may use the 5 per cent trim statistic, which removes the top 5 per cent and bottom 5 per cent of the scores. This way you can obtain a measure of central tendency that is unaffected by extreme scores.

- Always remember to recode negatively worded scale items.

- By selecting **Recode into Same Variable:** you will overwrite the original data. It is therefore useful to save a raw data file before transformation.

- Mean substitution is a useful mechanism for managing missing data.

- When working in the **Compute Variable** dialogue box, if previous settings remain, these can be cleared by pressing the **Reset** command pushbutton.

- When computing new variables, ensure that the new variable name is unique. Otherwise, existing variables with the same name will be overwritten.

- When there are violations of assumptions such as normality, it may be worth considering some of the nonparametric data analytical techniques available to you — refer to chapter 19 for more details of these techniques.

4

Descriptive statistics

Descriptive statistics are used to explore the data collected, as shown in chapter 3, and to summarise and describe those data.

Descriptive statistics may be particularly useful if one just wants to make some general observations about the data collected, for example the number of male and females, the age range and average (mean) age or the average length of residence in a community. Other statistics such as standard deviation and variance give more information about the distribution of each variable.

Frequency distributions

A frequency distribution is a display of the frequency of occurrence of each score value. The frequency distribution can be represented in tabular form or, with more visual clarity, in graphical form. For continuous variables, measured on ratio or interval scales, histograms or frequency polygons are appropriate. For categorical variables, measured on nominal or ordinal scales, bar charts are suitable.

Measures of central tendency and variability

The three main measures of central tendency are mode, median and mean. The measures of variability include range, interquartile range, standard deviation and variance. All of these measures of variability are more appropriate for interval or ratio data. You can also examine the normality of the distribution through the **Frequencies** procedure.

Working example

One hundred tennis players participated in a serving competition. Gender and number of aces were recorded for each player. The data file can be found in Work4.sav on the website that accompanies this title and is shown in the following figure.

To obtain a frequency table, measures of central tendency and variability

1   Select the **Analyze** menu.

2   Click on **Descriptive Statistics** and then on **Frequencies...** to open the **Frequencies** dialogue box.

3   Select the variable(s) you require (i.e. *aces*) and click on the ▶ button to move the variable into the **Variable(s):** box.

4   Click on the **Statistics...** command pushbutton to open the **Frequencies: Statistics** subdialogue box.

5   In the **Percentile Values** box, select the **Quartiles** check box.

6   In the **Central Tendency** box, select the **Mean**, **Median** and **Mode** check boxes.

7   In the **Dispersion** box, select the **Std. deviation**, **Variance**, **Range**, **Minimum** and **Maximum** check boxes.

8   Click on **Continue**.

9   Click on the **Charts...** command pushbutton to open the **Frequencies: Charts** subdialogue box.

10   Click on the **Histogram(s)** radio button. You will notice that you can also obtain a normal curve overlay, so click on the **Show normal curve on histogram** check box.

11   Click on **Continue** and then **OK**.

Statistics

aces

N	Valid	100
	Missing	0
Mean		5.1100
Median		5.0000
Mode		5.00
Std. Deviation		1.83620
Variance		3.372
Range		9.00
Minimum		1.00
Maximum		10.00
Percentiles	25	4.0000
	50	5.0000
	75	6.0000

aces

		Frequency	Percent	Valid Percent	Cumulative Percent
Valid	1.00	3	3.0	3.0	3.0
	2.00	6	6.0	6.0	9.0
	3.00	7	7.0	7.0	16.0
	4.00	15	15.0	15.0	31.0
	5.00	35	35.0	35.0	66.0
	6.00	15	15.0	15.0	81.0
	7.00	8	8.0	8.0	89.0
	8.00	6	6.0	6.0	95.0
	9.00	4	4.0	4.0	99.0
	10.00	1	1.0	1.0	100.0
	Total	100	100.0	100.0	

In the frequency table, the Frequency column summarises the total number of aces served. For example, only one person served ten aces. The Percent column displays this frequency in percentage form for *all* cases, including those that may be missing. The Valid Percent column is the proportion of scores only for those cases that are valid. Because you have no missing data in this example, the Percent and Valid Percent columns are identical. The Cumulative Percent column is the summation of the percentage for that score with the percentage for all lesser scores.

By obtaining the 25th and 75th percentiles for the distribution, the interquartile range can be calculated by subtracting one from the other. Therefore, in this example, the interquartile range is equal to 6 − 4 = 2.

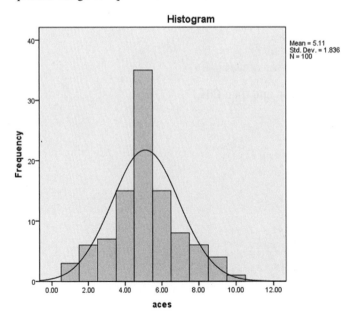

To obtain the appropriate output for a categorical variable

1   Select the **Analyze** menu.

2   Click on **Descriptive Statistics** and then on **Frequencies...** to open the **Frequencies** dialogue box.

3   Select the variable(s) you require (i.e. *gender*) and click on the ⊡ button to move the variable into the **Variable(s):** box.

4   Click on the **Statistics...** command pushbutton to open the **Frequencies: Statistics** subdialogue box.

5   In the **Central Tendency** box, click on the **Mode** check box.

6   Click on **Continue**.

7   Click on the **Charts...** command pushbutton to open the **Frequencies: Charts** subdialogue box.

8   Select the **Bar chart(s)** radio button.

9   Click on **Continue** and then **OK**.

gender

		Frequency	Percent	Valid Percent	Cumulative Percent
Valid	1.00	50	50.0	50.0	50.0
	2.00	50	50.0	50.0	100.0
	Total	100	100.0	100.0	

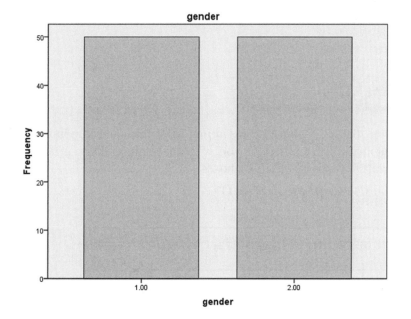

gender

The Descriptives command

It is also possible to obtain certain measures of central tendency and variability through the **Descriptives** command. In addition, this command allows you to save standardised values as variables. These standardised or Z-scores are useful for further analysis (e.g. interaction terms in multiple regression) or in comparing samples from different populations. Furthermore, inspection of Z-scores will allow identification of outlying cases, which is useful in data screening. Z-scores greater than +3 and less than −3 are considered to be outliers.

To obtain descriptive statistics and Z-scores

1   Select the **Analyze** menu.

2   Click on **Descriptive Statistics** and then **Descriptives...** to open the **Descriptives** dialogue box.

3   Select the variable(s) you require (i.e. *aces*) and click on the ⬛ button to move the variable into the **Variable(s):** box.

4   Select the **Save standardized values as variables** check box.

5   Click on the **Options** command pushbutton.

6   Note that the **Mean**, **Std. deviation**, **Minimum** and **Maximum** check boxes are automatically selected. If you wish to obtain additional descriptive statistics, select the appropriate check boxes.

7   Click on **Continue** and then **OK**.

Descriptive Statistics

	N	Minimum	Maximum	Mean	Std. Deviation
aces	100	1.00	10.00	5.1100	1.83620
Valid N (listwise)	100				

If you switch back to the Data Editor window, you will notice that the Z-scores have been saved as another variable: *Zaces*.

Handy hint
• If unwanted check boxes are selected, click on them to deselect them.

CHAPTER 5

Correlation

Correlation looks at the relationship between two variables in a linear fashion. A *Pearson product-moment correlation* coefficient describes the relationship between two continuous variables, and is available through the **Analyze** and **Correlate** menus.

A correlation between two dichotomous or categorical variables is called a *Phi coefficient*, and is available through the **Crosstabs** option from the **Analyze** and **Descriptive Statistics** menus.

A correlation between a continuous and a categorical variable is called a *point-biserial correlation*. This option is not available in the SPSS for Windows package. However, you can use a Pearson product-moment correlation to correlate a dichotomous and a continuous variable. The proportion of each category of the dichotomous variable must be approximately equal and variables must be coded as 0 and 1 though.

When the assumptions underlying correlation cannot be met adequately, a non-parametric alternative is *Spearman's rank-order correlation*.

In this chapter, you will perform bivariate and partial correlations using Pearson's product-moment correlation.

Simple bivariate correlation, also referred to as zero-order correlation, refers to the correlation between two continuous variables, and is the most common measure of linear relationship. This coefficient has a range of possible values from -1 to $+1$. The value indicates the strength of the relationship, while the sign ($+$ or $-$) indicates the direction.

Partial correlation provides a single measure of linear association between two variables while adjusting for the effects of one or more additional variables.

Assumption testing

Correlational analysis has several underlying assumptions:

1   **Related pairs:** data must be collected from related pairs; that is, if you obtain a score on an X variable, there must also be a score on the Y variable from the same participant.

2   **Scale of measurement:** data should be interval or ratio in nature.

3   **Normality:** the scores for each variable should be normally distributed.

4   **Linearity:** the relationship between the two variables must be linear.

5   **Homoscedasticity:** the variability in scores for one variable is roughly the same at all values of the other variable. That is, it is concerned with how the scores cluster uniformly about the regression line.

Assumptions 1 and 2 are a matter of research design. Assumption 3 can be tested using the procedures outlined in chapters 3 and 4. Assumptions 4 and 5 can be tested by examining scatterdots of the variables.

Working example

Twenty students wishing to enter university were given an intelligence test (IQ) and their tertiary entrance examination scores (TEE) were recorded. You suspect that a positive relationship exists between these two variables and wish to test this directional hypothesis (one-tailed).

At the end of the academic year, the course averages for the same twenty students were obtained. You also wish to determine whether the relationship between TEE scores and course average is significant when IQ is controlled in the analysis.

The data can be found in Work5.sav on the website that accompanies this title and are shown in the following figure.

	iq	tee	uniav
1	121	375.00	85
2	119	380.00	78
3	114	290.00	68
4	112	270.00	65
5	117	300.00	73
6	118	326.00	75
7	122	400.00	71
8	123	387.00	86
9	116	340.00	72
10	117	300.00	69
11	116	310.00	58
12	118	367.00	74
13	115	375.00	80
14	115	370.00	75
15	115	330.00	68
16	123	410.00	81
17	119	365.00	74
18	114	344.00	69
19	121	390.00	83
20	118	355.00	72
21	119	342.00	61
22	117	361.00	59
23	122	368.00	73
24	121	395.00	79

 To obtain a scatterdot

1   Select the **Graphs** menu.

2   Select the **Legacy Dialogs** option.

3   Click on **Scatter/dot...** to open the **Scatter/dot** dialogue box.

4   Ensure that the **Simple Scatter** option is selected.

5   Click on the **Define** command pushbutton to open the **Simple Scatter** sub-dialogue box.

6   Select the first variable (i.e. *tee*) and click on the ⏺ button to move the variable into the **Y Axis:** box.

7   Select the second variable (i.e. *iq*) and click on the ⏺ button to move the variable into the **X Axis:** box.

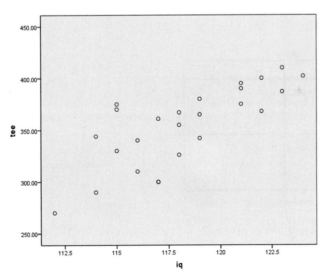

8   Click on **OK**.

As you can see from the scatterdot, there is a linear relationship between IQ and TEE scores. Given that the scores cluster uniformly around the regression line, the assumption of homoscedasticity has not been violated.

Similarly, the scatterdot was obtained for TEE scores and course average, indicating that assumptions of linearity and homoscedasticity were not violated. The output of this plot is not displayed.

▶ To obtain a bivariate Pearson product-moment correlation

1   Select the **Analyze** menu.

2   Click on **Correlate** and then **Bivariate...** to open the **Bivariate Correlations** dialogue box.

3   Select the variables you require (i.e. *iq* and *tee*) and click on the ⊡ button to move the variables into the **Variables:** box.

4   Ensure that the **Pearson** correlation option has been selected.

5   In the **Test of Significance** box, select the **One-tailed** radio button.

6   Click on **OK**.

Correlations

		iq	tee
iq	Pearson Correlation	1	.767**
	Sig. (1-tailed)		.000
	N	25	25
tee	Pearson Correlation	.767**	1
	Sig. (1-tailed)	.000	
	N	25	25

**. Correlation is significant at the 0.01 level (1-tailed).

To interpret the correlation coefficient, you examine the coefficient and its associated significance value (p). The output confirms the results of the scatterdot in that a significant positive relationship exists between IQ and TEE ($r = .767$, $p < .05$). Therefore, higher intelligence scores are associated with higher TEE scores.

Therefore, in reporting on your findings, you might say that a bivariate correlation was undertaken between students' intelligence scores and their tertiary entrance examination scores. It was hypothesised that a positive relationship would exist between these two variables. Results of the correlation indicate that higher intelligence scores are associated with higher TEE scores (r = .767, p < .05).

Handy hint
- Remember that the assumptions for correlation can be examined using different procedures in SPSS. These procedures have been outlined in chapters 3, 4 and 5.

t-tests

A t-test is used to determine whether there is a significant difference between two sets of scores. Three main types of t-test may be applied:

- one-sample
- independent groups
- repeated-measures.

Assumption testing

Each statistical test has certain assumptions that must be met before analysis. These assumptions need to be evaluated because the accuracy of test interpretation depends on whether assumptions are violated. Some of these assumptions are generic to all types of t-test but others are more specific.

The generic assumptions underlying all types of t-test are:

1   **Scale of measurement:** the data should be at the interval or ratio level of measurement.

2   **Random sampling:** the scores should be randomly sampled from the population of interest.

3   **Normality:** the scores should be normally distributed in the population.

Clearly, assumptions 1 and 2 are a matter of research design and not statistical analysis. Assumption 3 can be tested in different ways, as outlined in chapter 3.

Working example

A major oil company developed a petrol additive that was supposed to increase engine efficiency. Twenty-two cars were test driven both with and without the additive and the number of kilometres per litre was recorded. Whether the car was automatic or manual was also recorded and coded as 1 = manual and 2 = automatic.

During an earlier trial, 22 cars were test driven using the additive. The mean number of kilometres per litre was 10.5.

You are interested in answering the following questions:

1   Are the cars in the present trial running more efficiently than those in the earlier trial? The one-sample t-test will help answer this question.

2   Does engine efficiency improve when the additive is used? This is a repeated-measures t-test design.

3   Does engine efficiency with and without the additive differ between manual and automatic cars? This is an independent-groups t-test.

The data can be found in Work6.sav on the website that accompanies this title and are shown in the following figure.

	cartype	without	withadd	var	var	var	var	var	var	var	var	var
1	1	7	14									
2	2	14	16									
3	1	12	17									
4	1	11	13									
5	2	9	10									
6	2	4	8									
7	1	13	14									
8	2	16	19									
9	2	11	17									
10	1	7	11									
11	2	9	12									
12	2	9	14									
13	1	6	15									
14	1	7	13									
15	2	10	12									
16	1	6	17									
17	1	6	15									
18	2	5	11									
19	2	4	12									
20	1	4	12									
21	2	8	16									
22	1	9	17									
23												
24												

The one-sample t-test

The one-sample t-test is used when you have data from a single sample of participants and you wish to know whether the mean of the population from which the sample is drawn is the same as the hypothesised mean.

> **To conduct a one-sample t-test**

1   Select the **Analyze** menu.

2   Click on **Compare Means** and then **One-Sample T Test...** to open the **One-Sample T Test** dialogue box.

3   Select the variable you require (i.e. *withadd*) and click on the ⯆ button to move the variable into the **Test Variable(s):** box.

4   In the **Test Value:** box type the mean score (i.e. *10.5*).

One-Sample T Test dialog box:

Test Variable(s): withadd

Available variables: cartype, without

Test Value: 10.5

Buttons: OK, Paste, Reset, Cancel, Help, Options...

5   Click on **OK**.

It is possible to determine whether a difference exists between the sample mean and the hypothesised mean by consulting the t-value, degree of freedom (df) and two-tail significance. If the value for two-tail significance is less than .05 ($p < .05$), then the difference between the means is significant.

The output indicates that there is a significant difference in engine efficiency between the present trial and the earlier trial. That is, the cars in the present trial seem to have greater engine efficiency than those in the earlier trial — $t (21) = 5.74$, $p < .05$.

One-Sample Statistics

	N	Mean	Std. Deviation	Std. Error Mean
withadd	22	13.86	2.748	.586

One-Sample Test

	Test Value = 10.5					
				Mean	95% Confidence Interval of the Difference	
	t	df	Sig. (2-tailed)	Difference	Lower	Upper
withadd	5.741	21	.000	3.364	2.15	4.58

t-tests with more than one sample

In the previous section, a one-sample t-test was used to determine whether a single sample of scores was likely to have been drawn from a hypothesised population. This section will extend the understanding of sampling distributions to ask whether two sets of scores are random samples from the same or different populations. If they are random samples from the same population, then any differences across conditions or groups can be attributed to random sampling variability. However, if the two sets of scores are random samples from different populations, then you can attribute any difference between means across conditions to the independent variable or the treatment effect.

Repeated-measures t-test

The repeated-measures t-test, also referred to as the dependent-samples or paired t-test, is used when you have data from only one group of participants. In other words, an individual obtains two scores under different levels of the independent variable. Data that are collected from the same group of participants are also referred to as within-subjects, because the same subject performs in both conditions. Studies which employ a pretest–posttest design are commonly analysed using repeated-measures t-tests. In this form of design, the same participant obtains a score on the pretest and, after some intervention or manipulation, a score on the posttest. You wish to determine whether the difference between means for the two sets of scores is the same or different.

Before you attempt to answer this question, you must ensure that the assumptions of the repeated-measures t-test are met. You will remember from the section on assumption testing that some assumptions are generic to all types of t-test. The repeated-measures t-test has one additional assumption:

1   **Normality of population difference scores**: the difference between the scores for each participant should be normally distributed. Providing the sample size is not too small (30+), violations of this assumption are of little concern.

Testing this assumption involves the same procedures as used for the single-sample t-test. Because you have two dependent variables, you will need to test the normality of each variable separately, which will allow you to assume that the difference scores are normally distributed. Having evaluated the assumption of normality for both pretest and posttest measures, you are ready to conduct a repeated-measures t-test.

To conduct a repeated-measures t-test

1   Select the **Analyze** menu.

2   Click on **Compare Means** and then **Paired-Samples T Test...** to open the **Paired-Samples T Test** dialogue box.

3   Select the variables you require (i.e. *without* and *withadd*) and press the ⏎ button to move the variables into the **Paired Variables**: box.

4   Click on **OK**.

Paired Samples Statistics

		Mean	N	Std. Deviation	Std. Error Mean
Pair 1	without	8.50	22	3.335	.711
	withadd	13.86	22	2.748	.586

Paired Samples Correlations

		N	Correlation	Sig.
Pair 1	without & withadd	22	.559	.007

Paired Samples Test

		Paired Differences							
					95% Confidence Interval of the Difference				
		Mean	Std. Deviation	Std. Error Mean	Lower	Upper	t	df	Sig. (2-tailed)
Pair 1	without - withadd	-5.364	2.904	.619	-6.651	-4.076	-8.663	21	.000

By looking at the t-value, df and two-tail significance, you can determine whether the groups come from the same or different populations. The correct way to determine significance is to consult the critical t-tables that are available at the back of most statistical textbooks, using the dfs. However, significance can also be determined by looking at the probability level (p) specified under the heading 'two-tail significance' (sig (2-tailed)). If the probability value is less than the specified alpha value, then the observed t-value is significant. The 95 per cent confidence interval indicates that 95 per cent of the time the interval specified will contain the true difference between the population means.

As can be seen from the output, a significant difference exists between engine efficiency with and without the additive. The additive significantly improves the number of kilometres to the litre, t (21) = –8.66, p < .05.

The independent-groups t-test

The independent-groups t-test is appropriate when different participants have performed in each of the different conditions; in other words, when the participants in one condition are different from the participants in the other condition. This is commonly referred to as a between-subjects design.

Again, you wish to determine whether the difference between means for the two sets of scores is significant.

The independent-groups t-test has two additional assumptions.

1   **Independence of groups**: participants should appear in only one group and these groups should be unrelated.

2   **Homogeneity of variance**: the groups should come from populations with equal variances. To test for homogeneity of variance, SPSS uses the Levene test for equality of variances. If this test is significant (p < .05), then you reject the null hypothesis and accept the alternative hypothesis that the variances are unequal. In this instance, the unequal variance estimates are consulted. If the test is not significant (p > .05), then you accept the null hypothesis that there are no significant differences between the variances of the groups. In this case, you would consult the equal variance estimates. This explanation will make more sense when you consult the output of the independent-groups t-test.

Assumption 1 is a matter of research design, while assumption 2 is tested in the independent-groups analysis. Before proceeding you need to check the normality of the data. Because you have different participants in each condition, you need to check the normality of each set of scores separately. This is achieved through the **Explore** dialogue box using the **Factor List** option.

▶ **To screen for normality**

1   Select the **Analyze** menu.

2   Click on **Descriptive Statistics** and then **Explore...** to open the **Explore** dialogue box.

3   Select the dependent variable(s) (i.e. *without* and *withadd*) and click on the ⊡ button to move the variables into the **Dependent List**: box.

4   Select the grouping variable (i.e. *cartype*) and click on the ⊡ button to move this variable into the **Factor List**: box.

5   Click on **OK**.

Descriptives

	cartype			Statistic	Std. Error
without	manual	Mean		8.00	.863
		95% Confidence	Lower Bound	6.08	
		Interval for Mean	Upper Bound	9.92	
		5% Trimmed Mean		7.94	
		Median		7.00	
		Variance		8.200	
		Std. Deviation		2.864	
		Minimum		4	
		Maximum		13	
		Range		9	
		Interquartile Range		5	
		Skewness		.656	.661
		Kurtosis		−.704	1.279
	automatic	Mean		9.00	1.152
		95% Confidence	Lower Bound	6.43	
		Interval for Mean	Upper Bound	11.57	
		5% Trimmed Mean		8.89	
		Median		9.00	
		Variance		14.600	
		Std. Deviation		3.821	
		Minimum		4	
		Maximum		16	
		Range		12	
		Interquartile Range		6	
		Skewness		.355	.661
		Kurtosis		−.253	1.279
withadd	manual	Mean		14.36	.622
		95% Confidence	Lower Bound	12.98	
		Interval for Mean	Upper Bound	15.75	
		5% Trimmed Mean		14.40	
		Median		14.00	
		Variance		4.255	
		Std. Deviation		2.063	
		Minimum		11	
		Maximum		17	
		Range		6	
		Interquartile Range		4	
		Skewness		−.013	.661
		Kurtosis		−1.012	1.279
	automatic	Mean		13.36	1.002
		95% Confidence	Lower Bound	11.13	
		Interval for Mean	Upper Bound	15.60	
		5% Trimmed Mean		13.35	
		Median		12.00	
		Variance		11.055	
		Std. Deviation		3.325	
		Minimum		8	
		Maximum		19	
		Range		11	
		Interquartile Range		5	
		Skewness		.169	.661
		Kurtosis		−.749	1.279

In reviewing the descriptive statistics and the other output such as stem-and-leaf plots and boxplots (not shown), it is clear that there is minimal violation to the assumption of normality.

 **To conduct an independent-groups t-test**

1   Select the **Analyze** menu.

2   Click on **Compare Means** and then **Independent-Samples T Test...** to open the **Independent Samples T Test** dialogue box.

3   Select the test variable(s) (i.e. *without*) and then click on the ⏷ button to move the variables into the **Test Variable(s):** box.

4   Select the grouping variable (i.e. *cartype*) and click on the ⏷ button to move the variable into the **Grouping Variable:** box.

```
┌─────────────────────────────────────────────────────────┐
│ ▦ Independent-Samples T Test                      [ X ]  │
├─────────────────────────────────────────────────────────┤
│                          Test Variable(s):                │
│                                              ┌──────────┐ │
│   ◢ withadd                  ◢ without       │ Options. │ │
│                                              └──────────┘ │
│                        ┌───┐                              │
│                        │ ← │                              │
│                        └───┘                              │
│                                                           │
│                          Grouping Variable:               │
│                   ┌───┐  ┌──────────────────┐             │
│                   │ ← │  │ cartype(? ?)      │             │
│                   └───┘  └──────────────────┘             │
│                          ┌──────────────┐                 │
│                          │ Define Groups...│               │
│                          └──────────────┘                 │
│      ┌────┐ ┌──────┐ ┌──────┐ ┌────────┐ ┌──────┐         │
│      │ OK │ │Paste │ │Reset │ │ Cancel │ │ Help │         │
│      └────┘ └──────┘ └──────┘ └────────┘ └──────┘         │
└─────────────────────────────────────────────────────────┘
```

5   Click on the **Define Groups...** command pushbutton to open the **Define Groups** subdialogue box.

6   In the **Group 1:** box, type the lowest value for the variable (i.e. *1*), then tab. Enter the second value for the variable (i.e. *2*) in the **Group 2:** box.

```
┌──────────────────────────────────┐
│ ▦ Define Groups          [ X ]    │
├──────────────────────────────────┤
│  ◉ Use specified values           │
│      Group 1:  │ 1          │      │
│      Group 2:  │ 2          │      │
│  ○ Cut point:  │            │      │
│  ┌─────────┐ ┌────────┐ ┌──────┐  │
│  │Continue │ │ Cancel │ │ Help │  │
│  └─────────┘ └────────┘ └──────┘  │
└──────────────────────────────────┘
```

7   Click on **Continue** and then **OK**.

In the case of the independent-groups t-test, you have a grouping variable, so you can distinguish between groups 1 and 2 when comparing engine efficiency.

Group Statistics

	cartype	N	Mean	Std. Deviation	Std. Error Mean
without	manual	11	8.00	2.864	.863
	automatic	11	9.00	3.821	1.152

Independent Samples Test

		Levene's Test for Equality of Variances		t-test for Equality of Means					95% Confidence Interval of the Difference	
		F	Sig.	t	df	Sig. (2-tailed)	Mean Difference	Std. Error Difference	Lower	Upper
without	Equal variances assumed	.172	.683	-.695	20	.495	-1.000	1.440	-4.003	2.003
	Equal variances not assumed			-.695	18.539	.496	-1.000	1.440	-4.018	2.018

Given that Levene's test has a probability greater than .05, you can assume that the population variances are relatively equal. Therefore, you can use the t-value, df and two-tail significance for the equal variance estimates to determine whether car type differences exist. The two-tail significance for *without* additive indicates that $p > .05$ and, therefore, is not significant. You therefore accept the null hypothesis and reject the alternative hypothesis. The two groups must come from the same population because no significant differences exist — $t(20) = -.695$, $p > .05$.

Although it is possible to perform two t-tests with the one command, for the sake of clarity two separate procedures are shown.

Group Statistics

	cartype	N	Mean	Std. Deviation	Std. Error Mean
withadd	manual	11	14.36	2.063	.622
	automatic	11	13.36	3.325	1.002

Independent Samples Test

		Levene's Test for Equality of Variances		t-test for Equality of Means					95% Confidence Interval of the Difference	
		F	Sig.	t	df	Sig. (2-tailed)	Mean Difference	Std. Error Difference	Lower	Upper
withadd	Equal variances assumed	3.390	.080	.848	20	.407	1.000	1.180	-1.461	3.461
	Equal variances not assumed			.848	16.704	.409	1.000	1.180	-1.492	3.492

In relation to the *withadd* variable, Levene's test was not significant and so the equal variance estimates are interpreted. Consulting the t-value, df and two-tail significance, again no significant differences are apparent ($p > .05$). That is, there is no significant difference in engine efficiency between manual and automatic cars either with or without the additive — $t(20) = .848$, $p > .05$.

Handy hints

- Remember to test assumptions before analysis. Scale of measurement and random sampling are a matter of research design. Normality, however, can be tested in various ways, as outlined in chapter 3. For repeated-measures designs, there is the additional assumption of normality of population difference scores. For independent-groups t-tests, there are the additional assumptions of independence of groups and homogeneity of variance.

- Conduct a one-sample t-test when you have data from a single population and are interested in determining whether the sample population mean is the same as the hypothesised mean. You are determining whether a single sample of scores was likely to have been drawn from the hypothesised population.

- Conduct a repeated-measures t-test (also called a dependent-sampled, paired t-test or within-subject design) when considering data sourced from one group of participants, where each participant has two scores under different levels of the independent variable. You are considering whether two sets of random scores are from the same or different populations. If you observe that they are from the same population, differences can be attributed to random sampling variability. Alternatively, if observed from the same population, differences are due to the independent variable or treatment effect.

- Conduct an independent-groups t-test (also called a between-subjects design) when different participants have performed in each of the conditions.

One-way between-groups ANOVA with post-hoc comparisons

In the previous chapter, you tested the null hypothesis that two population means were equal. When you wish to compare the means of more than two groups or levels of an independent variable, a one-way analysis of variance (ANOVA) is appropriate.

At the heart of ANOVA is the notion of variance. The basic procedure is to derive two different estimates of population variance from the data, then calculate a statistic from the ratio of these two estimates. One of these estimates (between-groups variance) is a measure of the effect of the independent variable combined with error variance. The other estimate (within-groups variance) is of error variance by itself. The F-ratio is the ratio of between-groups variance to within-groups variance. A significant F-ratio indicates that the population means are probably not all equal. Because the null hypothesis is rejected if any pair of means is unequal, where the significant differences lie needs to be worked out. This requires post-hoc analysis.

Post-hoc analysis involves hunting through the data for any significance; that is, doing an entire set of comparisons. This type of testing carries risks of type I errors. Unlike planned comparisons, post-hoc tests are designed to protect against type I errors, given that all the possible comparisons are going to be made. These tests are stricter than planned comparisons, so it is harder to obtain significance.

Several post-hoc tests are available. The more options a test offers, the stricter its determination of significance. The Scheffe test, for example, allows every possible comparison to be made but is tough on rejecting the null hypothesis. In contrast, Tukey's honestly significant difference (HSD) test is more lenient but the types of comparison that can be made are restricted. This chapter illustrates Tukey's HSD post-hoc test.

Assumption testing

Before conducting the ANOVA, the necessary assumptions must be met. The assumptions for ANOVA are the same as those for the t-test.

The two assumptions of concern are:

1   **Population normality:** populations from which the samples have been drawn should be normal. Check this for each group using normality statistics such as skewness and Shapiro–Wilk.

2   **Homogeneity of variance:** the scores in each group should have homogeneous variances. As with the t-test, Levene's test determines whether variances are equal or unequal.

Working example

An economist wished to compare household expenditure on electricity and gas in four major cities in Australia. She obtained random samples of 25 two-person households from each city and asked them to keep records of their energy expenditure over a six-month period. Note that this is an independent-groups design because the different households are in different cities. If the same participants were in all conditions, then it would be a within-subjects or repeated-measures design. A repeated-measures design requires a different class of procedures, so it is discussed in chapter 10.

The data can be found in Work7.sav on the website that accompanies this title and are shown in the following figure.

	city	cost
1	1	545
2	1	470
3	1	445
4	1	574
5	1	463
6	1	383
7	1	452
8	1	573
9	1	529
10	1	471
11	1	538
12	1	587
13	1	466
14	1	621
15	1	429
16	1	487
17	1	460
18	1	504
19	1	500
20	1	450
21	1	505
22	1	436
23	1	555
24	1	496

To conduct a one-way ANOVA with post-hoc analysis

1   Select the **Analyze** menu.

2   Click on **Compare Means** and **One-Way ANOVA...** to open the **One-Way ANOVA** dialogue box.

3   Select the dependent variable (i.e. *cost*) and click on the button to move the variable into the **Dependent List:** box.

4   Select the independent variable (i.e. *city*) and click on the button to move the variable into the **Factor:** box.

5   Click on the **Options...** command pushbutton to open the **One-Way ANOVA: Options** subdialogue box.

6   Click on the check boxes for **Descriptive** and **Homogeneity of variance test**.

7   Click on **Continue**.

8   Click on the **Post Hoc...** command pushbutton to open the **One-Way ANOVA: Post Hoc Multiple Comparisons** subdialogue box. You will notice that a number of multiple comparison options are available. In this example, you will use Tukey's HSD multiple comparison test.

9   Click on the check box for **Tukey**.

One-Way ANOVA: Post Hoc Multiple Comparisons

Equal Variances Assumed

- [ ] LSD
- [ ] Bonferroni
- [ ] Sidak
- [ ] Scheffe
- [ ] R-E-G-W F
- [ ] R-E-G-W Q
- [ ] S-N-K
- [x] Tukey
- [ ] Tukey's-b
- [ ] Duncan
- [ ] Hochberg's GT2
- [ ] Gabriel
- [ ] Waller-Duncan
  - Type I/Type II Error Ratio: 100
- [ ] Dunnett
  - Control Category: Last
  - **Test**
    - (●) 2-sided (○) < Control (○) > Control

Equal Variances Not Assumed

- [ ] Tamhane's T2   [ ] Dunnett's T3   [ ] Games-Howell   [ ] Dunnett's C

Significance level: 0.05

[Continue] [Cancel] [Help]

10   Click on **Continue** and then **OK**.

Descriptives

cost of electricity and gas

	N	Mean	Std. Deviation	Std. Error	95% Confidence Interval for Mean		Minimum	Maximum
					Lower Bound	Upper Bound		
Adelaide	25	497.28	56.628	11.326	473.91	520.65	383	621
Hobart	25	515.84	56.529	11.306	492.51	539.17	397	647
Melbourne	25	531.20	63.976	12.795	504.79	557.61	397	677
Perth	25	555.12	72.576	14.515	525.16	585.08	429	739
Total	100	524.86	65.385	6.539	511.89	537.83	383	739

To interpret this output, you must first ensure that the homogeneity assumption has not been violated. Levene's test for homogeneity of variances is not significant ($p > .05$), so you can be confident that the population variances for each group are approximately equal.

Test of Homogeneity of Variances

cost of electricity and gas

Levene Statistic	df1	df2	Sig.
.817	3	96	.488

To determine whether you have a significant F-ratio, you use the degrees of freedom (dfs) (3,96), the F-ratio and the F-probability. Again, the correct way to determine significance is to use the critical F tables. Significance can also be determined by looking at the F-probability value. Given that $p < .05$, you can reject the null hypothesis and accept the alternative hypothesis that states that expenditure on electricity and gas is different across capital cities, $F(3,96) = 3.802$, $p < .05$.

ANOVA

cost of electricity and gas

	Sum of Squares	df	Mean Square	F	Sig.
Between Groups	44947.000	3	14982.333	3.802	.013
Within Groups	378299.040	96	3940.615		
Total	423246.040	99			

Having obtained a significant result, you can also go further and determine, using Tukey's HSD test, where the significance lies; that is, between which cities is there a significant difference in energy costs? You can see by looking at the results of the Tukey test in the table that follows that Adelaide and Perth have significantly different mean energy costs.

Multiple Comparisons

cost of electricity and gas

Tukey HSD

(I) city	(J) city	Mean Difference (I-J)	Std. Error	Sig.	95% Confidence Interval	
					Lower Bound	Upper Bound
Adelaide	Hobart	-18.560	17.755	.723	-64.98	27.86
	Melbourne	-33.920	17.755	.231	-80.34	12.50
	Perth	-57.840*	17.755	.008	-104.26	-11.42
Hobart	Adelaide	18.560	17.755	.723	-27.86	64.98
	Melbourne	-15.360	17.755	.823	-61.78	31.06
	Perth	-39.280	17.755	.127	-85.70	7.14
Melbourne	Adelaide	33.920	17.755	.231	-12.50	80.34
	Hobart	15.360	17.755	.823	-31.06	61.78
	Perth	-23.920	17.755	.535	-70.34	22.50
Perth	Adelaide	57.840*	17.755	.008	11.42	104.26
	Hobart	39.280	17.755	.127	-7.14	85.70
	Melbourne	23.920	17.755	.535	-22.50	70.34

*. The mean difference is significant at the 0.05 level.

Handy hint
- Remember to meet the assumptions of ANOVA, namely population normality and homogeneity of variance.

CHAPTER 8

One-way between-groups ANOVA with planned comparisons

Planned (or *a priori*) comparisons are used when you have specific expectations or predictions about some of the results. These comparisons are often of theoretical importance and are planned from the onset of the study. Post-hoc comparisons, on the other hand, such as Tukey's honestly significantly different (HSD) test outlined in chapter 7, are not theoretically driven. Instead, every possible comparison is performed to detect significant effects.

Both planned and post-hoc analyses have problems with type I and type II error properties. For example, in relation to planned comparisons, there are problems associated with performing multiple statistical tests on a set of data. This increases the vulnerability of the test to Type I errors. The more tests you perform, the greater the chances of Type I error on at least one of those tests. You should be familiar with two types of Type I error rate. These include:

1   **The per comparison error rate:** the error rate in a single comparison. For each comparison that you make, the alpha level is set at .05.

2   **The familywise error rate:** the cumulative effects of doing many separate tests. It is the probability that you have made at least one type I error in the complete set of comparisons you have undertaken. For example, if you wish to make three comparisons, each at an alpha level of .05, then the familywise error rate would be 0.15, which is equal to $3 \times .05$.

There is much debate whether the familywise error rate should be controlled when performing multiple planned comparisons. In most instances, you are permitted to perform one fewer comparison than the number of levels or groups of your independent variable. For example, with three levels, you could perform two comparisons without any difficulty. However, if further comparisons are required using the same data, then a more strict alpha level should be adopted. The Bonferroni test helps you determine the appropriate alpha level to be used to evaluate the significance of the comparisons. If you wish to conduct four comparisons using a familywise error rate of .15, then each comparison would have to be evaluated against an alpha level of .025, which is the closest alpha value to .0375 (.15/4).

In chapter 7 you discovered how post-hoc tests, such as Tukey's HSD test, can be used to locate significant differences among groups on a dependent variable. However, if you have theoretical reasons for hypothesising differences, you can also conduct planned comparisons to investigate the nature of those differences. A comparison between any two of the group means is referred to as a simple pairwise comparison. It is also possible to conduct more complex planned or post-hoc comparisons.

In analysis of variance (ANOVA), the null hypothesis states that all population means associated with each group or condition under investigation are the same. Furthermore, if the null hypothesis is true, the difference (comparison value) between any simple or complex comparison of population means must be zero. To specify the comparison between any mean (or average of a set of means) and any other mean (or average of a different set of means) requires that means for the appropriate groups are weighted using a set of coefficients. A description of how these coefficients are established is beyond the scope of this chapter, but information regarding coefficients can be obtained from any good statistical text.

Assumption testing

In relation to assumption testing, planned and post-hoc analyses are based on the analytic procedure that precedes them. In this chapter, you are addressing the use of planned comparisons with the one-way ANOVA procedure, so the assumptions underlying this test apply.

Working example

A dietary consultant has asked you to test the efficacy of three weight-reduction programs. Carbohydrates were restricted in program A, protein was restricted in program B and fats were restricted in program C. Ten overweight volunteers were randomly assigned to each of the programs, and their weight loss after eight weeks was recorded in kilograms. Positive scores signify a weight drop. The dietitian predicted that the diet type would influence the weight loss, and that the loss would be greatest for those restricting fats (program C). Before analysis, checks for normality were conducted and considered to be acceptable.

The data can be found in Work8.sav on the website that accompanies this title and are shown in the following figure.

Work8.sav [DataSet2] - PASW Statistics Data Editor

File Edit View Data Transform Analyze Graphs Utilities Add-ons Window Help

1 : diet   1   Visible: 2 of 2 Variables

	diet	wtloss	var	var	var	var	var	var	var	var	var	var	var
1	1	6											
2	1	5											
3	1	7											
4	1	3											
5	1	3											
6	1	3											
7	1	7											
8	1	5											
9	1	4											
10	1	6											
11	2	5											
12	2	6											
13	2	7											
14	2	4											
15	2	8											
16	2	3											
17	2	7											
18	2	5											
19	2	4											
20	2	6											
21	3	8											
22	3	9											
23	3	7											
24	3	11											

Data View Variable View

PASW Statistics Processor is ready

 To conduct a one-way ANOVA with a planned comparison

1   Select the **Analyze** menu.

2   Click on **Compare Means** and **One-Way ANOVA...** to open the **One-Way ANOVA** dialogue box.

3   Select the dependent variable (i.e. *wtloss*) and click on the ⏵ button to move the variable into the **Dependent List:** box.

4   Select the independent variable (i.e. *diet*) and click on the ⏵ button to move the variable into the **Factor:** box.

5   Click on the **Options...** command pushbutton to open the **One-Way ANOVA: Options** subdialogue box.

6   Select the check boxes for **Descriptive** and **Homogeneity of variance test**.

```
┌─────────────────────────────────────────┐
│ ▦ One-Way ANOVA: Options        [___x__] │
│ ┌─Statistics─────────────────────────┐   │
│ │ ☑ Descriptive                      │   │
│ │ ☐ Fixed and random effects         │   │
│ │ ☑ Homogeneity of variance test     │   │
│ │ ☐ Brown-Forsythe                   │   │
│ │ ☐ Welch                            │   │
│ └────────────────────────────────────┘   │
│   ☐ Means plot                            │
│ ┌─Missing Values─────────────────────┐   │
│ │ ◉ Exclude cases analysis by analysis│  │
│ │ ○ Exclude cases listwise            │  │
│ └────────────────────────────────────┘   │
│   [ Continue ]  [ Cancel ]  [ Help ]      │
└─────────────────────────────────────────┘
```

7   Click on **Continue.**

8   Click on the **Contrasts...** command pushbutton to open the **One-Way ANOVA: Contrasts** subdialogue box.

9   In the **Coefficients:** box, type the value of the coefficient for the first group (i.e. *−1*) and click on **Add** to move the coefficient into the box below.

10   In the **Coefficients:** box, type the value of the coefficient for the second group (i.e. *−1*) and click on **Add**.

11   In the **Coefficients:** box, type the value of the coefficient for the third group (i.e. *2*) and click on **Add**. If all the coefficients have been entered correctly, the **Coefficient Total:** should equal zero.

12   Click on **Continue** and then **OK**.

Descriptives

weight loss

	N	Mean	Std. Deviation	Std. Error	95% Confidence Interval for Mean Lower Bound	95% Confidence Interval for Mean Upper Bound	Minimum	Maximum
restricted carbohydrate	10	4.90	1.595	.504	3.76	6.04	3	7
restricted protein	10	5.50	1.581	.500	4.37	6.63	3	8
restricted fat	10	8.40	1.776	.562	7.13	9.67	5	11
Total	30	6.27	2.227	.407	5.43	7.10	3	11

An examination of the Levene test for homogeneity of variances (follows) suggests that this assumption has not been violated (p > .05) and, therefore, interpretation of the ANOVA can proceed.

Test of Homogeneity of Variances

weight loss

Levene Statistic	df1	df2	Sig.
.038	2	27	.963

ANOVA

weight loss

	Sum of Squares	df	Mean Square	F	Sig.
Between Groups	70.067	2	35.033	12.817	.000
Within Groups	73.800	27	2.733		
Total	143.867	29			

The F-ratio with an F-probability value less than .05 is significant, suggesting that type of diet does significantly influence weight loss, $F(2,27) = 12.817$, $p < .05$.

Means and standard deviations for each group are illustrated. The contrast coefficient matrix gives the coefficients that have been assigned for each group or level of the independent variable. For example, program A, program B and program C have coefficients of -1, -1 and 2 respectively.

Contrast Coefficients

Contrast	diet program restricted carbohydrate	diet program restricted protein	diet program restricted fat
1	-1	-1	2

Contrast Tests

	Contrast	Value of Contrast	Std. Error	t	df	Sig. (2-tailed)
weight loss Assume equal variances	1	6.40	1.281	4.998	27	.000
Does not assume equal variances	1	6.40	1.329	4.815	16.327	.000

You have not violated the assumption of homogeneity of variance, so you can consult the 'Assume equal variances' row for Contrast 1. To interpret this contrast you need to examine both the t-value and the t-probability value. A t-value of 4.988 is highly significant (t-probability < .05). Because you have made only one comparison, it is not necessary to adjust this significance level to evaluate the comparison.

An examination of the means for each of these groups, located in the descriptive statistics section of the output, indicates that a significantly greater reduction in weight was made by those in program C than in either of the other programs. Therefore, you can conclude that individuals restricting their fat intake lose significantly more weight than do those restricting either their protein or carbohydrate intake, $F(1,27) = 24.98$, $p < .05$.

As outlined, to report the planned comparison, the t-value is squared to obtain an F-value. Also note that the df1 for planned comparisons is always 1. The df2 value is that which corresponds to the within-groups estimate in the ANOVA summary table.

Handy hints
- Assumption testing depends on the analytical tests that were conducted before planned and post-hoc analysis. However, ensure population normality and homogeneity of variance (these assumptions should also be met for two-way between-groups ANOVA featured in chapter 9).
- Remember that the coefficient total should equal zero (e.g. $-1 + -1 + 2 = 0$).

CHAPTER 9

Two-way between-groups ANOVA

The two-way analysis of variance (ANOVA) operates in the same manner as the one-way ANOVA except that you are examining an additional independent variable. Each independent variable may possess two or more levels. In a two-factor between-groups design, each participant has been randomly assigned to only one of the different levels of each independent variable. Each of the different cells represents the unique combinations of the levels of the two factors.

Assumption testing

Before you can conduct the two-way ANOVA, you must ensure that the necessary assumptions are met. The assumptions for two-way ANOVA are the same as those for the one-way ANOVA:

1 **Population normality:** the populations from which the samples have been drawn should be normal. Check this for each group using normality statistics such as skewness and Shapiro–Wilk.

2 **Homogeneity of variance:** the scores in each group should have homogeneous variances.

You are primarily concerned with violations to the second assumption because these could mean that your data have been evaluated at a significance level greater than you initially assumed. Rather than being significant at the alpha level of .05, your results may really be significant at only an alpha level of .10. This is because violations of the homogeneity assumption distort the shape of the F-distribution so that the critical F-value no longer corresponds to a cut-off of 5 per cent.

> **Automated Data Preparation Module**
>
> In addition to the IBM SPSS Base, the IBM SPSS Data Preparation add-on module contains an Automated Data Preparation (ADP) procedure which can help you detect errors or anomalies in your data, as well as correct and impute missing values.
>
> The **automatic** feature of the ADP procedure automatically identifies and applies fixes to your data. It creates new *transformed* variables in addition to the original variables, allowing you to run the two-way ANOVA on two models — one on the prepared (transformed) data and the other on the unprepared (untransformed) data. You might find changes in significance of certain predictors between both the prepared and unprepared models. Nonparametric correlations analysis (e.g. Kendall's tau-b and Spearman's rho measures) may be performed to determine if predictors in the prepared model are more strongly correlated with the dependent variable, relative to the unprepared model. A stronger correlation between the prepared model and the observed values would suggest that running the automated data preparation has improved the overall model.

Working example

A toy distributor wished to determine which stores were the most successful in selling their stock. The distributor wished to compare the sales in different types of store in different locations: in discount toy stores, department stores and variety stores, and stores in either the central city district or in suburban shopping centres. Therefore, the first independent variable was store type, with three levels; the second independent variable was location, with two levels; and the dependent variable was the amount of toy sales in $1000s per week. Therefore, you have a 3×2 factorial design with six data cells ($3 \times 2 = 6$). Four stores were randomly chosen for each of the six cells ($n = 4$); sales from a total of 24 stores were recorded ($N = 24$).

The toy distributor wishes to ask three questions:

1 Does the type of store influence the sales of toys?

2 Does the location of the store influence the sales of toys?

3 Does the influence of the store type on toy sales depend on the location of the store?

Questions 1 and 2 refer to main effects, while question 3 examines the interaction of the two independent variables on the dependent variable.

The data can be found in Work9.sav on the website that accompanies this title and are shown in the following figure.

	location	type	sales
1	1	1	1
2	1	1	4
3	1	1	0
4	1	1	7
5	1	2	13
6	1	2	5
7	1	2	7
8	1	2	15
9	1	3	9
10	1	3	16
11	1	3	18
12	1	3	13
13	2	1	15
14	2	1	6
15	2	1	10
16	2	1	13
17	2	2	6
18	2	2	18
19	2	2	9
20	2	2	15
21	2	3	14
22	2	3	7
23	2	3	6
24	2	3	13

To conduct a two-way ANOVA

1 Select the **Analyze** menu.

2 Click on **General Linear Model** and then **Univariate...** to open the **Univariate** dialogue box.

3 Select the dependent variable (i.e. *sales*) and click on the ⊡ button to move the variable into the **Dependent Variable:** box.

4   Select the independent variables (i.e. *location* and *type*) and click on the ⏎ button to move the variables into the **Fixed Factor(s):** box.

5   Click on the **Options...** command pushbutton to open the **Univariate: Options** subdialogue box.

6   In the **Display** box, click on the **Descriptive statistics, Estimates of effect size, Observed power** and **Homogeneity tests** check boxes.

7   Click on **Continue** and then **OK**.

Descriptive Statistics

Dependent Variable:toy sales in $1000 per week

location of store	type of toy store	Mean	Std. Deviation	N
city central	variety store	3.00	3.162	4
	department store	10.00	4.761	4
	discount toy store	14.00	3.916	4
	Total	9.00	5.970	12
suburban shopping centre	variety store	11.00	3.916	4
	department store	12.00	5.477	4
	discount toy store	10.00	4.082	4
	Total	11.00	4.200	12
Total	variety store	7.00	5.398	8
	department store	11.00	4.870	8
	discount toy store	12.00	4.276	8
	Total	10.00	5.150	24

Levene's Test of Equality of Error Variances[a]

Dependent Variable:toy sales in $1000 per week

F	df1	df2	Sig.
1.000	5	18	.446

Tests the null hypothesis that the error variance of the dependent variable is equal across groups.

a. Design: Intercept + location + type + location * type

The Levene's test tells us that the homogeneity of variance assumption has not been violated. The output illustrates that the main effects for location and store type are not significant ($p > .05$). Therefore, neither store type nor location significantly influences the sales of toys.

Tests of Between-Subjects Effects

Dependent Variable:toy sales in $1000 per week

Source	Type III Sum of Squares	df	Mean Square	F	Sig.	Partial Eta Squared	Noncent. Parameter	Observed Power[b]
Corrected Model	280.000[a]	5	56.000	3.055	.036	.459	15.273	.742
Intercept	2400.000	1	2400.000	130.909	.000	.879	130.909	1.000
location	24.000	1	24.000	1.309	.268	.068	1.309	.192
type	112.000	2	56.000	3.055	.072	.253	6.109	.517
location * type	144.000	2	72.000	3.927	.038	.304	7.855	.630
Error	330.000	18	18.333					
Total	3010.000	24						
Corrected Total	610.000	23						

a. R Squared = .459 (Adjusted R Squared = .309)

b. Computed using alpha = .05

Because neither main effect is significant, post-hoc analyses are not required. If significant main effects had been obtained, a comparison of marginal means for each effect would have been necessary. You may have noticed that means can be displayed for particular factors in the **Univariate Options** dialogue box.

The output also shows that there is a significant interaction effect ($p < .05$) for location * type. That is, the influence of store type on sales does depend on the location of the store, $F(2,18) = 3.927$, $p < .05$.

With a significant interaction effect, you are interested in conducting a simple effects analysis, and simple comparisons if the simple effects are significant. In addition, interpretation is facilitated by plotting the cell means.

Effect sizes and observed power are also provided. Profile plots could be obtained as part of the analysis but the following procedure gives a clearer picture of the interaction.

▶ **To plot the cell means**

1   Select the **Graphs** menu.

2   Select the **Legacy Dialogs** option.

3   Click on **Line...** to open the **Line Charts** dialogue box.

4   Click on the **Multiple** box and ensure that the **Summaries for groups of cases** radio button has been selected.

5   Click on the **Define** command pushbutton to open the **Define Multiple Line: Summaries for Groups of Cases** subdialogue box.

6   In the **Lines Represent** box, select the **Other statistic (e.g., mean)** radio button.

7   Select the dependent variable (i.e. *sales*) and click on the ▶ button to move the variable into the **Variable:** box.

8   Select the independent variable with the most levels (i.e. *type*) and click on the button to move the variable into the **Category Axis:** box.

9   Select the other independent variable (i.e. *location*) and click on the button to move the variable into the **Define Lines by:** box. You will notice a **Titles...** command pushbutton in the top right-hand side of the window, which allows you to give titles to the lines of the graph. You can add a title for your graph if you want to.

Define Multiple Line: Summaries for Groups of Cases

Lines Represent
- ○ N of cases
- ○ Cum. N
- ◉ Other statistic (e.g., mean)
- ○ % of cases
- ○ Cum. %

Variable:
MEAN(toy sales in $1000 per w...

Change Statistic...

Category Axis:
type of toy store [type]

Define Lines by:
location of store [location]

Panel by

Rows:

☐ Nest variables (no empty rows)

Columns:

☐ Nest variables (no empty columns)

Template
☐ Use chart specifications from:
File...

Titles...
Options...

OK   Paste   Reset   Cancel   Help

10   Click on **OK**.

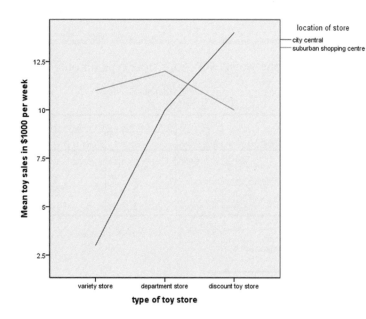

The graph shows that for suburban shopping centres, the type of store has no influence on the sale of toys. However, in the city centre, the type of store has considerable impact: discount toy stores have the highest sales.

When you have obtained a significant interaction, it is necessary to conduct an analysis of simple effects. That is, you need to look at the effect of one factor at only one level of the other factor. For example, you may be interested in looking at the effect of location on the variety stores, department stores or discount toy stores. Likewise, you could analyse the effect of the type of store just in the city centre or just for suburban shopping centres. In each case you would be analysing simple effects. If you were interested in looking at suburban shopping centres, you would first have to select only those cases in which stores were located in the suburbs. You can achieve this by using the **Select Cases** option in the **Data** menu or clicking the **Select Cases** tool.

	location	type	sales	filter_$
1	1	1	1	0
2	1	1	4	0
3	1	1	0	0
4	1	1	7	0
5	1	2	13	0
6	1	2	5	0
7	1	2	7	0
8	1	2	15	0
9	1	3	9	0
10	1	3	16	0
11	1	3	18	0
12	1	3	13	0
13	2	1	15	1
14	2	1	6	1
15	2	1	10	1
16	2	1	13	1
17	2	2	6	1
18	2	2	18	1
19	2	2	9	1
20	2	2	15	1
21	2	3	14	1
22	2	3	7	1
23	2	3	6	1
24	2	3	13	1

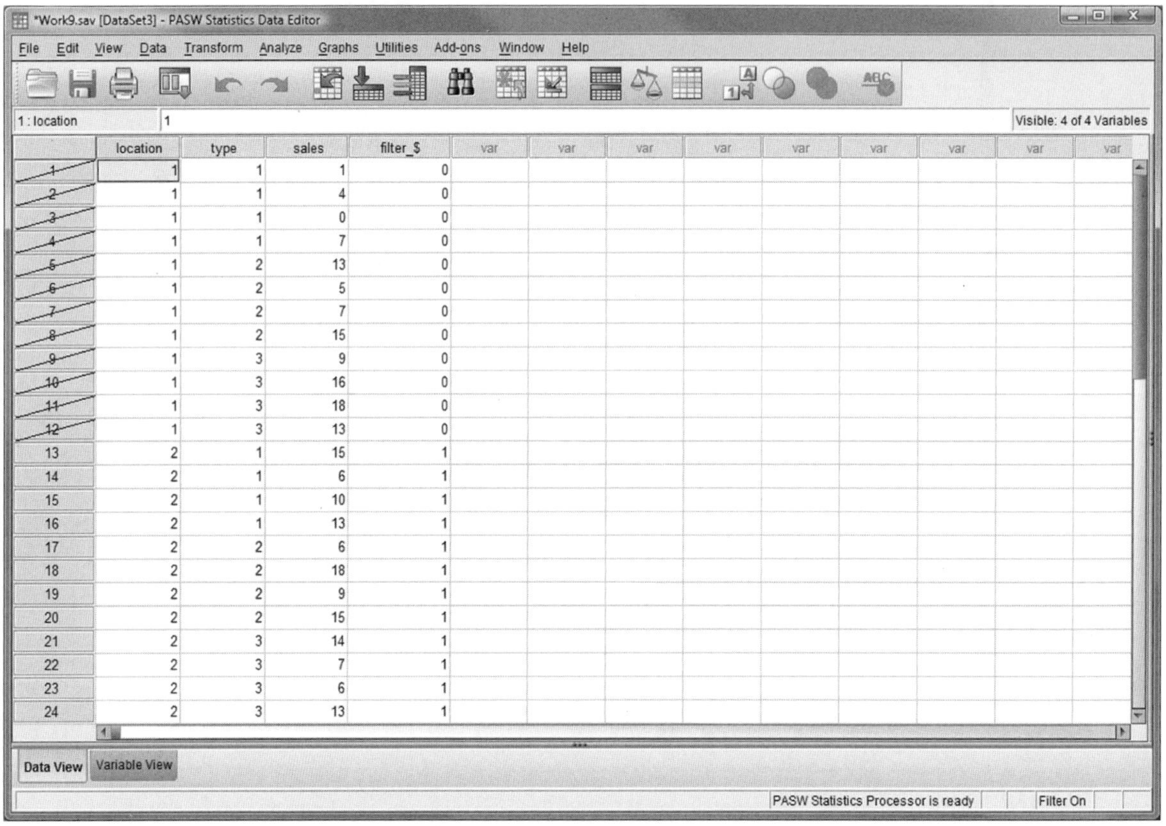

You would then conduct a one-way ANOVA for store type for only these selected cases.

Descriptives

toy sales in $1000 per week

	N	Mean	Std. Deviation	Std. Error	95% Confidence Interval for Mean		Minimum	Maximum
					Lower Bound	Upper Bound		
variety store	4	11.00	3.916	1.958	4.77	17.23	6	15
department store	4	12.00	5.477	2.739	3.28	20.72	6	18
discount toy store	4	10.00	4.082	2.041	3.50	16.50	6	14
Total	12	11.00	4.200	1.212	8.33	13.67	6	18

Test of Homogeneity of Variances

toy sales in $1000 per week

Levene Statistic	df1	df2	Sig.
1.050	2	9	.389

ANOVA

toy sales in $1000 per week

	Sum of Squares	df	Mean Square	F	Sig.
Between Groups	8.000	2	4.000	.194	.827
Within Groups	186.000	9	20.667		
Total	194.000	11			

Having conducted this analysis, you could take this simple effect and perform simple comparisons. However, simple comparisons are usually performed only if the relevant simple effect proves to be significant. In this case, the effect is not significant.

If simple comparisons were required, then appropriate coefficients would have to be determined. That is, you would need to establish which means you were interested in comparing. For example, if you have obtained a significant simple effect for store type in suburban shopping centres, then you may be interested in determining whether discount stores had higher sales than department or variety stores. Remember, you are still only dealing with suburban shopping centres.

Consistent with conducting trend analysis, it is also important to remember that the significance of the contrast F-ratio must be evaluated using the residual mean square from the omnibus test. That is, the residual mean square from the original two-way ANOVA summary table is used. For this example, the mean square residual for the two-way ANOVA is equal to *18.333*. Again, the first degree of freedom (df) for all contrasts is 1, while the second df is the value for the residual estimate from the two-way ANOVA summary table (i.e. *18*).

IBM SPSS can also be used to analyse data from more complex factorial designs with three or more independent variables. With these designs, the interpretation of interaction effects becomes extremely complex.

CHAPTER 10

One-way repeated-measures ANOVA

In chapter 7 you examined the analysis of an independent groups experimental design in which a different group of participants served in each of the conditions. That is, you used an independent-groups analysis of variance (ANOVA) to detect differences in group means.

You are now interested in refining the experimental design to increase its sensitivity to detecting differences in the dependent variable. A major source of experimental error is individual differences, which can be controlled by using a repeated-measures or within-subjects design. By having the same participants perform under every condition, you eliminate systematic bias attributable to participants in one group being different from the participants in other groups.

Assumption testing

Three of the four assumptions underlying the repeated-measures ANOVA are similar to those of the independent-groups design:

1   **Random selection:** the sample should be independently and randomly selected from the population of interest.

2   **Normality:** each population of scores should have a normal distribution.

3   **Homogeneity of variance:** the different populations of scores should have homogeneous variances. This is assessed by obtaining variances for each group and dividing the largest variance by the smallest variance to obtain an F-max value. If this ratio is greater than three, then the assumption has been violated and the resulting F-ratio must be evaluated at a more conservative alpha level.

4   **Sphericity:** the variance of the population difference scores for any two conditions should be the same as the variance of the population difference scores for any other two conditions.

Assumption 1 is a matter of research design, while assumption 2 can be tested by using statistics outlined in chapter 3. Assumptions 3 and 4 are assessed as part of the analysis.

Working example

You wish to determine whether practice increases the ability to solve anagrams. Eight participants were asked to solve as many anagrams as possible in ten minutes. They were then allowed to practise for an hour before being asked to complete another ten-minute timed task. Participants were then given another practice session and another timed task. The number of anagrams correctly solved was recorded.

The data can be found in Work10.sav on the website that accompanies this title and are shown in the following figure.

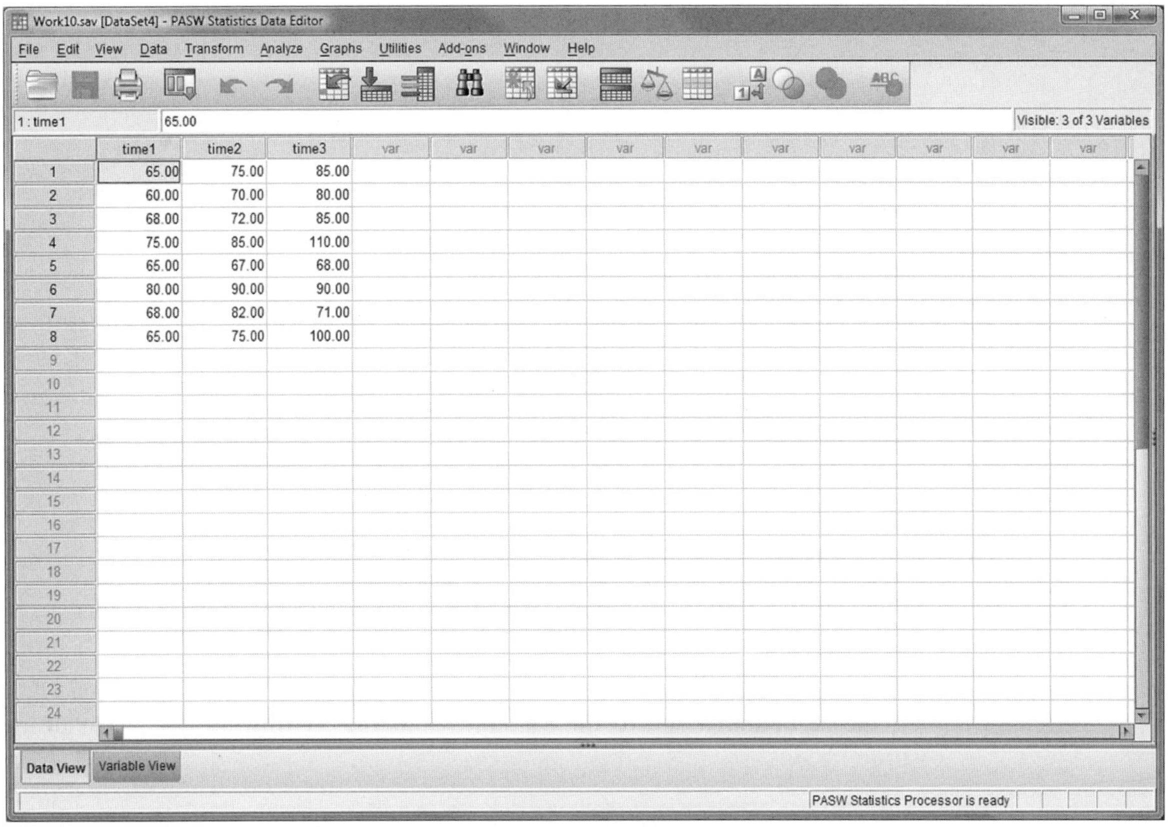

	time1	time2	time3
1	65.00	75.00	85.00
2	60.00	70.00	80.00
3	68.00	72.00	85.00
4	75.00	85.00	110.00
5	65.00	67.00	68.00
6	80.00	90.00	90.00
7	68.00	82.00	71.00
8	65.00	75.00	100.00

To conduct a repeated-measures ANOVA

1. Select the **Analyze** menu.
2. Click on **General Linear Model** and then **Repeated Measures...** to open the **Repeated Measures Define Factor(s)** dialogue box.
3. In the **Within-Subject Factor Name:** box, type the name for the within-subjects factor (i.e. *time*).
4. In the **Number of Levels:** box, type the number of levels of that particular factor (i.e. *3*).
5. Click on **Add** to move this information into the box below.

6 Click on the **Define** command pushbutton to open the **Repeated Measures** subdialogue box.

7 Select the three within-subjects variables (i.e. *time1*, *time2* and *time3*) and click on the ⊡ button to move the variables into the **Within-Subjects Variables (time):** box.

8 Click on the **Options...** command pushbutton to open the **Repeated Measures: Options** subdialogue box.

9 In the **Display** box, click on the **Descriptive statistics**, **Estimates of effect size** and **Observed power** check boxes.

Repeated Measures: Options

Estimated Marginal Means

Factor(s) and Factor Interactions:
(OVERALL)
time

Display Means for:

☐ Compare main effects

Confidence interval adjustment:
LSD(none)

Display

☑ Descriptive statistics   ☐ Transformation matrix
☑ Estimates of effect size ☐ Homogeneity tests
☑ Observed power   ☐ Spread vs. level plot
☐ Parameter estimates   ☐ Residual plot
☐ SSCP matrices   ☐ Lack of fit
☐ Residual SSCP matrix   ☐ General estimable function

Significance level: .05   Confidence intervals are 95.0 %

Continue   Cancel   Help

10 Click on **Continue** and then **OK**.

Before interpretation of the output, the assumption of homogeneity of variance was assessed by calculating F-max. No violation of this assumption was found.

For a one-way within-subjects ANOVA, IBM SPSS produces a lot of output: statistics for evaluating the sphericity assumption; traditional univariate ANOVA results and ANOVA results using multivariate tests. The summary tables for between-subjects effects and within-subjects contrasts are not discussed here.

Descriptive Statistics

	Mean	Std. Deviation	N
correct anagrams at time 1	68.2500	6.36396	8
correct anagrams at time 2	77.0000	7.92825	8
correct anagrams at time 3	86.1250	14.01466	8

Multivariate Tests^c

Effect		Value	F	Hypothesis df	Error df	Sig.	Partial Eta Squared	Noncent. Parameter	Observed Power^b
time	Pillai's Trace	.876	21.234^a	2.000	6.000	.002	.876	42.469	.994
	Wilks' Lambda	.124	21.234^a	2.000	6.000	.002	.876	42.469	.994
	Hotelling's Trace	7.078	21.234^a	2.000	6.000	.002	.876	42.469	.994
	Roy's Largest Root	7.078	21.234^a	2.000	6.000	.002	.876	42.469	.994

a. Exact statistic
b. Computed using alpha = .05
c. Design: Intercept
Within Subjects Design: time

Mauchly's Test of Sphericity[b]

Measure:MEASURE_1

Within Subjects Effect	Mauchly's W	Approx. Chi-Square	df	Sig.	Epsilon[a]		
					Greenhouse-Geisser	Huynh-Feldt	Lower-bound
time	.254	8.234	2	.016	.573	.612	.500

Tests the null hypothesis that the error covariance matrix of the orthonormalized transformed dependent variables is proportional to an identity matrix.

a. May be used to adjust the degrees of freedom for the averaged tests of significance. Corrected tests are displayed in the Tests of Within-Subjects Effects table.

b. Design: Intercept
Within Subjects Design: time

Before you can interpret the F-ratio of the within-subjects effect (time), you must first ensure that the assumption of sphericity has not been violated. The value for Mauchly is equal to .254 and is significant (p < .05). You must therefore evaluate the obtained F-ratio using new degrees of freedom (dfs), which are calculated using the Huynh-Feldt Epsilon (.612). The new dfs are 1.22 and 8.56 (2 × .61, 14 × .61), compared with 2 and 14. An examination of the critical F-tables (available in any good statistical text) indicates that the F-ratio is still significant when using the new dfs.

Tests of Within-Subjects Effects

Measure:MEASURE_1

Source		Type III Sum of Squares	df	Mean Square	F	Sig.	Partial Eta Squared	Noncent. Parameter	Observed Power[a]
time	Sphericity Assumed	1278.250	2	639.125	11.777	.001	.627	23.554	.979
	Greenhouse-Geisser	1278.250	1.145	1116.226	11.777	.008	.627	13.487	.876
	Huynh-Feldt	1278.250	1.223	1045.066	11.777	.006	.627	14.405	.894
	Lower-bound	1278.250	1.000	1278.250	11.777	.011	.627	11.777	.836
Error(time)	Sphericity Assumed	759.750	14	54.268					
	Greenhouse-Geisser	759.750	8.016	94.778					
	Huynh-Feldt	759.750	8.562	88.736					
	Lower-bound	759.750	7.000	108.536					

a. Computed using alpha = .05

You will notice that both the multivariate and univariate summary tables show that the result is significant. There is a large effect size but the study may be overpowered. However, you have demonstrated that practice brings about changes in the ability to solve anagrams, F(1.22,8.56) = 11.77, p < .05. The exact location of these differences requires that contrasts be performed. Post-hoc analysis of this nature is beyond the scope of this chapter.

CHAPTER 11

Two-way repeated-measures ANOVA

Assumption testing

In the two-way repeated measures design you have two independent variables, with two or more levels, which are within-subject in nature. That is, each participant performs in all conditions.

The assumptions underlying the two-way repeated-measures analysis of variance (ANOVA) are identical to those outlined in the one-way repeated-measures ANOVA.

Working example

To illustrate the two-way repeated-measures ANOVA, you can use an example similar to the one you used for the two-way independent-groups design. Here, manager productivity is considered, which is reflected in sales across various store types and locations. Each manager oversees six stores: one of each type in each location. Remember, you wish to determine the effect of store type (variety, department and discount) and location (city centre or suburbs) on productivity, measured as sales of toys. The first independent variable is type of store, with three levels, the second independent variable is location, with two levels, and the dependent variable is the amount of toy sales in $1000s per week. Therefore, you have a 3×2 factorial design with six data cells ($3 \times 2 = 6$). Given that four managers participated in each of the conditions, you have a total of 24 observations.

You wish to ask three questions:

1   Does the store type influence the amount of toy sales?

2   Does the store location influence the amount of toy sales?

3   Does the influence of store type on the amount of toy sales depend on the location of the store?

Questions 1 and 2 refer to main effects, while question 3 examines the effect of the interaction of the two independent variables on the dependent variable.

The data can be found in Work11.sav on the website that accompanies this title and are shown in the following figure.

	loc1typ1	loc1typ2	loc1typ3	loc2typ1	loc2typ2	loc2typ3	var	var	var	var	var	var	var
1	1	13	9	15	6	14							
2	4	5	16	6	18	7							
3	0	7	18	10	9	6							
4	7	15	13	13	15	13							

To conduct a two-way repeated-measures ANOVA

1   Select the **Analyze** menu.

2   Click on **General Linear Model** and then on **Repeated Measures...** to open the **Repeated Measures Define Factor(s)** dialogue box.

3   In the **Within-Subject Factor Name:** box, type the name for the first within-subjects factor (i.e. *location*).

4   In the **Number of Levels:** box, type the number of levels of that particular factor (i.e. *2*).

5   Click on **Add** to move this information into the box below.

6   In the **Within-Subject Factor Name:** box, type the name for the second within-subjects factor (i.e. *type*).

7   In the **Number of Levels:** box, type the number of levels of that particular factor (i.e. *3*).

8   Click on **Add** to move this information into the box below.

9 Click on the **Define** command pushbutton to open the **Repeated Measures** subdialogue box.

10 Select the six within-subjects variables (i.e. *loc1typ1*, *loc1typ2*, *loc1typ3*, *loc2typ1*, *loc2typ2*, *loc2typ3*) and click on the ▣ button to move the variables into their appropriate places within the **Within-Subjects Variables (location, type): box** (i.e. *loc1typ1 > {1,1}*, *loc1typ2 > {1,2}* and so on).

11 Click on the **Options...** command pushbutton to open the **Repeated Measures: Options** subdialogue box.

12 In the **Display** box, click on the **Descriptive statistics**, **Estimates of effect size** and **Observed power** check boxes.

13 Click on **Continue** and then **OK**.

Descriptive Statistics

	Mean	Std. Deviation	N
city, variety store	3.00	3.162	4
city department store	10.00	4.761	4
city discount store	14.00	3.916	4
suburb variety store	11.00	3.916	4
suburb department store	12.00	5.477	4
suburb discount store	10.00	4.082	4

Mauchly's Test of Sphericity[b]

Measure:MEASURE_1

Within Subjects Effect	Mauchly's W	Approx. Chi-Square	df	Sig.	Epsilon[a]		
					Greenhouse-Geisser	Huynh-Feldt	Lower-bound
location	1.000	.000	0	.	1.000	1.000	1.000
type	.918	.171	2	.918	.924	1.000	.500
location * type	.502	1.378	2	.502	.668	1.000	.500

Tests the null hypothesis that the error covariance matrix of the orthonormalized transformed dependent variables is proportional to an identity matrix.

a. May be used to adjust the degrees of freedom for the averaged tests of significance. Corrected tests are displayed in the Tests of Within-Subjects Effects table.

b. Design: Intercept

Within Subjects Design: location + type + location * type

Measure:MEASURE_1

Source		Type III Sum of Squares	df	Mean Square	F	Sig.	Partial Eta Squared	Noncent. Parameter	Observed Power[a]
location	Sphericity Assumed	24.000	1	24.000	6.000	.092	.667	6.000	.395
	Greenhouse-Geisser	24.000	1.000	24.000	6.000	.092	.667	6.000	.395
	Huynh-Feldt	24.000	1.000	24.000	6.000	.092	.667	6.000	.395
	Lower-bound	24.000	1.000	24.000	6.000	.092	.667	6.000	.395
Error(location)	Sphericity Assumed	12.000	3	4.000					
	Greenhouse-Geisser	12.000	3.000	4.000					
	Huynh-Feldt	12.000	3.000	4.000					
	Lower-bound	12.000	3.000	4.000					
type	Sphericity Assumed	112.000	2	56.000	10.723	.010	.781	21.447	.891
	Greenhouse-Geisser	112.000	1.849	60.589	10.723	.013	.781	19.823	.865
	Huynh-Feldt	112.000	2.000	56.000	10.723	.010	.781	21.447	.891
	Lower-bound	112.000	1.000	112.000	10.723	.047	.781	10.723	.600
Error(type)	Sphericity Assumed	31.333	6	5.222					
	Greenhouse-Geisser	31.333	5.546	5.650					
	Huynh-Feldt	31.333	6.000	5.222					
	Lower-bound	31.333	3.000	10.444					
location * type	Sphericity Assumed	144.000	2	72.000	1.929	.226	.391	3.857	.260
	Greenhouse-Geisser	144.000	1.335	107.857	1.929	.248	.391	2.575	.200
	Huynh-Feldt	144.000	2.000	72.000	1.929	.226	.391	3.857	.260
	Lower-bound	144.000	1.000	144.000	1.929	.259	.391	1.929	.168
Error(location*type)	Sphericity Assumed	224.000	6	37.333					
	Greenhouse-Geisser	224.000	4.005	55.926					
	Huynh-Feldt	224.000	6.000	37.333					
	Lower-bound	224.000	3.000	74.667					

a. Computed using alpha = .05

The main effect for location is not significant and, therefore, you can conclude that the location of the store does not influence the amount of toy sales.

Because the Mauchly test of sphericity for store type is not significant, you have not violated this assumption. The main effect for type of store is significant (p < .05), so you can conclude that toy sales are influenced by the type of store in which they are sold, $F(2,6) = 10.723$, p < .05. There is a large effect size and the power of the study is good.

Because the Mauchly test of sphericity for the interaction is not significant, you have not violated this assumption. The location by type of store interaction effect is not significant and, therefore, you can conclude that the differences in sales across type of store do not depend on the location of the store.

If post-hoc analysis was to follow, you would conduct a comparison of marginal means for the significant main effect, which can be calculated from the cell means in the output.

Handy hint
• Make sure that when conducting your two-way repeated-measures analysis that you move your within-subjects variables to their appropriate position in the **Within-Subjects Variables (location, type)** box.

Trend analysis

Sometimes, having determined that a significant effect exists, you may wish to determine the nature of the relationship by examining trends in the data. Post-hoc and planned comparisons could be performed between the treatment means, as discussed in chapters 7 and 8. This chapter discusses how you can test for different trends in the data, for example, a trend may be linear, quadratic or cubic. However, trend analysis is only appropriate when:

1   The levels of the independent variable can be considered to form an increasing or decreasing continuum.

2   The intervals between adjacent levels of the independent variable are equal or proportional.

When you conduct planned comparisons, you use coefficients to pick out and represent a particular combination of means you wish to compare. When you conduct trend analysis, you also use coefficients but those you select, when plotted, define the particular shape of the curve that you are testing. These coefficients can be found in the tables of any good statistical text but when conducting trend analysis within IBM SPSS for Windows, linear and quadratic trend options already exist. In essence, trend analysis is a special case of planned comparisons.

Assumption testing

As outlined in chapter 11, trend analysis follows analysis of variance (ANOVA) and, therefore, the assumptions of ANOVA must be met.

Working example

A cognitive psychologist was interested in whether reaction time (RT) declined as a function of age. She obtained random samples of 25 people from each of four age groups and measured the time it took each participant to press a button in response to a visual cue. The age groups she chose were 15–20 years, 35–40 years, 55–60 years and 75–80 years. The researcher expected that RT would increase consistently with age.

The data can be found in Work12.sav on the website that accompanies this title and are shown in the following figure.

To conduct a linear trend analysis

1   Select the **Analyze** menu.

2   Click on **Compare Means** and **One-Way ANOVA...** to open the **One-Way ANOVA** dialogue box.

3   Select the dependent variable (i.e. *rt*) and click on the ▶ button to move the variable into the **Dependent List:** box.

4   Select the independent variable (i.e. *age*) and click on the ▶ button to move the variable into the **Factor:** box.

5   Click on the **Options...** command pushbutton to open the **One-Way ANOVA: Options** subdialogue box.

6   Select the check boxes for **Descriptive** and **Homogeneity of variance test**.

7 Click on **Continue**.

8 Click on the **Contrasts...** command pushbutton to open the **One-Way ANOVA: Contrasts** subdialogue box.

9 Select the **Polynomial** check box.

10 In the **Degree:** drop-down list, ensure that the **Linear** trend is selected.

11 Click on **Continue** and then **OK**.

Descriptives

rt

	N	Mean	Std. Deviation	Std. Error	95% Confidence Interval for Mean		Minimum	Maximum
					Lower Bound	Upper Bound		
15-20	25	497.2800	56.62782	11.32556	473.9052	520.6548	383.00	621.00
35-40	25	515.8400	56.52925	11.30585	492.5059	539.1741	397.00	647.00
55-60	25	531.2000	63.97591	12.79518	504.7920	557.6080	397.00	677.00
75-80	25	555.1200	72.57601	14.51520	525.1621	585.0779	429.00	739.00
Total	100	524.8600	65.38511	6.53851	511.8862	537.8338	383.00	739.00

Test of Homogeneity of Variances

rt

Levene Statistic	df1	df2	Sig.
.817	3	96	.488

ANOVA

rt

			Sum of Squares	df	Mean Square	F	Sig.
Between Groups	(Combined)		44947.000	3	14982.333	3.802	.013
	Linear Term	Contrast	44594.568	1	44594.568	11.317	.001
		Deviation	352.432	2	176.216	.045	.956
Within Groups			378299.040	96	3940.615		
Total			423246.040	99			

Levene's test for homogeneity of variances is not significant (p > .05), indicating that the assumption has not been violated.

The ANOVA summary table shows a significant between-groups F-ratio ($p < .05$), so you can conclude that RT differs significantly across age groups, $F(3,96) = 3.802$, $p < .05$. Furthermore, by examining the linear term, which is also significant ($p < .05$), you can also conclude that RT increases consistently across age groups. Plotting these means illustrates a linear trend, as evident in the following figure. Remember, you can plot means using the **Graphs** menu and **Line Charts** submenu.

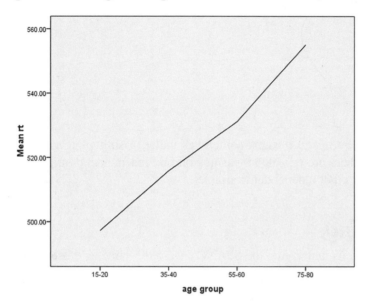

Trend analyses can also be conducted in the case of a one-way repeated-measures design or two-way independent and repeated-measures designs. First, the relevant simple effect must be extracted using the **Select Cases...** option in the **Data** menu or toolbar, then analysis for trend components is conducted using the **Contrasts...** procedure available in the **One-Way ANOVA** submenu. In the case of two-way designs, it is important to remember that the error term for the different trend F-ratios will be the within-groups or residual mean square from the overall ANOVA. That is, the mean square from the two-way ANOVA summary table is used.

Mixed/split plot design (SPANOVA)

In the two-way mixed designs sometimes called a split plot analysis of variance or SPANOVA, there are repeated measures on one independent variable and independent groups on the other independent variable.

Assumption testing

The assumptions underlying the SPANOVA are the same as those for the independent-groups and repeated-measures ANOVAs. A further assumption specifically applies to this analysis:

1   **Homogeneity of intercorrelations:** the pattern of intercorrelations among the various levels of the repeated measures factor(s) should be consistent from level to level of the between-subjects factor(s). This assumption is tested using Box's M statistic. This statistic is very sensitive, so it is recommended that an alpha level of .001 be used in its interpretation. Homogeneity is present when the statistic is not significant ($p > .001$).

Working example

A therapist wishes to determine the efficacy of a new treatment program for depression. She randomly assigns eight participants to either the treatment group or the control group. She asks each participant to complete a depression inventory before the treatment starts, immediately the treatment finishes and three months after completion. The first independent variable, time of test, is within-subjects in nature and has three levels. The second independent variable, treatment status, is a between-subjects factor with two levels. The dependent variable is the score on the depression inventory. Therefore, you have a 3×2 factorial design with six data cells ($3 \times 2 = 6$) and 48 observations.

The therapist wishes to ask three questions:

1   Do depression scores change with time?

2   Is the treatment more effective than the control?

3   Are there differential changes in depression scores for the treatment and control groups?

Questions 1 and 2 refer to main effects, while question 3 examines the effects of the interaction of the two independent variables on the dependent variable. The data can be found in Work13.sav on the website that accompanies this title and are shown in the following figure.

To conduct a SPANOVA

1 Select the **Analyze** menu.

2 Click on **General Linear Model** and then on **Repeated Measures...** to open the **Repeated Measures Define Factor(s)** dialogue box.

3 In the **Within-Subject Factor Name:** box, type a name for the within-subjects factor (i.e. *time*), then tab. In the **Number of Levels:** box, type the number of levels of this factor (i.e. *3*).

4 Click on **Add** to move this information into the box below.

5   Click on the **Define** command pushbutton to open the **Repeated Measures** subdialogue box.

6   Select the variables representing the within-subjects factor (i.e. *pretest*, *posttest* and *followup*) and click on the ⊡ button to move these variables into the **Within-Subjects Variables: (time)** box.

7   Select the between-subjects variable (i.e. *treat*) and click on the ⊡ button to move this variable into the **Between-Subjects Factor(s):** box.

8   Click on the **Options...** command pushbutton to open the **Repeated Measures: Options** subdialogue box.

9   In the **Display** box, click on the **Descriptive statistics**, **Estimates of effect size**, **Observed power** and **Homogeneity tests** check boxes.

Repeated Measures: Options

Estimated Marginal Means

Factor(s) and Factor Interactions:
(OVERALL)
treat
time
treat*time

Display Means for:

☐ Compare main effects

Confidence interval adjustment:
LSD(none)

Display

☑ Descriptive statistics   ☐ Transformation matrix
☑ Estimates of effect size   ☑ Homogeneity tests
☑ Observed power   ☐ Spread vs. level plot
☐ Parameter estimates   ☐ Residual plot
☐ SSCP matrices   ☐ Lack of fit
☐ Residual SSCP matrix   ☐ General estimable function

Significance level: .05   Confidence intervals are 95.0 %

Continue   Cancel   Help

10   Click on **Continue** and then **OK**.

Descriptive Statistics

	treatment status	Mean	Std. Deviation	N
pre treatment depression score	treatment group	37.00	3.162	4
	control group	29.00	3.916	4
	Total	33.00	5.398	8
post treatment depression score	treatment group	30.00	4.761	4
	control group	28.00	5.477	4
	Total	29.00	4.870	8
follow up depression score	treatment group	26.00	3.916	4
	control group	30.00	4.082	4
	Total	28.00	4.276	8

Box's Test of Equality of Covariance Matrices[a]

Box's M	9.081
F	.659
df1	6
df2	260.830
Sig.	.683

Tests the null hypothesis that the observed covariance matrices of the dependent variables are equal across groups.

a. Design: Intercept + treat
Within Subjects Design: time

Because Box's M statistic is not significant (p > .001), you have not violated the assumption of homogeneity of variance–covariance matrices.

The Mauchly test of sphericity for time (below) is also not significant (p > .05) and so you have not violated the sphericity assumption.

Mauchly's Test of Sphericity[b]

Measure:MEASURE_1

Within Subjects Effect	Mauchly's W	Approx. Chi-Square	df	Sig.	Epsilon[a]		
					Greenhouse-Geisser	Huynh-Feldt	Lower-bound
time	.577	2.749	2	.253	.703	1.000	.500

Tests the null hypothesis that the error covariance matrix of the orthonormalized transformed dependent variables is proportional to an identity matrix.

a. May be used to adjust the degrees of freedom for the averaged tests of significance. Corrected tests are displayed in the Tests of Within-Subjects Effects table.

b. Design: Intercept + treat
Within Subjects Design: time

Tests of Within-Subjects Effects

Measure:MEASURE_1

Source		Type III Sum of Squares	df	Mean Square	F	Sig.	Partial Eta Squared	Noncent. Parameter	Observed Power[a]
time	Sphericity Assumed	112.000	2	56.000	2.632	.113	.305	5.264	.424
	Greenhouse-Geisser	112.000	1.406	79.686	2.632	.137	.305	3.699	.340
	Huynh-Feldt	112.000	2.000	56.000	2.632	.113	.305	5.264	.424
	Lower-bound	112.000	1.000	112.000	2.632	.156	.305	2.632	.278
time * treat	Sphericity Assumed	144.000	2	72.000	3.384	.068	.361	6.768	.525
	Greenhouse-Geisser	144.000	1.406	102.453	3.384	.093	.361	4.756	.421
	Huynh-Feldt	144.000	2.000	72.000	3.384	.068	.361	6.768	.525
	Lower-bound	144.000	1.000	144.000	3.384	.115	.361	3.384	.341
Error(time)	Sphericity Assumed	255.333	12	21.278					
	Greenhouse-Geisser	255.333	8.433	30.277					
	Huynh-Feldt	255.333	12.000	21.278					
	Lower-bound	255.333	6.000	42.556					

a. Computed using alpha = .05

Levene's Test of Equality of Error Variances[a]

	F	df1	df2	Sig.
pre treatment depression score	.200	1	6	.670
post treatment depression score	.231	1	6	.648
follow up depression score	.273	1	6	.620

Tests the null hypothesis that the error variance of the dependent variable is equal across groups.

a. Design: Intercept + treat
Within Subjects Design: time

Levene's test for homogeneity of variance is not significant, so this assumption is also not violated.

The main effect for time is not significant (p > .05) and, therefore, you can conclude that depression scores did not change significantly from the pretest to the followup.

The main effect for treatment is also not significant (p > .05) and so those participants in the treatment group did not fare any better than those in the control group. Consequently, the therapist must be very disappointed!

Tests of Between-Subjects Effects

Measure:MEASURE_1

Transformed Variable:Average

Source	Type III Sum of Squares	df	Mean Square	F	Sig.	Partial Eta Squared	Noncent. Parameter	Observed Power[a]
Intercept	21600.000	1	21600.000	1735.714	.000	.997	1735.714	1.000
treat	24.000	1	24.000	1.929	.214	.243	1.929	.217
Error	74.667	6	12.444					

a. Computed using alpha = .05

Last, the interaction effect is not significant (p > .05). Had the main effect for time or the interaction been significant, you would have needed to locate the source of these differences using post-hoc analysis.

Handy hints

- Ensure that the assumption of homogeneity of intercorrelations is met. The assumption is tested using Box's M statistic and is very sensitive, so ensure an alpha level of .001 is adopted.

- When conducting a SPANOVA and working in the **Repeated Measures** sub-dialogue box, ensure that you move the variables into their appropriate places within the **Within-Subjects Variables (time)** box.

14

One-way analysis of covariance (ANCOVA)

Analysis of covariance (ANCOVA) provides an elegant means of reducing systematic bias, as well as within-groups error, in the analysis. To determine whether the independent variable is indeed having an effect, the influence of an extraneous variable (covariate) on the dependent variable is statistically controlled during the analysis. That is, you attempt to reduce error variance due to individual differences. ANCOVA requires that different participants perform in each condition, and because of this is suitable for only between or independent groups designs.

Assumption testing

There are six assumptions that you need to address before conducting an ANCOVA:

1   **Independence:** the individual's scores on both the dependent variable and the covariate should be independent of those scores for all the other participants.

2   **Normality:** the dependent variable should have a normal distribution for participants with the same score on the covariate and in the same group. You want to obtain normality at each score on the covariate. If the scores for the covariate alone are normally distributed, then ANCOVA is robust to this assumption.

3   **Linearity:** a linear relationship should exist between the dependent variable and the covariate for each group. This can be verified by inspecting scatterplots for each group.

4   **Homogeneity of regression slopes:** the relationship of the dependent variable to the covariate in each group should be the same.

5   **Independence of covariate and treatments:** when you remove the proportion of shared variability between the dependent variable and the covariate, you must be careful that you do not also remove some of the effect of the independent variable. You can avoid this, to some extent, by measuring the covariate before the beginning of the experiment and also by randomly allocating participants to the different levels of the independent variable.

6   **Reliability of the covariate:** the instrument used to measure the covariate should be reliable.

Assumptions 1, 5 and 6 relate to experimental design, while assumption 2 has been explored in chapter 3. To test assumptions 3 and 4, the procedures outlined in the research example can be used.

Working example

A sales manager wished to determine whether women or men were more successful salespeople. He recorded the sales made by 22 sales representatives over a 12-month period. However, he was aware that years of selling experience would also contribute to the representatives' success and he thought it would be fairer to make the comparison while taking into account this added factor. Therefore, the dependent variable is sales in $1000s per year, the independent variable is gender (coded as 1 = male and 2 = female) and the covariate is years of experience in selling.

The data can be found in Work14.sav on the website that accompanies this title and are shown in the following figure.

	gender	years	sales
1	1	7	110
2	1	12	117
3	1	11	113
4	1	13	114
5	1	7	111
6	1	6	114
7	1	7	111
8	1	6	112
9	1	6	110
10	1	4	109
11	1	9	117
12	2	14	116
13	2	9	110
14	2	4	108
15	2	16	119
16	2	11	117
17	2	9	112
18	2	9	114
19	2	10	112
20	2	5	111
21	2	4	112
22	2	8	116

 Test for linearity

Assumptions of linearity need to be assessed for each level or group of the independent variable separately. The **Split File...** option can be used to select specific groups from the data file.

1   Select the **Data** menu and click on **Split File...** or click on the **Split File** tool to open the **Split File** dialogue box.

2   Select the **Organize output by groups** radio button, then select the group variable (i.e. *gender*) and click on the ⮕ button to move the variable into the **Groups Based on:** box.

3   Click on **OK**.

4   Select the **Graphs** menu and **Legacy Dialogs** option.

5   Click on **Scatter/Dot** to open the **Scatter/Dot** dialogue box. Notice that the **Simple Scatter** option is outlined by default.

6   Click on the **Define** command pushbutton to open the **Simple Scatterplot** subdialogue box.

7   Select the first variable (i.e. *sales*) and click on the ⬆ button to move the variable into the **Y Axis:** box.

8   Select the second variable (i.e. *years*) and click on the ⬆ button to move the variable into the **X Axis:** box.

9   Click on **OK**.

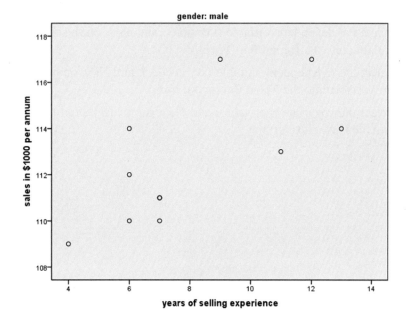

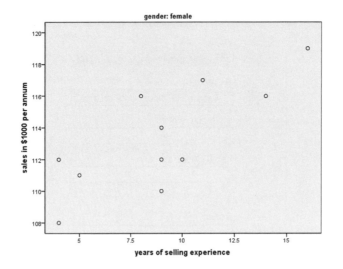

Both of these scatterplots indicate a linear relationship between the dependent variable (sales) and the covariate (years) for each group (male and female). In addition, it seems that the slope of the regression line is similar across groups. Therefore, you can confidently proceed with an ANCOVA.

Remember to turn the **Split File...** option off before conducting the ANCOVA. You do this by selecting the **Data** menu, clicking on **Split File...** to open the **Split File** dialogue box and selecting the **Analyse all cases, do not create groups** radio button. Click on **OK**. The split file option is now off and you are ready to continue.

 To conduct an ANCOVA

1   Select the **Analyze** menu.

2   Click on **General Linear Model** and then **Univariate...** to open the **Univariate** dialogue box.

3   Select the dependent variable (i.e. *sales*) and click on the ⊡ button to move the variable into the **Dependent Variable:** box.

4   Select the independent variable (i.e. *gender*), and click on the ⊡ button to move the variable into the **Fixed Factor(s):** box.

5   Select the covariate (i.e. *years*) and click on the ⊡ button to move the variable into the **Covariate(s):** box.

6   Click on the **Options...** command pushbutton to open the **Univariate: Options** subdialogue box.

7   In the **Display** box click on the **Descriptive statistics**, **Estimates of effect size**, **Observed power** and **Homogeneity tests** check boxes.

8   Click on **Continue** and then **OK**.

Descriptive Statistics

Dependent Variable:sales in $1000 per annum

gender	Mean	Std. Deviation	N
male	112.55	2.734	11
female	113.36	3.325	11
Total	112.95	3.000	22

Levene's Test of Equality of Error Variances[a]

Dependent Variable:sales in $1000 per annum

F	df1	df2	Sig.
.022	1	20	.884

Tests the null hypothesis that the error variance of the dependent variable is equal across groups.

a. Design: Intercept + years + gender

Levene's test is not significant (p > .05), indicating that the homogeneity of variance assumption has not been violated.

Tests of Between-Subjects Effects

Dependent Variable:sales in $1000 per annum

Source	Type III Sum of Squares	df	Mean Square	F	Sig.	Partial Eta Squared	Noncent. Parameter	Observed Power[b]
Corrected Model	106.353[a]	2	53.176	12.232	.000	.563	24.463	.988
Intercept	31745.528	1	31745.528	7302.092	.000	.997	7302.092	1.000
years	102.671	1	102.671	23.616	.000	.554	23.616	.996
gender	.116	1	.116	.027	.872	.001	.027	.053
Error	82.602	19	4.347					
Total	280881.000	22						
Corrected Total	188.955	21						

a. R Squared = .563 (Adjusted R Squared = .517)

b. Computed using alpha = .05

The output indicates no main effect (p > .05) for gender; but a significant relationship exists between sales and years of experience, $F(1,19) = 23.616$, p < .05. So it can be said that when you statistically control for years of experience, gender has no influence on the amount of sales made per year. The sales manager's hunch that sales success is related to years of selling experience is also confirmed.

If you had obtained a significant F-ratio for gender, and if you had more than two levels of the independent variable, then you would have had to tease out the source of the significance. Planned and post-hoc comparisons could be used to achieve this.

Handy hints

- Ensure that you address the assumptions of independence, normality, linearity, homogeneity of regression slopes, independence of covariate and treatments and reliability of the covariate before proceeding with your analysis. You have learned how to test these assumptions in this chapter and also in chapter 3. Independence, independence of covariate and treatments and reliability of the covariate are a matter of research design.

- Remember to turn the **Split File...** option off before conducting the ANCOVA. Do so by ensuring that the **Analyse all cases, do not create groups** radio button is selected in the **Split File** dialogue box.

CHAPTER 15

Reliability analysis

There are several different reliability coefficients. One of the most commonly used is Cronbach's alpha, which is based on the average correlation of items within a test if the items are standardised. If the items are not standardised, it is based on the average covariance among the items. Because Cronbach's alpha can be interpreted as a correlation coefficient, it ranges in value from 0 to 1. IBM SPSS output also provides a standardised item alpha that is the value that would be obtained if all the items were standardised. Items usually possess comparable variances, so there is little difference between these two alphas.

In addition to Cronbach's alpha, IBM SPSS allows us to compute several other reliability models:

- split-half reliability
- Guttman
- parallel
- strictly parallel.

However, discussion in this chapter is limited to Cronbach's alpha.

Working example

One-hundred-and-five members of the community completed a ten-item attitudes-to-help-seeking instrument. You wish to determine the internal consistency of this scale using Cronbach's alpha. Item 5 was negatively worded and was recoded before analysis.

The data can be found in Work15.sav on the website that accompanies this title and are shown in the following figure.

To conduct a reliability analysis

1   Select the **Analyze** menu.

2   Click on **Scale** and then **Reliability Analysis...** to open the **Reliability Analysis** dialogue box.

3   Select the variables you require (i.e. *hs1* to *hs10*) and click on the ☑ button to move the variables into the **Items:** box.

4   Ensure that *Alpha* is displayed in the **Model:** drop-down list.

5   Click on the **Statistics...** command pushbutton to open the **Reliability Analysis: Statistics** subdialogue box.

6   In the **Descriptives for** box, select the **Scale** and **Scale if item deleted** check boxes.

7   In the **Inter-Item** box, select the **Correlations** check box.

8   Click on **Continue** and **OK**.

Reliability Statistics

Cronbach's Alpha	Cronbach's Alpha Based on Standardized Items	N of Items
.768	.792	10

Inter-Item Correlation Matrix

	hs1	hs2	hs3	hs4	hs5	hs6	hs7	hs8	hs9	hs10
hs1	1.000	.297	.552	.454	.542	.355	.179	.390	.538	.148
hs2	.297	1.000	.449	.087	.376	.225	.101	.013	.107	.199
hs3	.552	.449	1.000	.297	.541	.377	.287	.418	.445	.238
hs4	.454	.087	.297	1.000	.274	.242	.197	.323	.271	.027
hs5	.542	.376	.541	.274	1.000	.314	.288	.266	.442	.313
hs6	.355	.225	.377	.242	.314	1.000	.170	.157	.331	.143
hs7	.179	.101	.287	.197	.288	.170	1.000	.063	.200	-.057
hs8	.390	.013	.418	.323	.266	.157	.063	1.000	.385	.278
hs9	.538	.107	.445	.271	.442	.331	.200	.385	1.000	.167
hs10	.148	.199	.238	.027	.313	.143	-.057	.278	.167	1.000

Item-Total Statistics

	Scale Mean if Item Deleted	Scale Variance if Item Deleted	Corrected Item-Total Correlation	Squared Multiple Correlation	Cronbach's Alpha if Item Deleted
hs1	17.94	21.862	.648	.528	.720
hs2	17.39	23.048	.345	.301	.764
hs3	18.19	22.348	.693	.533	.719
hs4	17.72	22.836	.379	.259	.758
hs5	17.75	21.977	.646	.464	.721
hs6	17.86	23.220	.425	.209	.749
hs7	17.39	25.029	.246	.158	.772
hs8	18.45	24.692	.415	.339	.752
hs9	18.15	24.265	.526	.389	.743
hs10	17.44	23.710	.253	.193	.781

When you examine the characteristics of a scale, you want to look at the individual items, the overall scale and the relationship between the individual items and the overall scale.

You could have obtained means and standard deviations for each item by selecting the **Item** check box in the **Descriptives for** box. However, to minimise the output, this option was not chosen.

In relation to the **Item-total Statistics** you have a number of important columns:

- **Scale Mean if Item Deleted:** this column tells us the average score for the scale if the item was excluded from the scale.

- **Scale Variance if Item Deleted:** this column tells us the scale variance if the item was eliminated.

- **Corrected Item-Total Correlation:** this column gives the Pearson correlation coefficient between the score on the individual item and the sum of the scores on the remaining items.

- **Squared Multiple Correlation:** this column gives the result of a multiple regression equation with the item of interest as the dependent variable and all of the other items as independent variables.

- **Cronbach's Alpha if Item Deleted:** this column gives the alpha coefficient that would result if the item was removed from the scale.

An examination of the items comprising the attitudes to help-seeking scale indicates that items 7 and 10 have the lowest corrected item–total correlations. The Cronbach's alpha for the overall scale is equal to .768. If these two items were removed from the scale, the **Cronbach's Alpha if Item Deleted** column shows that overall reliability would increase slightly. When you remove these items and recalculate the reliability coefficient, Cronbach's alpha is raised to .7845. Therefore, deletion of these items may be considered appropriate.

CHAPTER 16

Factor analysis

Factor analysis is a data reduction technique used to reduce a large number of variables to a smaller set of underlying factors that summarise the essential information contained in the variables. More frequently, factor analysis is used as an exploratory technique when the researcher wishes to summarise the structure of a set of variables. However, for testing a theory about the structure of a particular domain, confirmatory factor analysis is appropriate.

When the researcher's goal is to construct a reliable test, factor analysis is an additional means of determining whether items are tapping into the same construct.

The **Factor** menu in IBM SPSS allows seven methods of factor extraction:

- principal components (PC)
- unweighted least squares
- generalised least squares
- maximum likelihood
- principal axis factoring (PAF)
- alpha factoring
- image factoring.

The most frequently used of these methods are PC and PAF. There is much debate in the literature over which method is the most appropriate. This chapter demonstrates only PAF.

Several steps comprise a factor-analytic procedure:

1   **Computation of the correlation matrix:** to determine the appropriateness of the factor-analytic model

2   **Factor extraction:** to determine the number of factors necessary to represent the data

3   **Rotation:** to make the factor structure more interpretable. Rotation may be orthogonal (factors are uncorrelated with one another) or oblique (factors are correlated). The choice of rotation is both empirically and theoretically driven. The criteria for making this selection can be found in any good multivariate statistics text.

Assumption testing

There are several assumptions and practical considerations underlying the application of PAF and PC.

1   **Sample size:** a minimum of five subjects per variable is required for factor analysis. A sample of 100 subjects is acceptable but sample sizes of 200+ are preferable.

2   **Normality:** factor analysis is robust to assumptions of normality. However, if variables are normally distributed, then the solution is improved.

3   **Linearity:** because factor analysis is based on correlation, linearity is important. If linearity is not present, the solution may be degraded.

4   **Outliers among cases:** factor analysis is sensitive to outlying cases. These cases need to be identified and either removed from the data set or brought into the distribution by transformation or recode options.

5   **Multicollinearity and singularity:** this assumption is not relevant for PC. However, in the case of PAF, singularity and multicollinearity can be identified if any of the squared multiple correlations are near or equal to 1. If this is the case, the inclusion of the offending variables needs to be reconsidered.

6   **Factorability of the correlation matrix:** a correlation matrix that is appropriate for factor analysis will have several sizeable correlations. Inspect the matrix for correlations in excess of .3 and, if none is found, reconsider the use of PAF. The anti-image correlation matrix is used to assess the sampling adequacy of each variable. The measures of sampling adequacy are displayed on the diagonal of the anti-image correlation matrix. Variables with a measure of sampling accuracy that falls below the acceptable level of .5 should be excluded from the analysis. Bartlett's test of sphericity and the Kaiser–Meyer–Olkin measure of sampling adequacy are both tests that can be used to determine the factorability of the matrix as a whole. If Bartlett's test of sphericity is large and significant, and the Kaiser–Meyer–Olkin measure is greater than .6, then factorability is assumed.

7   **Outliers among variables:** a variable with a low squared multiple correlation with all other variables, and low correlations with all important factors, is an outlier among the variables. These outliers may need to be deleted from the analysis.

Working example

Three hundred and eighty-eight participants responded to a survey regarding organ donation. They completed a 16-item scale that was designed to measure attitudes towards organ donation. The researcher wished to determine the underlying factor structure of this scale, and decided to conduct a PAF analysis.

A sample size of 388 for a 16-item scale more than meets the desired cases-to-variables ratio for PAF. Furthermore, you are assuming that assumptions of normality and linearity have been satisfied before analysis. No outlying cases were detected. The remainder of the assumptions will be examined as they occur in the output.

The data can be found in Work16.sav on the website that accompanies this text and are shown in the following figure.

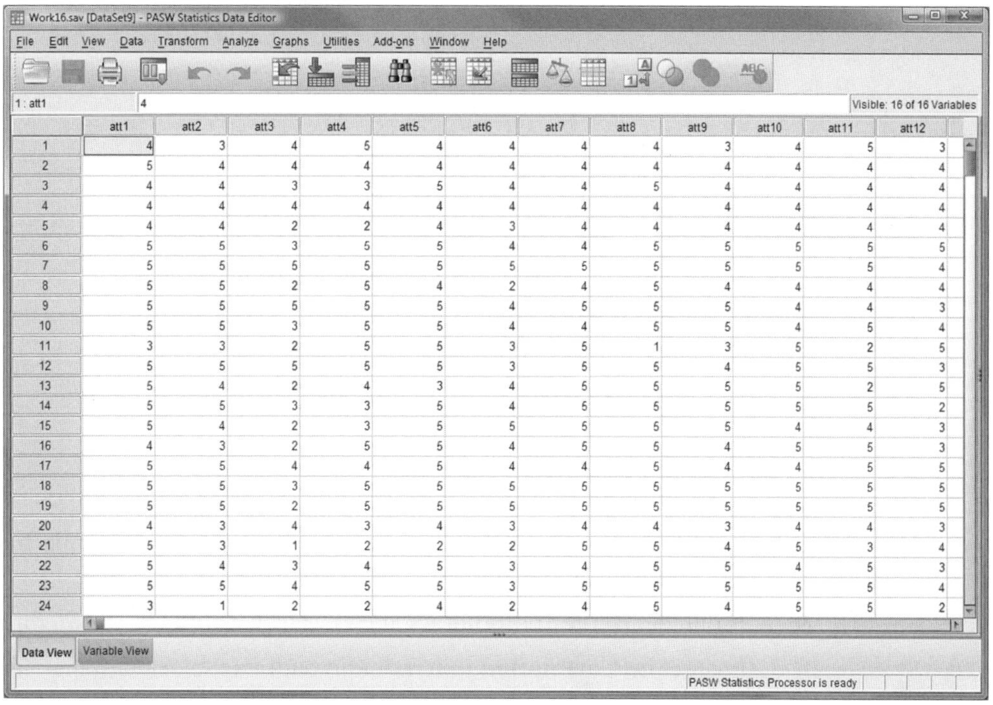

	att1	att2	att3	att4	att5	att6	att7	att8	att9	att10	att11	att12
1	4	3	4	5	4	4	4	4	3	4	5	3
2	5	4	4	4	4	4	4	4	4	4	4	4
3	4	4	3	3	5	4	4	5	4	4	4	4
4	4	4	4	4	4	4	4	4	4	4	4	4
5	4	4	2	2	4	3	4	4	4	4	4	4
6	5	5	3	5	5	4	4	5	5	5	5	5
7	5	5	5	5	5	5	5	5	5	5	5	4
8	5	5	2	5	4	2	4	5	4	4	4	4
9	5	5	5	5	5	4	5	5	5	4	4	3
10	5	5	3	5	5	4	4	5	5	4	5	4
11	3	3	2	5	5	3	5	1	3	5	2	5
12	5	5	5	5	5	3	5	5	4	5	5	3
13	5	4	2	4	3	4	5	5	5	5	2	5
14	5	5	3	3	5	4	5	5	5	5	5	2
15	5	4	2	3	5	5	5	5	5	4	4	3
16	4	3	2	5	5	4	5	5	4	5	5	3
17	5	5	4	4	5	4	4	5	4	4	5	5
18	5	5	3	5	5	5	5	5	5	5	5	5
19	5	5	2	5	5	5	5	5	5	5	5	5
20	4	3	4	3	4	3	4	4	3	4	4	3
21	5	3	1	2	2	2	5	5	4	5	3	4
22	5	4	3	4	5	3	4	5	5	4	5	3
23	5	5	4	5	5	3	5	5	5	5	5	4
24	3	1	2	2	4	2	4	5	4	5	5	2

To conduct a PAF analysis

1. Select the **Analyze** menu.
2. Click on **Dimension Reduction** and then on **Factor...** to open the **Factor Analysis** dialogue box.
3. Select the variables you require (i.e. *att1* to *att16*) and click on the button to move the variables into the **Variables:** box.

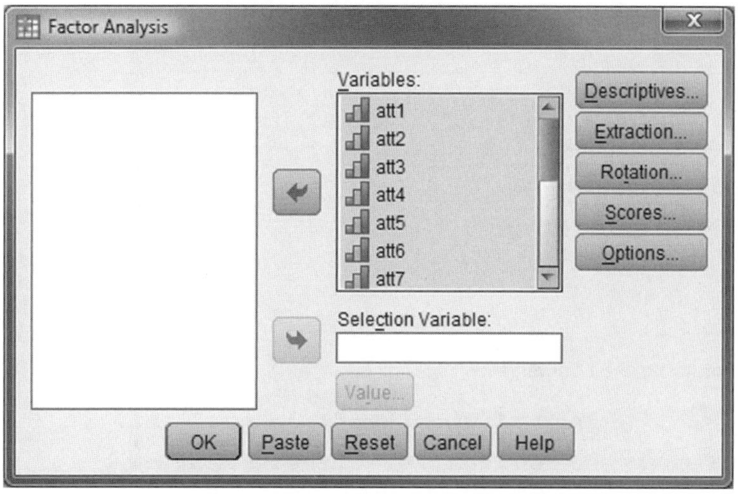

4. Click on the **Descriptives...** command pushbutton to open the **Factor Analysis: Descriptives** subdialogue box.
5. In the **Statistics** box, ensure that the **Initial solution** check box has been selected.

6   In the **Correlation Matrix** box, select the **Coefficients**, **KMO and Bartlett's test of sphericity** and **Anti-image** check boxes.

```
┌──────────────────────────────────────────────┐
│ ▦ Factor Analysis: Descriptives          X    │
│ ┌─Statistics──────────────────────────────┐  │
│ │  ☐ Univariate descriptives               │  │
│ │  ☑ Initial solution                      │  │
│ └──────────────────────────────────────────┘  │
│ ┌─Correlation Matrix──────────────────────┐  │
│ │  ☑ Coefficients        ☐ Inverse         │  │
│ │  ☐ Significance levels ☐ Reproduced      │  │
│ │  ☐ Determinant         ☑ Anti-image      │  │
│ │  ☑ KMO and Bartlett's test of sphericity │  │
│ └──────────────────────────────────────────┘  │
│       [ Continue ]  [ Cancel ]  [ Help ]       │
└──────────────────────────────────────────────┘
```

7   Click on **Continue**.

8   Click on the **Extraction...** command pushbutton to open the **Factor Analysis: Extraction** subdialogue box.

9   From the **Method:** drop-down menu, select *Principal axis factoring*.

10   Ensure the **Correlation matrix** radio button is selected in the **Analyze** box.

11   In the **Extract** box, ensure that the **Based on Eigenvalue** radio button has been selected and that *1* is displayed in the **Eigenvalues greater than:** box.

12   In the **Display** box, ensure that the **Unrotated factor solution** and **Scree plot** check boxes are selected.

```
┌──────────────────────────────────────────────────────┐
│ ▦ Factor Analysis: Extraction                    X     │
│                                                        │
│  Method:  [ Principal axis factoring      ▼ ]          │
│  ┌─Analyze──────────────┐ ┌─Display─────────────────┐ │
│  │ ⦿ Correlation matrix │ │ ☑ Unrotated factor      │ │
│  │ ○ Covariance matrix  │ │   solution              │ │
│  │                      │ │ ☑ Scree plot            │ │
│  └──────────────────────┘ └─────────────────────────┘ │
│  ┌─Extract──────────────────────────────────────────┐ │
│  │ ⦿ Based on Eigenvalue                             │ │
│  │     Eigenvalues greater than: [ 1 ]               │ │
│  │ ○ Fixed number of factors                         │ │
│  │     Factors to extract: [   ]                     │ │
│  └───────────────────────────────────────────────────┘ │
│  Maximum Iterations for Convergence: [ 25 ]            │
│        [ Continue ]  [ Cancel ]  [ Help ]              │
└──────────────────────────────────────────────────────┘
```

13   Click on **Continue**.

14   Click on the **Rotation...** command pushbutton to open the **Factor Analysis: Rotation** subdialogue box.

15   In the **Method** box, select the **Varimax** radio button.

16 In the **Display** box, ensure that the **Rotated solution** check box has been selected.

[Factor Analysis: Rotation dialogue box showing:]

Method
- ◯ None
- ◉ Varimax
- ◯ Direct Oblimin
- ◯ Quartimax
- ◯ Equamax
- ◯ Promax

Delta: 0   Kappa 4

Display
- ☑ Rotated solution   ☐ Loading plot(s)

Maximum Iterations for Convergence: 25

[Continue] [Cancel] [Help]

17 Click on **Continue**.

18 Click on the **Options...** command pushbutton to open the **Factor Analysis: Options** subdialogue box.

19 In the **Coefficient Display Format** box, select the **Sorted by size** and **Suppress small coefficients** check boxes. With the latter check box you are then prompted to enter the appropriate **Absolute value below:** value you require, which is usually *.3*. You will also notice that in the previous subdialogue box you have the option of replacing missing values with the mean of each of the items. This procedure is useful when you have an incomplete data set. By default, missing cases are deleted listwise, meaning that the whole case is excluded from the analysis.

[Factor Analysis: Options dialogue box showing:]

Missing Values
- ◉ Exclude cases listwise
- ◯ Exclude cases pairwise
- ◯ Replace with mean

Coefficient Display Format
- ☑ Sorted by size
- ☑ Suppress small coefficients
  - Absolute value below: .3

[Continue] [Cancel] [Help]

20 Click on **Continue** and then **OK**.

You will be aware that there are many more options available within factor analysis. However, only the basic commands required will be addressed in this chapter. For example, a number of other rotation options were given in the **Rotation** subdialogue box. These included *Equamax*, *Quartimax*, *Direct Oblimin* and *Promax*. Similarly, the option to save factor loadings as variables is available in the **Scores** subdialogue box.

An examination of the correlation matrix (opposite) indicates that a considerable number of correlations exceed .3, so the matrix is suitable for factoring.

KMO and Bartlett's Test

Kaiser-Meyer-Olkin Measure of Sampling Adequacy.		.914
Bartlett's Test of Sphericity	Approx. Chi-Square	2491.010
	df	120
	Sig.	.000

You can see that the Bartlett test of sphericity is significant and that the Kaiser–Meyer–Olkin measure of sampling adequacy is far greater than .6.

Measures of sampling adequacy are printed on the diagonal. Inspection of the anti-image correlation matrix (opposite) reveals that all our measures of sampling adequacy are well above the acceptable level of .5.

Correlation Matrix

		att1	att2	att3	att4	att5	att6	att7	att8	att9	att10	att11	att12	att13	att14	att15	att16
Correlation	att1	1.000	.664	.250	.435	.490	.315	.378	.328	.574	.336	.575	.338	.176	.436	.379	.560
	att2	.664	1.000	.383	.506	.444	.456	.345	.260	.525	.316	.468	.414	.320	.533	.480	.674
	att3	.250	.383	1.000	.457	.210	.321	.216	.054	.217	.206	.231	.225	.429	.425	.314	.296
	att4	.435	.506	.457	1.000	.351	.352	.336	.240	.415	.352	.405	.416	.331	.558	.439	.529
	att5	.490	.444	.210	.351	1.000	.210	.318	.194	.303	.216	.603	.330	.188	.296	.238	.352
	att6	.315	.456	.321	.352	.210	1.000	.358	.128	.379	.475	.329	.290	.276	.421	.311	.486
	att7	.378	.345	.216	.336	.318	.358	1.000	.256	.373	.344	.332	.320	.175	.333	.265	.397
	att8	.328	.260	.054	.240	.194	.128	.256	1.000	.348	.209	.215	.128	.128	.200	.231	.265
	att9	.574	.525	.217	.415	.303	.379	.373	.348	1.000	.437	.368	.383	.203	.492	.398	.609
	att10	.336	.316	.206	.352	.216	.475	.344	.209	.437	1.000	.366	.296	.181	.325	.289	.419
	att11	.575	.468	.231	.405	.603	.329	.332	.215	.368	.366	1.000	.338	.176	.382	.333	.445
	att12	.338	.414	.225	.416	.330	.290	.320	.128	.383	.296	.338	1.000	.186	.377	.266	.386
	att13	.176	.320	.429	.331	.188	.276	.175	.128	.203	.181	.176	.186	1.000	.391	.233	.318
	att14	.436	.533	.425	.558	.296	.421	.333	.200	.492	.325	.382	.377	.391	1.000	.428	.579
	att15	.379	.480	.314	.439	.238	.311	.265	.231	.398	.289	.333	.266	.233	.428	1.000	.559
	att16	.560	.674	.296	.529	.352	.486	.397	.265	.609	.419	.445	.386	.318	.579	.559	1.000

Anti-image Matrices

		att1	att2	att3	att4	att5	att6	att7	att8	att9	att10	att11	att12	att13	att14	att15	att16
Anti-image Covariance	att1	.399	-.141	-.001	-.012	-.051	.047	-.042	-.058	-.112	-.005	-.120	.029	.048	-.002	.014	-.016
	att2	-.141	.366	-.057	-.013	-.054	-.080	.030	-.010	-.004	.051	.016	-.060	-.030	-.024	-.045	-.102
	att3	-.001	-.057	.647	-.135	-.004	-.062	-.023	.075	.021	-.001	.006	.016	-.189	-.074	-.066	.063
	att4	-.012	-.013	-.135	.519	-.027	.021	-.017	-.052	.011	-.046	-.024	-.097	-.019	-.107	-.057	-.047
	att5	-.051	-.054	-.004	-.027	.570	.040	-.068	-.010	-.010	.034	-.224	-.063	-.038	.021	.028	.009
	att6	.047	-.080	-.062	.021	.040	.605	-.090	.041	-.024	-.183	-.002	-.004	-.033	-.046	.017	-.060
	att7	-.042	.030	-.023	-.017	-.068	-.090	.719	-.089	-.102	-.061	-.002	-.075	.008	-.015	.001	-.035
	att8	-.058	-.010	.075	-.052	-.010	.041	-.089	.817	-.102	-.032	.002	.053	-.055	.016	-.054	.017
	att9	-.112	-.004	.021	.011	-.010	-.024	-.102	-.102	.482	-.099	.039	-.071	.022	-.072	-.013	-.095
	att10	-.005	.051	-.001	-.046	.034	-.183	-.061	-.032	-.099	.647	-.082	-.040	.020	.023	-.014	-.029
	att11	-.120	.016	.006	-.024	-.224	-.002	-.002	.002	.039	-.082	.491	-.025	.006	-.029	-.034	-.015
	att12	.029	-.060	.016	-.097	-.063	-.004	-.075	.053	-.071	-.040	-.025	.711	-.038	-.094	.011	.004
	att13	.048	-.030	-.189	-.019	-.038	-.033	.008	-.055	.022	.020	.006	-.038	.737	-.094	.016	-.040
	att14	-.002	-.024	-.074	-.107	.021	-.046	-.015	.016	-.072	.023	-.029	-.094	-.094	.501	-.026	-.064
	att15	.014	-.045	-.066	-.057	.028	.017	.001	-.054	-.013	-.014	-.034	.011	.016	-.026	.632	-.125
	att16	-.016	-.102	.063	-.047	.009	-.060	-.035	.017	-.095	-.029	-.015	.004	-.040	-.064	-.125	.362
Anti-image Correlation	att1	.897a	-.369	-.002	-.026	-.107	.095	-.079	-.101	-.256	-.009	-.271	.055	.089	-.005	.028	-.042
	att2	-.369	.911a	-.118	-.030	-.118	-.169	.059	-.019	-.008	.105	.037	-.118	-.058	-.055	-.095	-.280
	att3	-.002	-.118	.865a	-.234	-.006	-.099	-.034	.104	.037	-.001	.011	.024	-.274	-.130	-.104	.131
	att4	-.026	-.030	-.234	.939a	-.050	.037	-.027	-.079	.023	-.079	-.047	-.159	-.031	-.209	-.100	-.107
	att5	-.107	-.118	-.006	-.050	.875a	.069	-.106	-.015	.018	.056	-.423	-.098	-.058	.039	.047	.021
	att6	.095	-.169	-.099	.037	.069	.907a	-.136	.058	-.019	-.293	-.072	-.007	-.049	-.083	.027	-.127
	att7	-.079	.059	-.034	-.027	-.106	-.136	.950a	-.117	-.041	-.089	-.003	-.106	.011	-.025	.002	-.070
	att8	-.101	-.019	.104	-.079	-.015	.058	-.117	.894a	-.162	-.044	.003	.069	-.071	.024	-.075	.032
	att9	-.256	-.008	.037	.023	.018	-.019	-.041	-.162	.921a	-.177	.080	-.121	.036	-.147	-.023	-.229
	att10	-.009	.105	-.001	-.079	.056	-.293	-.089	-.044	-.177	.901a	-.145	-.059	-.008	.041	-.022	-.061
	att11	-.271	.037	.011	-.047	-.423	-.072	-.003	.003	.080	-.145	.883a	-.042	.034	-.057	-.060	-.036
	att12	.055	-.118	.024	-.159	-.098	-.007	-.106	.069	-.121	-.059	-.042	.944a	.009	-.063	.016	.008
	att13	.089	-.058	-.274	-.031	-.058	-.049	.011	-.071	.036	-.008	.034	.009	.887a	-.154	.023	-.078
	att14	-.005	-.055	-.130	-.209	.039	-.083	-.025	.024	-.147	.041	-.057	-.063	-.154	.946a	-.047	-.150
	att15	.028	-.095	-.104	-.100	.047	.027	.002	-.075	-.023	-.022	-.060	.016	.023	-.047	.943a	-.262
	att16	-.042	-.280	.131	-.107	.021	-.127	-.070	.032	-.229	-.061	-.036	.008	-.078	-.150	-.262	.922a

a. Measures of Sampling Adequacy (MSA)

The table that follows displays the communality of the items and you will notice that *att8* has the lowest communality.

Communalities

	Initial	Extraction
att1	.601	.617
att2	.634	.606
att3	.353	.526
att4	.481	.514
att5	.430	.645
att6	.395	.360
att7	.281	.278
att8	.183	.164
att9	.518	.598
att10	.353	.308
att11	.509	.576
att12	.289	.274
att13	.263	.320
att14	.499	.550
att15	.368	.356
att16	.638	.682

Extraction Method: Principal Axis Factoring.

The table that follows displays the total variance explained at three stages. At the initial stage, it shows the factors and their associated eigenvalues, the percentage of variance explained and the cumulative percentages. In reference to the eigenvalues, you would expect three factors to be extracted because they have eigenvalues greater than 1. If three factors were extracted, then 46 per cent of the variance would be explained.

Total Variance Explained

Factor	Initial Eigenvalues			Extraction Sums of Squared Loadings			Rotation Sums of Squared Loadings		
	Total	% of Variance	Cumulative %	Total	% of Variance	Cumulative %	Total	% of Variance	Cumulative %
1	6.452	40.324	40.324	5.959	37.243	37.243	3.346	20.915	20.915
2	1.340	8.373	48.697	.833	5.206	42.449	2.150	13.438	34.353
3	1.062	6.639	55.336	.582	3.637	46.086	1.877	11.733	46.086
4	.951	5.942	61.278						
5	.841	5.253	66.531						
6	.756	4.727	71.257						
7	.656	4.101	75.359						
8	.643	4.017	79.376						
9	.577	3.608	82.985						
10	.528	3.298	86.283						
11	.499	3.118	89.401						
12	.421	2.633	92.033						
13	.389	2.431	94.464						
14	.348	2.176	96.640						
15	.302	1.889	98.529						
16	.235	1.471	100.000						

Extraction Method: Principal Axis Factoring.

The following scree plot graphically displays the eigenvalues for each factor and suggests that there is one predominant factor.

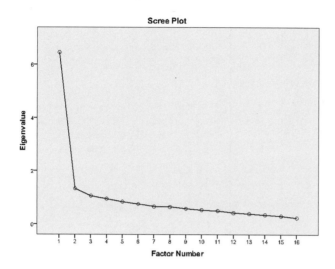

Scree Plot

The factor matrix is a matrix of loadings or correlations between the variables and factors. Pure variables have loadings of .3 or greater on only one factor. Complex variables may have high loadings on more than one factor, and they make interpretation of the output difficult. Rotation may therefore be necessary.

Factor Matrix[a]

	Factor		
	1	2	3
att16	.797		
att2	.778		
att1	.725	-.301	
att14	.702		
att9	.696		-.324
att4	.688		
att11	.643	-.333	
att15	.581		
att6	.569		
att5	.562	-.401	.410
att10	.526		
att12	.522		
att7	.519		
att3	.487	.441	.308
att13	.412	.345	
att8	.352		

Extraction Method: Principal Axis Factoring.

a. 3 factors extracted. 18 iterations required.

Rotated Factor Matrix[a]

	Factor		
	1	2	3
att9	.732		
att16	.710	.359	
att1	.567		.525
att2	.555	.391	.382
att10	.498		
att6	.464	.366	
att15	.462	.344	
att7	.424		
att8	.370		
att12	.361		
att3		.709	
att13		.545	
att14	.470	.544	
att4	.403	.527	
att5			.770
att11	.341		.655

Extraction Method: Principal Axis Factoring.

Rotation Method: Varimax with Kaiser Normalization.

a. Rotation converged in 6 iterations.

Varimax rotation, where the factor axes are kept at right angles to each other, is most frequently chosen. Ordinarily, rotation reduces the number of complex variables and improves interpretation. However, in the example, the rotated solution still includes several complex variables. Factor 1 comprises ten items with factor loadings ranging from .36 to .73. Factor 2 comprises four items with factor loadings ranging from .53 to .71. Factor 3 comprises two items with loadings of .65 and .77. Some items have dual or triple loadings greater than .3 on more than one factor, for example *att4, att16, att2, att6, att15, att14, att11*. These items must be interpreted with caution because simple structure is not apparent.

Factor Transformation Matrix

Factor	1	2	3
1	.717	.515	.470
2	-.113	.751	-.650
3	-.688	.412	.597

Extraction Method: Principal Axis Factoring.

Rotation Method: Varimax with Kaiser Normalization.

It is not surprising that this ambiguous structure has been obtained from varimax/orthogonal rotation. Items 1–16 were designed to measure a single construct and therefore it is expected that the factors extracted would be highly correlated. In this instance an oblique rotation (*Direct Oblimin*) would have been a more appropriate choice.

Pattern Matrix[a]

	Factor		
	1	2	3
att9	.837		
att16	.767		
att10	.552		
att1	.511		.410
att2	.506		
att6	.494		
att15	.477		
att14	.445	.409	
att7	.419		
att8	.409		
att12	.318		
att3		.724	
att13		.535	
att4	.329	.408	
att5			.836
att11			.640

Extraction Method: Principal Axis Factoring.
Rotation Method: Oblimin with Kaiser Normalization.

a. Rotation converged in 9 iterations.

Structure Matrix

	Factor		
	1	2	3
att16	.818	.483	.468
att9	.767		.418
att2	.734	.506	.581
att1	.707		.681
att14	.648	.624	.392
att4	.607	.606	.455
att15	.571	.424	.333
att6	.564	.441	
att10	.554		.307
att7	.515		.388
att12	.487	.339	.403
att8	.388		
att3	.336	.722	
att13	.313	.563	
att5	.420		.800
att11	.551		.745

Extraction Method: Principal Axis Factoring.
Rotation Method: Oblimin with Kaiser Normalization.

Factor Correlation Matrix

Fa...	1	2	3
1	1.000	.473	.579
2	.473	1.000	.289
3	.579	.289	1.000

Extraction Method: Principal Axis Factoring.
Rotation Method: Oblimin with Kaiser Normalization.

The oblique rotation provides a far more interpretable solution than that of the varimax rotation. Two matrices are produced: a pattern and a structure matrix. The difference between high and low loadings is more apparent in the pattern matrix, so this matrix is interpreted. The loadings in the pattern matrix represent the unique relationship between the factor and the variable. As illustrated in the output, the pattern matrix has fewer complex variables and simpler structure. The factor correlation matrix indicates the relationship between factors. All factors appear moderately related.

The final step in factor analysis involves determining how many factors to interpret and then assigning a label to these factors. The number of factors to be interpreted largely depends on the underlying purpose of the analysis. In the present study, the purpose was to confirm the factor structure of a scale. In other instances, factor analysis may be used to summarise the data set.

From the output, you can see that a single-factor solution may be more appropriate in this analysis. You will remember from examining the Total Variance Explained table (earlier in the output) that factor 1 had an eigenvalue of 5.96, whereas factors 2 and 3 had eigenvalues below 1.000 (.833 and .582 respectively). The scree plot also confirmed the dominance of a single factor represented by 11 items.

Examination of the items indicates that these items represent a conceptually distinct aspect of attitudes to organ donation that can be labelled 'altruistic issues'. A final step would be to determine Cronbach's alpha coefficient of internal consistency to ensure that the items comprising factor 1 produce a reliable scale. Reliability and factor analysis are complementary procedures in scale construction and definition.

Handy hints

- Make sure you have no missing variables in your data. By default, missing data are deleted listwise, resulting in the whole case being excluded from the analysis. To avoid this, either conduct mean substitution or you can get IBM SPSS to do this for you automatically in the **Factor Analysis: Options** subdialogue box.

- When considering the type of rotation to be adopted, refer to a sound multivariate statistic text to explore the selection of either an orthogonal or oblique rotation. Adopt the rotation that will make your factor structure more interpretable.

- Ensure that you address the assumptions of sample size, normality, linearity, outliers among cases, multicollinearity and singularity, factorability of the correction matrix and outliers among variables before analysis.

CHAPTER 17

Multiple regression

Multiple regression is an extension of bivariate correlation. The result of regression is an equation that represents the best prediction of a dependent variable from several independent variables. Regression analysis is used when independent variables are correlated with one another and with the dependent variable. Independent variables can be either continuous or categorical. However, in the latter case, these variables must be coded as dummy variables. In contrast, the dependent variable must be measured on a continuous scale. If the dependent variable is not continuous, then discriminant function analysis is appropriate.

There are three major regression models: standard or simultaneous, hierarchical and stepwise regression. These models differ in two ways: first, in the treatment of overlapping variability because of correlation of the independent variables, and second, in terms of the order of entry of the independent variables into the equation.

In the standard or simultaneous model, all independent variables enter the regression equation at once because you want to examine the relationship between the whole set of predictors and the dependent variable. In hierarchical multiple regression, you determine the order of entry of the independent variables based on theoretical knowledge.

In stepwise regression, the number of independent variables entered and the order of entry are determined by statistical criteria generated by the stepwise procedure. Method of entry can be forwards, backwards or a combination of both. Forwards selection involves the entry of predictors one at a time. The order of entry and whether the predictor is eventually accepted are decided on the basis of whether the F-test exceeds a certain critical value (FIN) and whether a critical alpha level (PIN) is met. Backward selection starts with all the variables in the equation and gradually deletes poor performers on the basis of whether the partial F-value is less than a critical value (FOUT). The default criterion (POUT) must also be met. Stepwise selection is a combination of the forward and backward procedures. It allows for the later removal of variables that were previously entered.

The choice of technique largely depends on the researcher's goals.

Assumption testing

A number of assumptions underpin the use of regression:

1   **Ratio of cases to independent variables:** the number of cases needed depends on the type of regression model to be used. For standard or hierarchical regression, you should ideally have 20 times more cases than predictors, whereas even more cases are required for stepwise regression. The minimum requirement is to have at least five times more cases than independent variables.

2   **Outliers:** extreme cases have considerable impact on the regression solution and should be deleted or modified to reduce their influence. Univariate outliers can be detected during data screening as described in chapter 3. Multivariate outliers can be detected using statistical methods such as Mahalanobis distance (see chapter 18) and graphical methods such as residual scatterplots. The decision to remove outliers from the data set must be made with care because their deletion often results in the generation of further outlying cases.

3   **Multicollinearity and singularity:** multicollinearity refers to high correlations among the independent variables, whereas singularity occurs when perfect correlations among independent variables exist. These problems affect how you interpret any relationships between the predictors (IVs) and the dependent variable, and they can be detected by examining the correlation matrix, squared multiple correlations and tolerances. Most computer programs have default values for multicollinearity and will not admit variables that are a problem.

4   **Normality, linearity, homoscedasticity and independence of residuals:** an examination of residual scatterplots allows these assumptions to be tested. It is assumed that the differences between the obtained and predicted dependent variable scores are normally distributed. Furthermore, it is assumed that the residuals have a linear relationship with the predicted dependent variable scores, and that the variance of the residuals is the same for all predicted scores. Mild deviations from linearity are not serious. Moderate to extreme deviations may lead to a serious underestimation of a relationship.

Assumption 1 relates to research design. Assumptions 2, 3 and 4 are assessed through regression analysis.

Working example

A marketing manager of a large supermarket chain wanted to determine the effect of shelf space and price on the sales of pet food. A random sample of 15 equally sized shops was selected, and the sales, shelf space in square metres and price per kilogram were recorded.

To demonstrate the application of the three regression models you will use the same data set to ask three questions:

1   What contribution do both shelf space and price make to the prediction of sales of pet food?

2   Which is the best predictor of sales of pet food?

3   Previous research has suggested that shelf space is the salient predictor of sales of pet food. Is this hypothesis correct?

The data can be found in Work17.sav on the website that accompanies this title and are shown in the following figure.

▶ **To conduct a standard (simultaneous) regression analysis**

1   Select the **Analyze** menu.

2   Click on **Regression** and then on **Linear...** to open the **Linear Regression** dialogue box.

3   Select the dependent variable (i.e. *sales of pet food*) and click on the ➡ button to move the variable into the **Dependent:** box.

4   Select the independent variables (i.e. *space* and *price*) and click on the ➡ button to move the variables into the **Independent(s):** box.

5   In the **Method:** drop-down list, ensure that **Enter** is selected.

6 Click on the **Statistics...** command pushbutton to open the **Linear Regression: Statistics** subdialogue box and ensure the **Estimates** and **Model fit** check boxes are selected in the **Regression Coefficients** box. In the **Residuals** box, select the **Casewise diagnostics** check box. Ensure the **Outliers outside** radio button has been selected. The default value of three standard deviations is most frequently used.

7 Click on **Continue**.

8 Click on the **Plots...** command pushbutton to open the **Linear Regression: Plots** subdialogue box.

9 Select ***ZRESID** and click on the ⯆ button to move the item into the **Y:** box.

10 Select ***ZPRED** and click on the ⯆ button to move the item into the **X:** box.

11 In the **Standardized Residual Plots** box, select the **Normal probability plot** check box.

12   Click on **Continue**.

13   Click on the **Save...** command pushbutton to open the **Linear Regression: Save** subdialogue box.

14   In the **Distances** box, select the **Mahalanobis** check box.

15   Click on **Continue** and then **OK**.

Variables Entered/Removed[b]

Model	Variables Entered	Variables Removed	Method
1	price, space[a]		Enter

a. All requested variables entered.

b. Dependent Variable: sales of pet food

Model Summary[b]

Model	R	R Square	Adjusted R Square	Std. Error of the Estimate
1	.922[a]	.850	.825	6.05904

a. Predictors: (Constant), price, space

b. Dependent Variable: sales of pet food

Both independent variables together explain 85 per cent of the variance (R Square) in sales of pet food, which is highly significant, as indicated by the F-value of 34.081 in the table below.

ANOVA[b]

Model		Sum of Squares	df	Mean Square	F	Sig.
1	Regression	2502.390	2	1251.195	34.081	.000[a]
	Residual	440.543	12	36.712		
	Total	2942.933	14			

a. Predictors: (Constant), price, space

b. Dependent Variable: sales of pet food

An examination of the t-values indicates that price contributes to the prediction of sales.

Coefficients[a]

Model		Unstandardized Coefficients		Standardized Coefficients	t	Sig.
		B	Std. Error	Beta		
1	(Constant)	2.029	5.126		.396	.699
	space	.057	2.613	.006	.022	.983
	price	10.500	3.262	.916	3.219	.007

a. Dependent Variable: sales of pet food

Because no univariate outliers were found, casewise plots were not necessary. If they had been produced, then these plots would have identified outlying cases with standard deviations greater than three.

From the scatterplot of residuals against predicted values, you can see that there is no clear relationship between the residuals and the predicted values, consistent with the assumption of linearity.

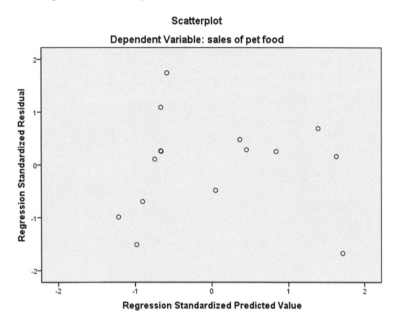

The normal plot of regression standardised residuals for the dependent variable also indicates a relatively normal distribution.

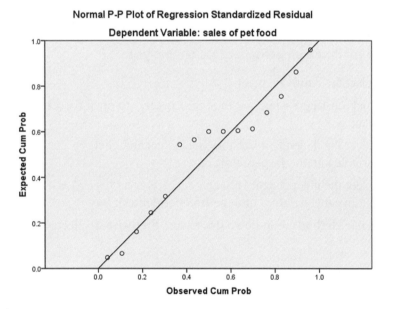

If you go back to your data file, you will also notice that IBM SPSS has added another new variable *MAH_1* to it.

An examination of the Mahalanobis distance values indicates that there are no multi-variate outliers among the independent variables; that is, no values are greater than or equal to the critical chi-square value of 13.8 at an alpha level of .001.

The image shows a PASW Statistics Data Editor window titled "*Work17.sav [DataSet10] - PASW Statistics Data Editor" with menu items File, Edit, View, Data, Transform, Analyze, Graphs, Utilities, Add-ons, Window, Help. The cell reference shows "1 : sales" with value "15.00". Visible: 4 of 4 Variables.

	sales	price	space	MAH_1	var	var	var	var	var	var	var	var
1	15.00	2.10	1.00	1.63616								
2	15.00	1.80	1.00	1.55206								
3	21.00	2.20	1.00	1.82652								
4	28.00	2.40	2.00	.60740								
5	30.00	2.50	2.00	.44322								
6	35.00	2.50	2.00	.44322								
7	40.00	2.60	2.00	.36021								
8	35.00	3.40	3.00	.00226								
9	30.00	2.50	3.00	3.20982								
10	45.00	3.80	3.00	.68686								
11	50.00	4.40	4.00	.76074								
12	60.00	5.10	4.00	4.30611								
13	45.00	3.90	5.00	5.47333								
14	60.00	5.40	5.00	2.88285								
15	50.00	5.50	6.00	3.80923								

Therefore, in answer to research question 1, you can say that price significantly predicts sales of pet food, $F(2,12) = 34.081$, $p < .05$. However, the shelf space allocated is not a significant predictor.

To conduct a stepwise regression analysis

1   Select the **Analyze** menu.

2   Click on **Regression** and then on **Linear...** to open the **Linear Regression** dialogue box.

3   Select the dependent variable (i.e. *sales*) and click on the ⬛ button to move the variable into the **Dependent:** box.

4   Select the independent variables (i.e. *space* and *price*) and click on the ⬛ button to move the variables into the **Independent(s):** box.

5   In the **Method:** drop-down list, ensure **Stepwise** is selected.

6   Click on the **Statistics...** command pushbutton to open the **Linear Regression: Statistics** subdialogue box and ensure the **Estimates** and **Model fit** check boxes are selected.

7   Click on **Continue** and then **OK**.

Variables Entered/Removed[a]

Model	Variables Entered	Variables Removed	Method
1	price	.	Stepwise (Criteria: Probability-of-F-to-enter <= .050, Probability-of-F-to-remove >= .100).

a. Dependent Variable: sales of pet food

Model Summary[b]

Model	R	R Square	Adjusted R Square	Std. Error of the Estimate
1	.922[a]	.850	.839	5.82145

a. Predictors: (Constant), price

b. Dependent Variable: sales of pet food

ANOVA[b]

Model		Sum of Squares	df	Mean Square	F	Sig.
1	Regression	2502.373	1	2502.373	73.840	.000[a]
	Residual	440.561	13	33.889		
	Total	2942.933	14			

a. Predictors: (Constant), price

b. Dependent Variable: sales of pet food

Coefficients[a]

Model		Unstandardized Coefficients		Standardized Coefficients	t	Sig.
		B	Std. Error	Beta		
1	(Constant)	1.977	4.373		.452	.659
	price	10.566	1.230	.922	8.593	.000

a. Dependent Variable: sales of pet food

Excluded Variables[b]

Model		Beta In	t	Sig.	Partial Correlation	Collinearity Statistics Tolerance
1	space	.006[a]	.022	.983	.006	.154

a. Predictors in the Model: (Constant), price

b. Dependent Variable: sales of pet food

You will notice from the output that only the variable price has been entered into the regression equation, and this variable explains 85 per cent of the variability in sales of pet food, $F(1,13) = 73.84$, $p < .05$. The second independent variable, shelf space, failed to meet the selection criteria, as indicated by the nonsignificant t-value ($p > .05$).

To conduct a hierarchical regression analysis

1 Select the **Analyze** menu.

2 Click on **Regression** and then on **Linear...** to open the **Linear Regression** dialogue box.

3 Select the dependent variable (i.e. *sales*) and click on the ⬥ button to move the variable into the **Dependent:** box.

4 Select the independent variable you have chosen to enter first (i.e. *space*) and click on the ⬥ button to move the variable into the **Independent(s):** box.

5 Click on **Next**.

6 Select the next independent variable you have chosen to enter (i.e. *price*) and click on the ⬥ button to move the variable into the **Independent(s):** box. You will notice that the box above in your output (not shown in the clip) reads **Block 2 of 2**.

Linear Regression dialogue box.

7   Click on the **Statistics** command pushbutton to open the **Linear Regression: Statistics** subdialogue box and ensure the **Estimates**, **Model fit** and **R squared change** check boxes are selected.

8   Click on **Continue** and then **OK**.

Variables Entered/Removed[b]

Model	Variables Entered	Variables Removed	Method
1	space		. Stepwise (Criteria: Probability-of-F-to-enter <= .050, Probability-of-F-to-remove >= .100).
2	price[a]		. Enter

a. All requested variables entered.

b. Dependent Variable: sales of pet food

Model Summary[c]

Model	R	R Square	Adjusted R Square	Std. Error of the Estimate	Change Statistics				
					R Square Change	F Change	df1	df2	Sig. F Change
1	.849[a]	.721	.700	7.94653	.721	33.604	1	13	.000
2	.922[b]	.850	.825	6.05904	.129	10.361	1	12	.007

a. Predictors: (Constant), space

b. Predictors: (Constant), space, price

c. Dependent Variable: sales of pet food

You will notice that shelf space on its own contributes 72 per cent of the variance in sales of pet food and is a significant predictor. At the second step, you will notice from the R Square Change statistic and the Sig. F Change value that price makes a significant unique contribution of 13 per cent to the variance of sales of pet food after shelf space.

ANOVA^c

Model		Sum of Squares	df	Mean Square	F	Sig.
1	Regression	2122.017	1	2122.017	33.604	.000^a
	Residual	820.916	13	63.147		
	Total	2942.933	14			
2	Regression	2502.390	2	1251.195	34.081	.000^b
	Residual	440.543	12	36.712		
	Total	2942.933	14			

a. Predictors: (Constant), space

b. Predictors: (Constant), space, price

c. Dependent Variable: sales of pet food

Coefficients^a

Model		Unstandardized Coefficients		Standardized Coefficients	t	Sig.
		B	Std. Error	Beta		
1	(Constant)	14.405	4.446		3.240	.006
	space	7.794	1.344	.849	5.797	.000
2	(Constant)	2.029	5.126		.396	.699
	space	.057	2.613	.006	.022	.983
	price	10.500	3.262	.916	3.219	.007

a. Dependent Variable: sales of pet food

However, examination of the preceding table indicates that shelf space is no longer a significant predictor when both independent variables are entered into the regression equation. In other words, these variables must be significantly correlated so that price subsumes shelf space.

Therefore, in answer to the third research question, you can say that shelf space on its own is a salient predictor of sales of pet food, $F(1,13) = 33.604$, $p < .05$. However, in combination with price, its effect is insignificant.

Handy hints

• Ensure that you have assessed the assumptions of ratio of cases to independent variables, outliers, multicollinearity and singularity, and normality, linearity, homoscedasticity and independence of residuals. The assumption of ratio of cases to independent variables relates to research design. The remaining assumptions are assessed through regression analysis.

• If univariate outliers were found, casewise plot would have been necessary.

CHAPTER 18

Multiple analysis of variance (MANOVA)

The extension of univariate analysis of variance (ANOVA) to the involvement of multiple dependent variables is termed multivariate analysis of variance (MANOVA). The hypotheses tested with MANOVA are similar to those tested with ANOVA except that sets of means replace the individual means specified in ANOVA. In a one-way MANOVA design, for example, the hypothesis tested is that the populations from which the samples are selected have the same means for all dependent variables.

The MANOVA command also allows you to perform a stepdown analysis if you have theoretical reasons for ordering your dependent variables. The ordering of these dependent variables can be tested using prior dependent variables as covariates. The choice between univariate and stepdown F may be difficult. When there is little correlation among the dependent variables, univariate F is acceptable. However, when dependent variables are highly correlated, stepdown F is preferable.

Bartlett's test of sphericity may help you decide whether stepdown analysis is appropriate. If Bartlett's test is significant at an alpha level of .05, this indicates that the dependent variables are related, so MANOVA with stepdown analysis should be conducted. If Bartlett's test is not significant, this indicates that the dependent variables are unrelated and that univariate ANOVAs, with adjustment for familywise error, would be more appropriate.

Assumption testing

Some assumptions underpin the use of MANOVA:

1   **Cell sizes:** it is necessary to have more subjects in each cell than the number of dependent variables. When cell size is greater than 30, assumptions of normality and equal variances are of little concern. If cell sizes are small and unequal, then assumption testing becomes more critical. Although equal cell size is ideal, it is not essential. However, ratios of smallest to largest size greater than 1:1.5 may cause problems.

2   **Univariate and multivariate normality:** MANOVA is sensitive to violations of univariate and multivariate normality. To test for univariate normality, the techniques described in chapter 3 can be used for each group or level of the independent variable using the **Split File** option. Multivariate outliers that influence normality can be identified using Mahalanobis distance in the **Regression** submenu. Mahalanobis distance is evaluated as chi-square with degrees of freedom equal to the number of dependent variables. The critical chi-square levels can be found in any critical values of chi-square table. An alpha level of .001 is recommended.

3   **Linearity:** linear relationships among all pairs of dependent variables must be assumed. Within-cell **scatterplots** must be conducted to test this assumption.

4   **Homogeneity of regression:** this assumption is related to stepdown analysis, and must be tested if stepdown analysis is required. It is assumed that the relationship between covariates and dependent variables in one group is the same as the relationship in other groups.

5   **Homogeneity of variance–covariance matrices:** this assumption is similar to the assumption of homogeneity of variance for individual dependent variables. In multivariate designs, this assumption is more complex. At the univariate level, Cochran's C and Bartlett-Box F tests can be used. If these tests are not significant ($p > .05$), then homogeneity of variance is assumed. Multivariate homogeneity of the variance–covariance matrices is tested using Box's M test, which must also be nonsignificant ($p > .001$). This test is very sensitive, so the alpha level of .001 is recommended.

6   **Multicollinearity and singularity:** when correlations among dependent variables are high, problems of multicollinearity and singularity exist. When the determinant of the within-cell correlation matrix is near zero ($< .0001$) or when the log (determinant) is less than -9.21034, singularity or multicollinearity may be present.

Working example

A social scientist wished to compare those respondents who had lodged an organ donor card with those who had not. Three hundred and eighty-eight new drivers completed a questionnaire that measured their attitudes towards organ donation, their feelings about organ donation and their previous exposure to the issue. It was hypothesised that individuals who agreed to be donors would have more positive attitudes towards organ donation, more positive feelings towards organ donation and greater previous exposure to the issue. Therefore, the independent variable was whether a donor card had been signed, and the dependent variables were attitudes towards organ donation, feelings towards organ donation and previous exposure to organ donation. Attitudes and feelings were measured on traditional scales, with a Likert-scale response format. Exposure was measured in terms of media exposure and personal experience. Conceptually and theoretically, these dependent variables were believed to be related, so MANOVA was the analysis of choice.

The data can be found in Work18.sav on the website that accompanies this title and are shown in the following figure.

File   Edit   View   Data   Transform   Analyze   Graphs   Utilities   Add-ons   Window   Help

1 : id   1   Visible: 5 of 5 Variables

	id	donor	exposure	attitude	feelings	var	var	var	var	var	var	var
1	1	1	12	75	35							
2	2	1	6	84	33							
3	3	1	6	87	35							
4	4	1	4	90	32							
5	5	1	6	113	41							
6	6	1	10	102	22							
7	7	1	60	113	17							
8	8	1	6	73	32							
9	9	1	30	64	22							
10	10	1	3	143	26							
11	11	1	4	48	43							
12	12	1	8	68	28							
13	13	1	6	87	29							
14	14	1	6	45	28							
15	15	1	10	.	29							
16	16	1	3	86	31							
17	17	1	20	48	23							
18	18	1	2	.	21							
19	19	1	5	69	22							
20	20	1	6	81	40							
21	21	1	10	52	48							
22	22	1	2	.	32							
23	23	1	23	45	20							
24	24	1	2	.	50							

Data View   Variable View

PASW Statistics Processor is ready

Data screening

1   *Cell sizes:* equality of cell size is often regulated by the type of design chosen. When using experimental designs, for example, the researcher is able to assign a set number of subjects to each condition. However, in quasiexperimental designs, equal *n* across cells is outside of the researcher's control. In this research example, cell sizes were approximately equal.

2   (a) *Univariate normality:* the data for each dependent measure by group were screened using the **Explore** option described in chapter 3. Assumptions of univariate normality were not violated.

     (b) *Multivariate outliers:* these were assessed using Mahalanobis distance in the **Regression** submenu. This is achieved by using the identification number in the data file as the dependent variable, in a simultaneous regression model, with all other variables as independent variables.

To detect multivariate outliers

1   Select the **Analyze** menu.

2   Click on **Regression** and then **Linear...** to open the **Linear Regression** dialogue box.

3   Select the dependent variable (i.e. *id*) and click on the ⮕ button to move the variable into the **Dependent:** box.

4   Select the independent variables (i.e. *attitude, exposure, feelings*) and click on the ⮕ button to move the variables into the **Independent(s):** box.

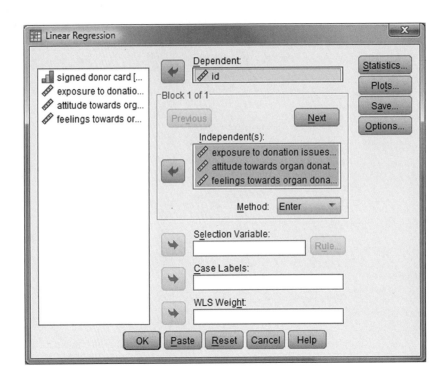

5 Click on the **Save...** command pushbutton to open the **Linear Regression: Save** subdialogue box.

6 In the **Distances** box, select the **Mahalanobis** check box.

7   Click on **Continue** and then **OK**.

You will notice that these distances have been added to your data file.

The critical value of chi-square, for three dependent variables, at an alpha level of .001 is 16.2. Using this value, you have seven outlying cases, which is not unexpected in a sample size of 388. Consequently, these outliers were retained in the data set. If a large number of outlying cases were identified, then their inclusion would need to be considered carefully.

3   *Linearity:* linearity among dependent measures was confirmed using scatterplots among pairs of dependent variables across groups.

4   *Homogeneity of regression:* this assumption is tested using the general factorial ANOVA model submenu, involving a fairly arduous process of modifying syntax files. Because you have no theoretical grounds for ordering the dependent variables, stepdown analysis will not be carried out in this example.

Assumptions 5 (*homogeneity of variance–covariance matrices*) and 6 (*multicollinearity and singularity*) will be tested in the MANOVA analysis.

To conduct a MANOVA

1   Select the **Analyze** menu.

2   Click on **General Linear Model** and then **Multivariate...** to open the **Multivariate** dialogue box.

3   Select the dependent variables (i.e. *attitudes, feelings, exposure*) and click on the ⊡ button to move the variables into the **Dependent Variables:** box.

4   Select the independent variable(s) (i.e. *donor*) and click on the ⊡ button to move the variable into the **Fixed Factor(s):** box.

5 Click on the **Model...** command pushbutton to open the **Multivariate: Model** subdialogue box.

6 In the **Specify Model** box, ensure the **Full factorial** radio button is selected and **Type III** is selected from the **Sum of squares:** drop-down list. The full factorial model contains all main effects, covariate main effects and all factor-by-factor interactions but does not contain covariate interactions. Type III is the default and the most commonly used method of calculating sum of squares for balanced/ unbalanced models with no missing cells.

7 Click on **Continue**.

8 Click on the **Options...** command pushbutton to open the **Multivariate: Options** subdialogue box.

9 In the **Estimated Marginal Means** box, under the heading **Factor(s) and Factor Interactions:**, click on the independent variable (i.e. *donor*) and click on the ▸ button to move the variable into the **Display Means for:** box.

10 In the **Display** box, select the **Descriptive statistics** and the **Homogeneity tests** check boxes.

11 Click on **Continue** and then **OK**.

Box's Test of Equality of Covariance Matrices[a]

Box's M	19.260
F	3.182
df1	6
df2	1018790.282
Sig.	.004

Tests the null hypothesis that the observed covariance matrices of the dependent variables are equal across groups.

a. Design: Intercept + donor

Box's M tests the homogeneity of the variance–covariance matrices. You have homogeneity of variance because this test is not significant at an alpha level of .001.

Levene's Test of Equality of Error Variances[a]

	F	df1	df2	Sig.
exposure to donation issues	2.936	1	375	.087
attitude towards organ donation	15.346	1	375	.000
feelings towards organ donation	1.284	1	375	.258

Tests the null hypothesis that the error variance of the dependent variable is
equal across groups.

a. Design: Intercept + donor

The univariate tests for homogeneity of variance for each of the dependent measures indicate that homogeneity of variance has not been violated for exposure to organ donation issues and feelings towards organ donation. However, for attitude towards organ donation, the Levene's test of equality of error variances is significant. If the univariate F-test for this variable is also significant, then you must interpret this finding at a more conservative alpha level.

Multivariate Tests[b]

Effect		Value	F	Hypothesis df	Error df	Sig.
Intercept	Pillai's Trace	.935	1790.688[a]	3.000	373.000	.000
	Wilks' Lambda	.065	1790.688[a]	3.000	373.000	.000
	Hotelling's Trace	14.402	1790.688[a]	3.000	373.000	.000
	Roy's Largest Root	14.402	1790.688[a]	3.000	373.000	.000
donor	Pillai's Trace	.033	4.255[a]	3.000	373.000	.006
	Wilks' Lambda	.967	4.255[a]	3.000	373.000	.006
	Hotelling's Trace	.034	4.255[a]	3.000	373.000	.006
	Roy's Largest Root	.034	4.255[a]	3.000	373.000	.006

a. Exact statistic

b. Design: Intercept + donor

The multivariate tests of significance test whether there are significant group differences on a linear combination of the dependent variables. You will notice that several multivariate statistics are available. Pillai's Trace criterion is considered to have acceptable power and to be the most robust statistic against violations of assumptions. Having obtained a significant multivariate effect for donor — that is, a significance of $F < .05$ — you can now interpret the univariate/between-subjects effects given below.

An examination of the univariate F-tests for each dependent variable indicates which individual dependent variables contribute to the significant multivariate effect. It is advisable to evaluate these effects using a Bonferroni-type adjustment. Adjusting for familywise or experimentwise error decreases the chance of type I error. The simple formula that may be applied is: alpha/number of tests. In this example the adjusted alpha is equal to .017 (0.05/3). Using this alpha level, you have a significant univariate main effect for feelings towards organ donation ($p < .017$).

Source	Dependent Variable	Type III Sum of Squares	df	Mean Square	F	Sig.
Corrected Model	exposure to donation issues	903.925[a]	1	903.925	3.830	.051
	attitude towards organ donation	12372.705[b]	1	12372.705	3.960	.047
	feelings towards organ donation	922.187[c]	1	922.187	11.100	.001
Intercept	exposure to donation issues	39489.506	1	39489.506	167.331	.000
	attitude towards organ donation	3105144.376	1	3105144.376	993.910	.000
	feelings towards organ donation	331042.346	1	331042.346	3984.772	.000
donor	exposure to donation issues	903.925	1	903.925	3.830	.051
	attitude towards organ donation	12372.705	1	12372.705	3.960	.047
	feelings towards organ donation	922.187	1	922.187	11.100	.001
Error	exposure to donation issues	88498.590	375	235.996		
	attitude towards organ donation	1171563.820	375	3124.170		
	feelings towards organ donation	31153.824	375	83.077		
Total	exposure to donation issues	128924.000	377			
	attitude towards organ donation	4288063.000	377			
	feelings towards organ donation	363028.000	377			
Corrected Total	exposure to donation issues	89402.515	376			
	attitude towards organ donation	1183936.525	376			
	feelings towards organ donation	32076.011	376			

a. R Squared = .010 (Adjusted R Squared = .007)

b. R Squared = .010 (Adjusted R Squared = .008)

c. R Squared = .029 (Adjusted R Squared = .026)

Therefore, you can conclude that a person's decision to act as a donor is significantly influenced by their feelings towards organ donation, $F(1,375) = 11.100$, $p < .017$. No significant main effects were found for the other dependent measures (exposure to or attitude towards organ donation).

An examination of the estimated marginal means for feelings towards organ donation and the variable donor indicates that those individuals who had signed a donor card had more positive feelings towards organ donation than those individuals who had not signed a donor card.

Estimated Marginal Means

signed donor card

Dependent Variable	signed donor card	Mean	Std. Error	95% Confidence Interval	
				Lower Bound	Upper Bound
exposure to donation issues	yes	11.783	1.117	9.586	13.980
	no	8.686	1.120	6.483	10.889
attitude towards organ donation	yes	85.026	4.066	77.032	93.021
	no	96.484	4.077	88.468	104.500
feelings towards organ donation	yes	28.069	.663	26.765	29.372
	no	31.197	.665	29.890	32.504

When independent variables involve more than two levels, further analytic comparisons are needed to find out which levels are significantly different on the individual dependent variable. These comparisons can be planned (when you have prior reason for anticipating specific or planned differences) or post hoc (when you have no prior reason for expecting differences but wish to explore the data further).

More than one independent variable and the presence of an interaction effect complicate the process of making comparisons and are beyond the scope of this chapter. However, the new general linear model procedure does allow you to perform contrasts using the **Contrasts...** and **Post Hoc...** command pushbuttons in the **General Factorial** dialogue box.

It is important to remember that MANOVA is an intricate analysis and is more straightforward when there is only one independent variable and only a few dependent variables. As the number of independent and dependent variables increases, the analysis becomes more complex. When the dependent variables are measured on the same scale, a special form of MANOVA (referred to as profile analysis) is more appropriate.

Handy hint
- Ensure that you have met the assumptions of cell sizes, univariate and multivariate normality, linearity, homogeneity of regression, homogeneity of variance–covariance matrices, multicollinearity and singularity.

CHAPTER 19

Nonparametric techniques

When you have serious violations of the distribution assumptions of parametric tests, alternative nonparametric techniques can be used. These tests tend to be less powerful than their parametric counterparts; however, some nonparametric tests are appropriate for data measured on scales that are not interval or ratio.

IBM SPSS has a wide selection of nonparametric techniques available, of which the following will be discussed:

- chi-square test for goodness of fit
- chi-square test for independence or relatedness
- Mann–Whitney test (Wilcoxon rank sum)
- Wilcoxon signed-rank test
- Kruskal–Wallis test
- Friedman test
- Spearman's rank-order correlation.

Assumption testing for nonparametric techniques is not as critical as for parametric methods. However, generic assumptions apply:

1   **random sampling**

2   **similar shape and variability across distributions**

3   **independence:** for between-subjects designs, independence (that is, subjects appear in only one group and the groups are not related in any way) must be ensured.

Chi-square tests

There are two main types of chi-square test. The chi-square test for goodness of fit applies to the analysis of a single categorical variable, and the chi-square test for independence or relatedness applies to the analysis of the relationship between two categorical variables.

Assumption testing

There are three assumptions you need to deal with before conducting chi-square tests.

1   **Random sampling:** observations should be randomly sampled from the population of all possible observations.

2   **Independence of observations:** each observation should be generated by a different subject and no subject is counted twice.

3   **Size of expected frequencies:** when the number of cells is less than ten and particularly when the total sample size is small, the lowest expected frequency required for a chi-square test is five. However, the observed frequencies can be any value, including zero.

Working example — chi-square test for goodness of fit

The following table outlines the attitudes of 60 people towards US military bases in Australia. A chi-square test for goodness of fit will allow us to determine if differences in frequency exist across response categories.

Attitude towards US military bases in Australia	Frequency of response
In favour	8
Against	20
Undecided	32

The data can be found in Work19a.sav on the website that accompanies this title and are shown in the following figure.

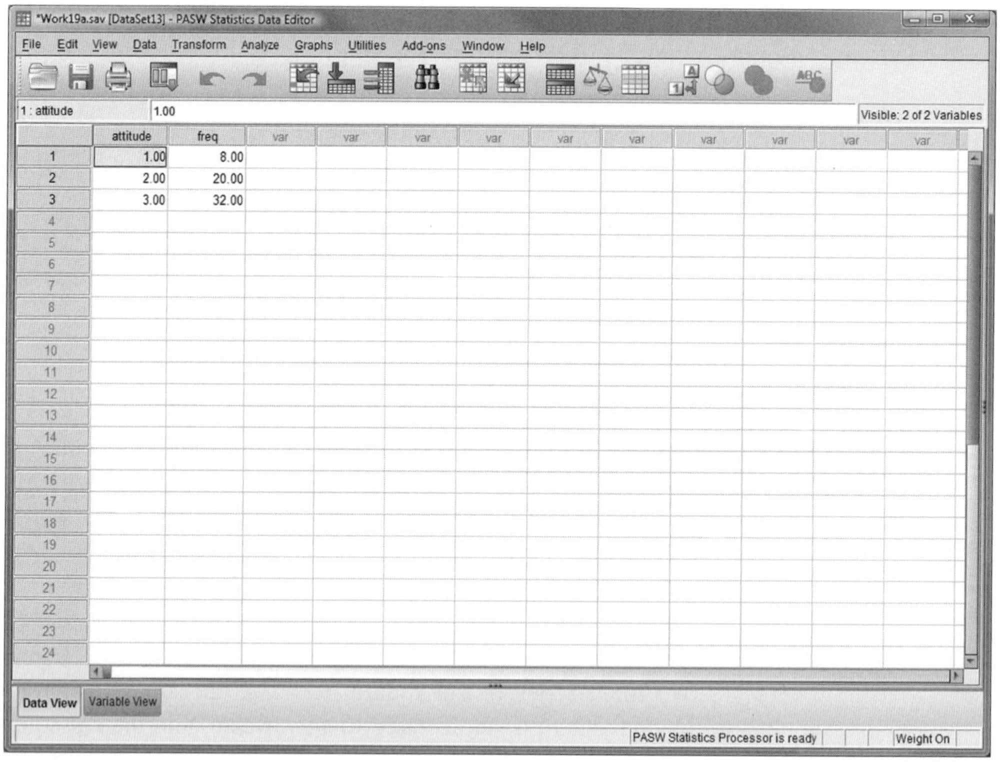

Initially, you have to tell the program that the data for frequency are in the form of frequency counts not scores. Using the **Weight Cases** option, you can do this quickly and easily and then you can perform the chi-square test.

▶ **To conduct a chi-square test for goodness of fit**

1   Select the **Data** menu.

2   Click on **Weight Cases...** to open the **Weight Cases** dialogue box.

3   Click on the **Weight cases by** radio button.

4   Select the variable you require (i.e. *freq*) and click on the ⬇ button to move the variable into the **Frequency Variable:** box.

5   Click on **OK**.

6   Select the **Analyze** menu.

7   Click on **Nonparametric Tests, Legacy Dialogs** and then **Chi-Square...** to open the **Chi-square Test** dialogue box.

8   Select the variable you require (i.e. *attitude*) and click on the ⬇ button to move the variable into the **Test Variable List:** box.

9   Click on **OK**.

attitude towards US military bases

	Observed N	Expected N	Residual
in favour	8	20.0	-12.0
against	20	20.0	.0
undecided	32	20.0	12.0
Total	60		

Test Statistics

	attitude towards US military bases
Chi-square	14.400[a]
df	2
Asymp. Sig.	.001

a. 0 cells (.0%) have expected frequencies less than 5. The minimum expected cell frequency is 20.0.

You can see from the output that the chi-square value is significant (p < .05). Therefore, it can be concluded that there are significant differences in the frequency of attitudes towards military bases in Australia, and the results show that people are largely undecided on this issue, $\chi^2(2, N = 60) = 14.4$, p < .05.

IBM SPSS version 18 offers some new features to its nonparametric statistics tests. For instance, the program may assist you in choosing the most appropriate nonparametric test based on your data characteristics, enabling you to make multiple comparisons about your data and choose the most accurate outcomes. The following steps illustrate an example of this new feature, using the same example dataset as above.

After you have weighted your cases (Steps 1 to 5 on pages 162–3),

1   Select the **Analyze** menu.

2   Click on **Nonparametric Tests** and select **One Sample...** instead of **Legacy Dialogs**.

Clicking on **Run** will enable you to obtain a **Hypothesis Test Summary** in the Output Viewer, as shown below. This summary provides a quick overview of whether to accept or reject your null hypothesis. It does not provide any specific analysis output details such as your chi-square value and degrees of freedom. Therefore, if you need to report on these values, you will have to run the analysis via the **Legacy Dialogs** option as illustrated earlier.

Hypothesis Test Summary

	Null Hypothesis	Test	Sig.	Decision
1	The categories of attitude towards US military bases occur with equal probabilities.	One-Sample Chi-Square Test	.001	Reject the null hypothesis.

Asymptotic significances are displayed. The significance level is .05.

Optionally, you can also specify an objective in the **Objective** tab of the **One Sample** application window; specify field assignments on the **Fields** tab; or specify expert settings on the **Settings** tab. For instance, the objectives allow you to quickly specify different but commonly used test settings:

- **Automatically compare observed data to hypothesized**: this objective applies the binomial test to categorical fields with only two categories; the chi-square test to all other categorical fields; and the Kolmogorov-Smirnov test to continuous fields.

- **Test sequence for randomness:** this objective uses the runs test to test the observed sequence of data values for randomness.

- **Custom analysis:** select this option if you want to manually amend the test settings on the **Settings** tab.

 To conduct a chi-square test for goodness of fit with unequal expected frequencies

It should be noted that the expected frequencies in the previous example represent a 1/3:1/3:1/3 split. Sometimes the expected frequencies are not evenly balanced across categories. For example, the expected frequency for each category might be 15, 15 and 30. IBM SPSS allows you to specify expected values that may not be equivalent. This technique will be demonstrated using already weighted cases.

1   Select the **Analyze** menu.

2   Click on **Nonparametric Tests, Legacy Dialogs** and then **Chi-Square...** to open the **Chi-square Test** dialogue box.

3   Select the variable you require (i.e. *attitude*) and click on the ☑ button to move the variable into the **Test Variable List:** box.

4   In the **Expected Values** box, click the **Values:** radio button.

5   Type *15* in the box and click on **Add**.

6   Type another *15* in the box and click on **Add**.

7   Type *30* in the box and click on **Add**.

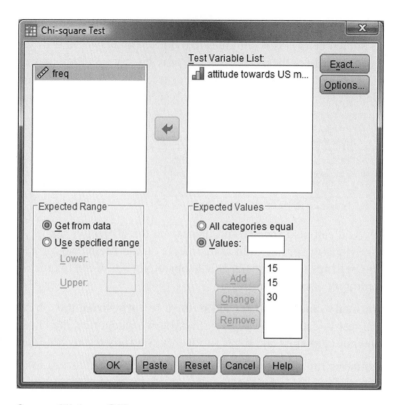

8   Click on **OK**.

attitude towards US military bases

	Observed N	Expected N	Residual
in favour	8	15.0	-7.0
against	20	15.0	5.0
undecided	32	30.0	2.0
Total	60		

Test Statistics

	attitude towards US military bases
Chi-square	5.067[a]
df	2
Asymp. Sig.	.079

a. 0 cells (.0%) have expected frequencies less than 5. The minimum expected cell frequency is 15.0.

You will notice that with the different cell frequencies, the chi-square statistic is no longer significant ($p > .05$).

Working example — chi-square test for relatedness or independence

A magazine publisher wished to determine whether preference for certain publications depended on geographic location of the reader. Of those preferring the *Financial Review*, 32 are urban readers and 24 are from the country. Of those who chose *Newsweek*, 28 are city readers while four are rural readers.

The data can be found in Work19b.sav on the website that accompanies this title and are shown in the following figure.

To conduct a chi-square test for relatedness or independence

1   Select the **Analyze** menu.

2   Click on **Descriptive Statistics** and then on **Crosstabs...** to open the **Crosstabs** dialogue box.

3   Select a row variable (i.e. *pref*) and click on the ☐ button to move the variable into the **Row(s):** box.

4   Select a column variable (i.e. *location*) and click on the ☐ button to move the variable into the **Column(s):** box.

5 Click on the **Statistics...** command pushbutton to open the **Crosstabs: Statistics** subdialogue box.

6 Click on the **Chi-square** check box.

7 Click on **Continue**.

8 Click on the **Cells...** command pushbutton to open the **Crosstabs: Cell Display** subdialogue box.

9 In the **Counts** box, click on the **Observed** and **Expected** check boxes.

10 In the **Percentages** box, click on the **Row**, **Column** and **Total** check boxes.

11 Click on **Continue** and then **OK**.

preference for magazine * location of reader Crosstabulation

			location of reader — urban	location of reader — rural	Total
preference for magazine	Financial Review	Count	32	24	56
		Expected Count	38.2	17.8	56.0
		% within preference for magazine	57.1%	42.9%	100.0%
		% within location of reader	53.3%	85.7%	63.6%
		% of Total	36.4%	27.3%	63.6%
	Newsweek	Count	28	4	32
		Expected Count	21.8	10.2	32.0
		% within preference for magazine	87.5%	12.5%	100.0%
		% within location of reader	46.7%	14.3%	36.4%
		% of Total	31.8%	4.5%	36.4%
Total		Count	60	28	88
		Expected Count	60.0	28.0	88.0
		% within preference for magazine	68.2%	31.8%	100.0%
		% within location of reader	100.0%	100.0%	100.0%
		% of Total	68.2%	31.8%	100.0%

Chi-Square Tests

	Value	df	Asymp. Sig. (2-sided)	Exact Sig. (2-sided)	Exact Sig. (1-sided)
Pearson Chi-Square	8.650[a]	1	.003		
Continuity Correction[b]	7.308	1	.007		
Likelihood Ratio	9.487	1	.002		
Fisher's Exact Test				.004	.003
Linear-by-Linear Association	8.552	1	.003		
N of Valid Cases	88				

a. 0 cells (.0%) have expected count less than 5. The minimum expected count is 10.18.

b. Computed only for a 2x2 table

To interpret the chi-square printout, you need to look at the Pearson statistic, which is short for Pearson's chi-square. In this example, Pearson has a value of 8.650 with a significance of .003. This significance value is well below the alpha level of .05 and is therefore significant.

You can also see in the notes below the Chi-square Tests table that the minimum expected cell frequency is 10, which is > 5, and, therefore, you can be confident that you have not violated one of the main assumptions of chi-square.

In examining the observed cell frequencies, it can be concluded that the rural readers prefer to read the *Financial Review* while the urban readers do not show a marked preference for either publication, $\chi^2(1, N = 88) = 8.65$, p < .05.

Mann–Whitney U test (Wilcoxon rank sum W test)

The Mann–Whitney U test tests the hypothesis that two independent samples come from populations having the same distribution. This test is equivalent to the independent groups t-test.

Working example

The productivity levels of factories A and B are to be compared. The monthly output, in tonnes of produce, was recorded for 22 consecutive months. The data violate the stringent assumptions of an independent groups t-test, so you have decided to perform a Mann–Whitney test. The data file can be found in Work19c.sav.

![Work19c.sav PASW Statistics Data Editor screenshot]

	factory	produce
1	1	14.00
2	2	16.00
3	1	17.00
4	1	13.00
5	2	10.00
6	2	8.00
7	1	14.00
8	2	19.00
9	2	17.00
10	1	11.00
11	2	12.00
12	2	14.00
13	1	15.00
14	1	13.00
15	2	12.00
16	1	17.00
17	1	15.00
18	2	11.00
19	2	12.00
20	1	12.00
21	2	16.00
22	1	17.00

To conduct a Mann–Whitney U test

1   Select the **Analyze** menu.

2   Click on **Nonparametric Tests, Legacy Dialogs** and then on **2 Independent Samples...** to open the **Two-Independent-Samples Tests** dialogue box.

3   Select the dependent variable (i.e. *produce*) and click on the ► button to move the variable into the **Test Variable List:** box.

4   Select the independent variable (i.e. *factory*) and click on the ► button to move the variable into the **Grouping Variable:** box.

5 Click on the **Define Groups...** command pushbutton to open the **Two Independent Samples: Define Groups...** subdialogue box.

6 In the **Group 1:** box, enter the first value for the independent variable (*sex*) (i.e. *1*), then tab. Enter the second value for the independent variable (i.e. *2*) in the **Group 2:** box.

7 Click on **Continue**.

8 Ensure the **Mann–Whitney U** check box has been selected.

9 Click on **OK**.

Ranks

	factory	N	Mean Rank	Sum of Ranks
tonnes of produce per month	A	11	12.77	140.50
	B	11	10.23	112.50
	Total	22		

Test Statistics[b]

	tonnes of produce per month
Mann-Whitney U	46.500
Wilcoxon W	112.500
Z	-.927
Asymp. Sig. (2-tailed)	.354
Exact Sig. [2*(1-tailed Sig.)]	.365[a]

a. Not corrected for ties.

b. Grouping Variable: factory

To interpret the output from the Mann–Whitney U test you need to consider the Z-score and two-tailed p-value, which have been corrected for ties.

The output indicates that the result, with correction for ties and Z-score conversion, was not significant, $Z = -.927$, $p > .05$, and, therefore, no significant differences in productivity exist between factories A and B.

Optionally, you may also obtain a **Hypothesis Test Summary** by selecting **Independent Samples...** instead of **Legacy Dialogs** from the **Nonparametric Tests** option in the **Analyze** menu. In the **Fields** tab, move the dependent variable (i.e. *produce*) into the **Test Fields:** box and the independent variable (i.e. *factory*) into the **Groups:** box.

Clicking on **Run** will produce the **Hypothesis Test Summary** in the Output Viewer. Consistent with the earlier output, the **Hypothesis Test Summary** has suggested to retain the null hypothesis given non-significant findings.

Hypothesis Test Summary

	Null Hypothesis	Test	Sig.	Decision
1	The distribution of tonnes of produce per month is the same across categories of factory.	Independent-Samples Mann-Whitney U Test	.354	Retain the null hypothesis.

Asymptotic significances are displayed. The significance level is .05.

Wilcoxon signed-rank test

The Wilcoxon signed-rank test, also referred to as the Wilcoxon t-test, is used when you would use a repeated measures or paired t-test, that is, when the same participants perform under each level of the independent variable.

Working example

A factory manager wished to compare productivity in his factory for the first and second halves of the year. He observed the productivity from 22 workstations and recorded their output in tonnes. The data violate the stringent assumptions of a paired t-test, so he decided to perform a Wilcoxon signed-rank test. The data file can be found in Work19d.sav.

To conduct a Wilcoxon signed-rank test

1   Select the **Analyze** menu.

2   Click on **Nonparametric Tests, Legacy Dialogs** and then on **Two Related Samples...** to open the **Two-Related-Samples Tests** dialogue box.

3   Select the variables you require (i.e. *output1* and *output2*) and click on the ► button to move the variables into the **Test Pair(s) List:** box.

4   Ensure that the **Wilcoxon** check box has been selected.

5   Click on the **Options...** command pushbutton to open the **Two-Related-Samples: Options** subdialogue box.

6   Ensure that the **Descriptive** check box has been selected.

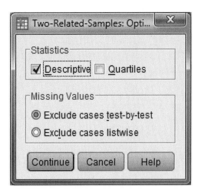

7   Click on **Continue** and then **OK**.

Ranks

		N	Mean Rank	Sum of Ranks
output2 - output1	Negative Ranks	0ᵃ	.00	.00
	Positive Ranks	22ᵇ	11.50	253.00
	Ties	0ᶜ		
	Total	22		

a. output2 < output1

b. output2 > output1

c. output2 = output1

Test Statisticsᵇ

	output2 - output1
Z	-4.113ᵃ
Asymp. Sig. (2-tailed)	.000

a. Based on negative ranks.

b. Wilcoxon Signed Ranks Test

To interpret the Wilcoxon signed-rank test, you need to examine the Z-score value and the two-tailed p-value.

Descriptive Statistics

	N	Mean	Std. Deviation	Minimum	Maximum
output1	22	8.5000	3.33452	4.00	16.00
output2	22	13.8636	2.74808	8.00	19.00

The output indicates that there is a significant difference in factory output for the first and second halves of the year, $Z = -4.113$, $p < .05$, with higher productivity in the second part of the year.

To view the **Hypothesis Test Summary**, select **Related Samples...** instead of **Legacy Dialogs** from the **Nonparametric Tests** option in the **Analyze** menu. In the **Fields** tab, move the variables into the **Test Fields:** box and click **Run**.

Hypothesis Test Summary

	Null Hypothesis	Test	Sig.	Decision
1	The median of differences between output1 and output2 equals 0.	Related-Samples Wilcoxon Signed Ranks Test	.000	Reject the null hypothesis.

Asymptotic significances are displayed. The significance level is .05.

Kruskal–Wallis test

The Kruskal–Wallis test is equivalent to the one-way between-groups analysis of variance (ANOVA), so it allows possible differences between two or more groups to be examined.

Working example

A personnel manager of a large insurance company wished to evaluate the effectiveness of three different sales training programs that had been designed for new employees. Seventy-five new graduates were randomly assigned to one of the programs, and then their annual sales figures (in $1000s) were compared 12 months later. The data violate the stringent assumptions of a one-way ANOVA, so the manager decided to perform a Kruskal–Wallis test. The data can be found in Work19e.sav on the website that accompanies this title and are shown in the following figure.

	training	sales
1	1	545
2	1	470
3	1	445
4	1	574
5	1	463
6	1	383
7	1	452
8	1	573
9	1	529
10	1	471
11	1	538
12	1	587
13	1	466
14	1	621
15	1	429
16	1	487
17	1	460
18	1	504
19	1	500
20	1	450
21	1	505
22	1	436
23	1	555
24	1	496

 To conduct a Kruskal–Wallis test

1   Select the **Analyze** menu.

2   Click on **Nonparametric Tests, Legacy Dialogs** and then on **K Independent Samples...** to open the **Tests for Several Independent Samples** box.

3   Select the dependent variable (i.e. *sales*) and click on the ⊡ button to move the variable into the **Test Variable List:** box.

4   Select the independent variable (i.e. *training*) and click on the ⊡ button to move the variable into the **Grouping Variable:** box.

5   Click on the **Define Range...** command pushbutton to open the **Several Independent Samples: Define Range** subdialogue box.

6   Enter the first value for the independent variable (*training*) (i.e. *1*) in the **Minimum:** box, then tab. Enter the greatest value for the independent variable (i.e. *3*) in the **Maximum:** box.

7   Click on **Continue**.

8   Ensure the **Kruskal–Wallis H** check box has been selected.

9   Click on **OK**.

Ranks

	training method	N	Mean Rank
sales in $1000	A	25	31.38
	B	25	38.98
	C	25	43.64
	Total	75	

Test Statistics[a,b]

	sales in $1000
Chi-square	4.032
df	2
Asymp. Sig.	.133

a. Kruskal Wallis Test

b. Grouping Variable: training method

To interpret the output from the Kruskal–Wallis test, you need to look at the chi-square value, degree of freedom (df) and significance, which has been corrected for ties.

These values indicate that sales do not significantly differ across the three training programs, $\chi^2(2, N = 75) = 4.032$, p > .05.

To obtain a **Hypothesis Test Summary**, select **Independent Samples...** instead of **Legacy Dialogs** from the **Nonparametric Tests** option in the **Analyze** menu. In the **Objective** tab, select **Customize analysis**.

In the **Fields** tab, move the independent variable (i.e. *sales*) into the into the **Test Fields:** box and the Dependent Variable (i.e. *training*) into the **Groups:** box.

In the **Settings** tab, select **Customize tests** and ensure the **Kruskal-Wallis 1-way ANOVA (k samples)** check box has been selected. Then click **Run**.

Hypothesis Test Summary

	Null Hypothesis	Test	Sig.	Decision
1	The distribution of sales in $1000 is the same across categories of training method.	Independent-Samples Kruskal-Wallis Test	.133	Retain the null hypothesis.

Asymptotic significances are displayed. The significance level is .05.

Friedman test

The Friedman test is used to compare two or more related samples, and is equivalent to the repeated-measures or within-subjects ANOVA.

Working example

Reaction times for eight subjects were measured under a placebo condition, a drug X condition and a drug Y condition. It was hypothesised that reaction times would differ significantly across drug conditions. The data violate the stringent assumptions of a repeated measures ANOVA, so it was decided that a Friedman test should be performed. The data can be found in Work19f.sav on the website that accompanies this title and are shown in the following figure.

To conduct a Friedman test

1   Select the **Analyze** menu.

2   Click on **Nonparametric Tests, Legacy Dialogs** and then on **K Related Samples...** to open the **Tests for Several Related Samples** box.

3   Select the variables you require (i.e. *drugx*, *drugy* and *placebo*) and click on the ➡ button to move the variables into the **Test Variables:** box.

4   Ensure the **Friedman** check box has been selected.

5   Click on **OK**.

Ranks

	Mean Rank
placebo	1.38
drugx	1.63
drugy	3.00

Test Statistics[a]

N	8
Chi-square	12.250
df	2
Asymp. Sig.	.002

a. Friedman Test

The results of the Friedman test indicate that significant differences do exist in reaction time across drug conditions, $\chi^2(2, N = 8) = 12.25$, p < .05, and that drug Y appears to slow reaction time considerably.

Alternatively, to obtain a **Hypothesis Test Summary**, select **Related Samples...** instead of **Legacy Dialogs** from **Nonparametric Tests** in the **Analyze** menu. In the **Objective** tab, select **Customize analysis** and in the **Fields** tab, move all the variables into the **Test Fields:** box.

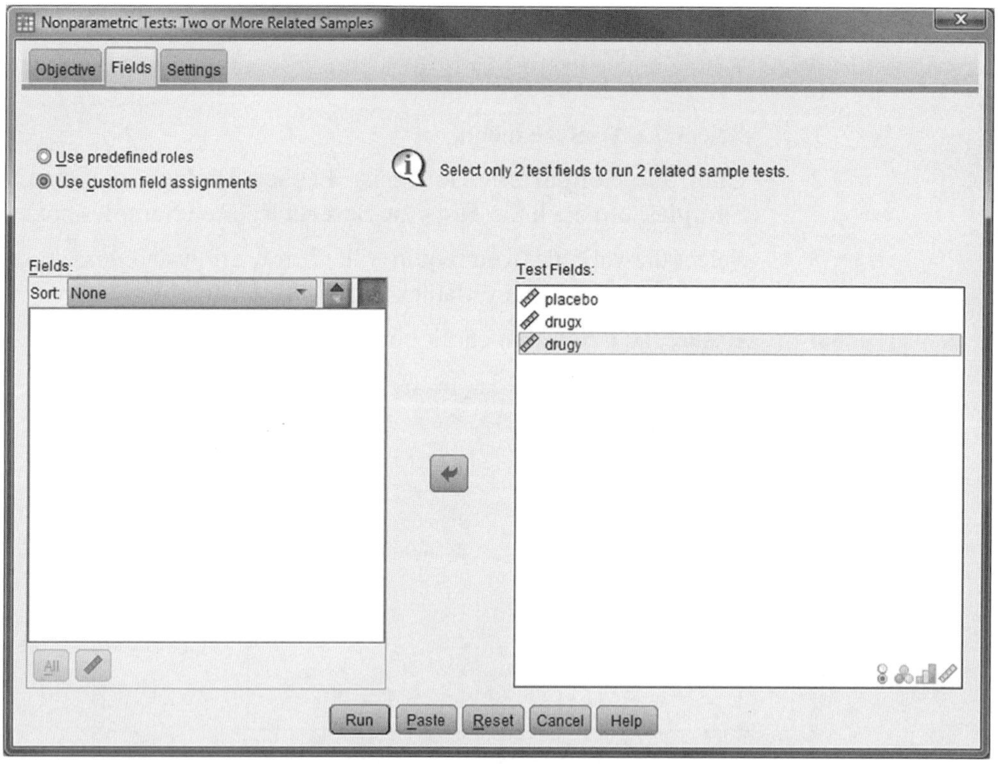

In the **Settings** tab, select **Customize tests** and ensure the **Friedman's 2-way ANOVA by ranks (k samples)** check box is selected. Click **Run**.

Hypothesis Test Summary

	Null Hypothesis	Test	Sig.	Decision
1	The distributions of placebo, drugx and drugy are the same.	Related-Samples Friedman's Two-Way Analysis of Variance by Ranks	.002	Reject the null hypothesis.

Asymptotic significances are displayed. The significance level is .05.

Spearman's rank-order correlation

A nonparametric alternative to the parametric bivariate correlation (Pearson's r) is Spearman's rho.

Working example

To examine the relationship between sales performance and employee income, data were collected from 20 sales representatives. The data violate the stringent assumptions of a Pearson's r, so it was decided a Spearman's rho should be performed. The data can be found in Work19g.sav on the website that accompanies this title and are shown in the following figure.

	sales	income	var	var	var	var	var	var	var	var	var	var
1	121	375.00										
2	119	380.00										
3	114	290.00										
4	112	270.00										
5	117	300.00										
6	118	326.00										
7	122	400.00										
8	123	387.00										
9	116	340.00										
10	117	300.00										
11	116	310.00										
12	118	367.00										
13	115	375.00										
14	115	370.00										
15	115	330.00										
16	123	410.00										
17	119	365.00										
18	114	344.00										
19	121	390.00										
20	118	355.00										
21	119	342.00										
22	117	361.00										
23	122	368.00										
24	121	395.00										

To conduct a Spearman's rank-order correlation

1   Select the **Analyze** menu.

2   Click on **Descriptive Statistics** and then on **Crosstabs...** to open the **Crosstabs** dialogue box.

3   Select the first variable (i.e. *sales*) and click on the ⮕ button to move the variable into the **Row(s):** box.

4   Select the second variable (i.e. *income*) and click on the ⮕ button to move the variable into the **Column(s):** box.

5   Click on the **Statistics...** command pushbutton to open the **Crosstabs: Statistics** subdialogue box.

6   Select the **Correlations** check box.

7   Click on **Continue** and then **OK**.

Symmetric Measures

		Value	Asymp. Std. Error[a]	Approx. T[b]	Approx. Sig.
Interval by Interval	Pearson's R	.767	.083	5.728	.000[c]
Ordinal by Ordinal	Spearman Correlation	.757	.110	5.554	.000[c]
N of Valid Cases		25			

a. Not assuming the null hypothesis.

b. Using the asymptotic standard error assuming the null hypothesis.

c. Based on normal approximation.

You can see from the output that Spearman's rank-order correlation is significant, $r(25) = .757$, $p < .05$, and so you can conclude that higher sales are associated with higher incomes.

Spearman's rho can also be obtained through the **Correlate-Bivariate** option in the **Analyze** menu.

Handy hint

- Although assumption testing is not as critical for nonparametric techniques, general assumptions apply, namely, random sampling, similar shape and variability across distributions and independence.

- If you are not required to report on detailed values of the analysis outputs, you may simply obtain a **Hypothesis Test Summary** which summarises the null hypothesis, sig. value, and suggests whether to retain or reject the null hypothesis.

CHAPTER 20

Multiple response analysis and multiple dichotomy analysis

Multiple response and multiple dichotomy analysis are commonly used in the analysis of questionnaire or survey data.

Multiple response analysis

Multiple response analysis is commonly used for the analysis of open-ended questions. For example, a questionnaire item may be:

Q: 'What do you think are the important things that need to be considered when developing higher density housing in your neighbourhood?'

You must do two things on receiving all your questionnaires back from the field, before analysing the information. These are:

1 Look at the responses to the open-ended question and determine the maximum responses to the question. In this example, are people giving one, two, three or more responses to the question?

2 Make sure you have some understanding of the range of possible responses. Will the number of different responses be less than 100, in which case you can code all responses from 01 to 99? If there seems to be more than 100 different responses, then you may have to use a three-digit code and code from 001 to 999.

Let us assume that in the example given you have decided that there is a maximum of four responses given to the question and that there are fewer than 100 different responses. Therefore, it is possible to use a two-digit code for these data. The next step is to code all your questionnaires. This coding system is defined using the **Value Labels** option. However, it is more efficient to use the **Template** option, given that there are likely to be multiple variables. Possible codes, in this example, could include:

01 — Privacy of residents

02 — Sewerage

03 — Noise from traffic

04 — Access to public transport.

In acknowledging a maximum of four possible responses to this open-ended question, it is accepted that four variables will be coded. Within IBM SPSS, these variables could be defined as *open1*, *open2*, *open3* and *open4*.

Working example

A sample of 364 farmers were asked to identify the selection criteria they used when choosing rams for their breeding program. The maximum responses obtained from an individual was four, and 14 possible criteria were identified. If an individual identified only two criteria, then a code of 88 would be used for variables 3 and 4. The data from the first four participants may look as follows:

Participant 1 01040288 (This participant has given three responses.)

Participant 2 05888888 (This participant has given one response.)

Participant 3 06011107 (This participant has given four responses.)

Participant 4 88888888 (This participant did not respond to the question.)

You wish to obtain a frequency analysis of the multiple responses of your entire sample for the question outlined on page 184.

These data can be found in Work20a.sav on the website that accompanies this title and are shown in the following figure.

	crit1	crit2	crit3	crit4
1	2	3	4	6
2	2	4	5	6
3	1	2	4	5
4	1	2	3	4
5	88	88	88	88
6	4	6	10	11
7	1	2	3	4
8	88	88	88	88
9	88	88	88	88
10	1	2	3	4
11	1	2	3	4
12	2	3	4	5
13	1	2	3	4
14	1	2	3	4
15	2	4	6	8
16	1	2	3	4
17	2	3	4	5
18	2	4	5	6
19	1	2	3	4
20	1	2	4	5
21	2	3	4	5
22	2	3	4	5
23	1	2	3	4
24	88	88	88	88

 To conduct a multiple response analysis

1   Select the **Analyze** menu.

2   Click on **Multiple Response** and then on **Define Sets...** to open the **Define Multiple Response Sets** dialogue box.

3   Select the four variables you require (i.e. *crit1* to *crit4*) and click on the ▶ button to move the variables into the **Variables in Set:** box.

4   In the **Variables Are Coded As** box, click on the **Categories** radio button.

5   In the **Range:** box, type the lowest code (i.e. *1*), press tab and then type the highest code (i.e. *14*).

6   In the **Name:** box, type a suitable variable name (i.e. *criteria*) and in the **Label:** box type a description of this variable (i.e. *Selection criteria*).

7 Click on the **Add** command pushbutton; you will notice that a new variable has been created (i.e. *$criteria*) in the **Multiple Response Sets:** box.

8 Click on **Close**.

9 Select the **Analyze** menu.

10 Click on **Multiple Response and Frequencies...** to open the **Multiple Response Frequencies** dialogue box.

11 Select the variable (i.e. *$criteria*) and click on the ⊡ button to move the variable into the **Table(s) for:** box.

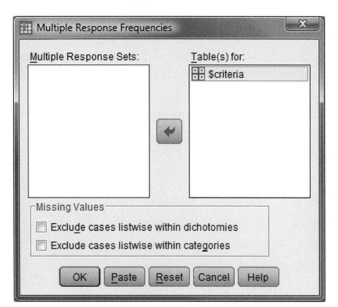

12 Click on **OK**.

Case Summary

	Cases					
	Valid		Missing		Total	
	N	Percent	N	Percent	N	Percent
$criteria[a]	276	75.8%	88	24.2%	364	100.0%

a. Group

$criteria Frequencies

		Responses		Percent of Cases
		N	Percent	
Selection criteria[a]	Fleece style	33	4.3%	12.0%
	Fibre diameter	85	11.0%	30.8%
	Greasy fleece weight	85	11.0%	30.8%
	Clean fleece weight	180	23.3%	65.2%
	Live weight	48	6.2%	17.4%
	Reproduction records	76	9.8%	27.5%
	Disease resistance	15	1.9%	5.4%
	Frame size	47	6.1%	17.0%
	Constitution	42	5.4%	15.2%
	Skin charactersitics	79	10.2%	28.6%
	Staple strength	15	1.9%	5.4%
	Feet	37	4.8%	13.4%
	Hocks, jaws	26	3.4%	9.4%
	Wool handle	4	.5%	1.4%
Total		772	100.0%	279.7%

a. Group

The frequency table of the multiple response set indicates that clean fleece weight is the most frequently used selection criterion.

Percentage of responses refers to the proportion of a given response in relation to the count; for example, 33 people cited fleece style as a selection criterion, and this is 33/772 per cent of the total responses (4.3 per cent).

Percentage of cases refers to the proportion of a given response in relation to the number of valid cases; for example, 79 people cited skin characteristics as a selection criterion and this is 79/276 per cent of the valid cases (28.6 per cent).

Multiple dichotomy analysis

Multiple dichotomy analysis is very similar to the multiple response analysis. The following questionnaire item, for example, could be analysed using a multiple dichotomy analysis.

Q: Would you object to any of the following developments being built next to your property?'

– Single house

– Group housing — duplex

– Group housing — villa units (four units or fewer)

– Group housing — villa units (five or more units)

– Group housing — townhouses (four townhouses or fewer)

– Group housing — townhouses (five or more)

– Flats or home units (three storeys or fewer)

– Flats or home units (four storeys or more)

In this example, each item would be given a variable label and a code. The codes normally used in these cases are 1 if the item is ticked and 0 if it is not ticked. If the person failed to place a tick alongside at least one item, then the missing value code of 9 might be assigned to all items. The data from the first four participants may look as follows:

Participant 1 00001111 (This participant did not tick the first four items.)

Participant 2 10000000 (This participant ticked only the first item.)

Participant 3 01111011 (This participant ticked variably across items.)

Participant 4 11111111 (This participant ticked all eight items.)

Working example

A sample of 388 home owners were asked to indicate which native trees were growing in their gardens. They were given five species to select from. Determine the species most frequently chosen by home owners. The data can be found in Work20b.sav and are shown in the following figure.

To conduct a multiple dichotomy analysis

1   Select the **Analyze** menu.

2   Click on **Multiple Response and Define Sets...** to open the **Define Multiple Response Sets** dialogue box.

3   Select the five variables (i.e. *banksia, bottle, gum, wattle, wax*) and click on the ⤷ button to move the variables into the **Variables in Set:** box.

4   In the **Variables Are Coded As** box, ensure that the **Dichotomies** radio button is selected.

5   In the **Counted value:** box, type the value that you have assigned to those items that were ticked by respondents (i.e. *1*).

6   In the **Name:** box, type a suitable variable name (i.e. *trees*) and in the **Label:** box, type a description of this variable (i.e. *native trees growing*).

7 Click on the **Add** command pushbutton. You will notice that a new variable has been created (i.e. *$trees*) in the **Multiple Response Sets:** box.

8 Click on **Close**.

9 Select the **Analyze** menu.

10 Click on **Multiple Response and Frequencies...** to open the **Multiple Response Frequencies** dialogue box.

11 Select the variable (i.e. *$trees*) and click on the ⊡ button to move the variable into the **Table(s) for:** box.

12 Click on **OK**.

Case Summary

	Cases					
	Valid		Missing		Total	
	N	Percent	N	Percent	N	Percent
$trees[a]	295	76.0%	93	24.0%	388	100.0%

a. Dichotomy group tabulated at value 1.

$trees Frequencies

		Responses		Percent of Cases
		N	Percent	
native growing trees[a]	bottle	281	92.7%	95.3%
	gum	11	3.6%	3.7%
	wattle	1	.3%	.3%
	banksia	3	1.0%	1.0%
	Geraldton wax	7	2.3%	2.4%
Total		303	100.0%	102.7%

a. Dichotomy group tabulated at value 1.

Inspection of the frequency table for the multiple dichotomous set indicates that bottle brushes are the most frequently chosen native species of tree in the garden.

Having defined multiple response or multiple dichotomous sets, it is possible to also perform crosstabs analysis, by means of which response sets or categorical variables can be presented in tabular form.

Handy hints

- Multiple response sets can also be defined in the data drop-down menu under the option **Define Multiple Response Sets**. However, this procedure does not allow the user to perform further analysis as sets defined here are not available in the **Multiple Response Frequencies** and **Crosstabs** procedures. Furthermore, the **Variable Coding** option does not allow the user to specify a range when working with variables coded as categories.

- Like earlier versions, IBM SPSS Version 18 allows the option of performing significance testing on multiple response sets. This is achievable by using the **Custom Table** function and performing a crosstabs analysis with an independent variable in the row of the table.

Multidimensional scaling

Multidimensional scaling (MDS) starts with a data set of 'proximities', which indicate the degree of 'similarity' or 'dissimilarity' among elements in a defined set. The proximity measures may be either 'direct' or 'derived' measures of proximity. If the measures are direct, then respondents have usually provided a direct estimate of the degree of (dis)similarity between any pair of elements, through either a rating or classification task. Derived proximities, on the other hand, usually consist of some measure of association (e.g. correlation) among elements within a set.

The objective of MDS is to take the proximities data and represent the elements in multi-dimensional space, so that the distances among the elements in the space accurately represent the original proximity measures. This chapter provides a basic overview of the concept of MDS. IBM SPSS also provides several alternative data analysis options that can be further developed and explored after a basic knowledge of MDS has been developed.

Working example

As part of a study into tourist perceptions of Australia, you are interested in under-standing how tourists from other countries comprehend travel distances among some of the major cities in Australia.

You provide a group of three visiting tourists with the names of eight Australian cities they are likely to visit. You indicate to the group that the distance between Sydney and Perth is 100 units and that they are to make judgements about what they think are the distances between all the remaining pairs of cities relative to the distance between Sydney and Perth.

The judgements made by all three tourists are averaged. The data can be found in Work21.sav on the website that accompanies this title. The data file represents the average of all the three judgements and is shown as a lower triangular matrix (see the following figure).

File   Edit   View   Data   Transform   Analyze   Graphs   Utilities   Add-ons   Window   Help

1 : Perth   1.00   Visible: 9 of 9 Variables

	Perth	Adelaide	Melbourne	Hobart	Sydney	Brisbane	Darwin	Cairns	Broome	var	var	var
1	1.00	.	.	.	.	.	.	.	.			
2	50.00	1.00	.	.	.	.	.	.	.			
3	75.00	30.00	1.00	.	.	.	.	.	.			
4	90.00	50.00	20.00	1.00	.	.	.	.	.			
5	100.00	55.00	35.00	50.00	1.00	.	.	.	.			
6	120.00	65.00	85.00	80.00	25.00	1.00	.	.	.			
7	80.00	100.00	110.00	130.00	70.00	55.00	1.00	.	.			
8	160.00	100.00	90.00	120.00	70.00	50.00	55.00	1.00	.			
9	50.00	110.00	130.00	140.00	100.00	80.00	40.00	80.00	1.00			
10												
11												
12												

Data View   Variable View

PASW Statistics Processor is ready

To conduct an MDS analysis

1   Select the **Analyze** menu.

2   Click on **Scale** and **Multidimensional Scaling... (PROXSCAL)** to open the **Multidimensional Scaling: Data Format** dialogue box.

3   In the **Data Format** box, select **The data are proximities** radio button.

4   In the **Number of Sources** box, make sure that the **One matrix source** radio button is selected.

5   In the **One Source** box, select **The proximities are in a matrix across columns** option.

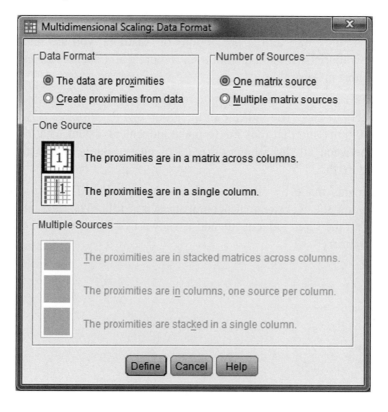

6   Click on the **Define** command pushbutton to open the **Multidimensional Scaling (Proximities in Matrices Across Columns)** dialogue box.

7   Select the nine variables representing each of the cities and click on the ⏎ button to move the variables into the **Proximities:** box.

8   Click on the **Model...** command pushbutton to open the **Multidimensional Scaling: Model** subdialogue box.

9   In the **Shape** box, select the **Lower-triangular matrix** radio button.

10   In the **Proximities** box, select the **Dissimilarities** radio button.

11   In the **Proximity Transformations** box, make sure that the **Ordinal** radio button is selected.

12   In the **Dimensions** box ensure that you have entered 2 for the **Minimum:** and 2 for the **Maximum:**.

13 Click on **Continue** to return to the **Multidimensional Scaling (Proximities in Matrices Across Columns)** dialogue box.

14 Click on the **Plots** command pushbutton to open the **Multidimensional Scaling: Plots** subdialogue box.

15 In the **Plots** box, ensure that the **Common space** and **Transformed proximities vs. distances** check boxes are both selected. The **All sources** radio button should also be selected in the **Source Plots** box.

16 Click on **Continue** once again to return to the **Multidimensional Scaling (Proximities in Matrices Across Columns)** dialogue box.

17 Click on the **Options** command pushbutton to open the **Multidimensional Scaling: Options** subdialogue box.

18 In the **Initial Configuration** box, ensure that the **Simplex** radio button is selected.

19 In the **Iteration Criteria** box, ensure that **Stress convergence:** is *.0001*, **Minimum stress:** is *.0001* and the **Maximum iterations:** is *100*.

20 Again, click on **Continue** to return to the **Multidimensional Scaling (Proximities in Matrices Across Columns)** dialogue box.

21 Click on the **Output** command pushbutton to open the **Multidimensional Scaling: Output** subdialogue box.

22 In the **Display** box, ensure that you select the **Common space coordinates**, **Iteration history** and **Multiple stress measures** check boxes.

23 Click on **Continue** and then **OK**.

MDS analysis has the potential to produce considerable output. The analysis that has been described is for a simple MDS solution in a two-dimensional space. Once an understanding is developed of the output of this simple solution, commands may be changed to produce more extended output, including increasing the dimensional space to three or more dimensions.

It is important before any inspection of the analyses to confirm that the data have been entered and analysed correctly. The case-processing summary shown in the following indicates that there were nine cases (towns), one source or matrix was analysed and, when excluding the diagonal, this matrix consisted of 36 proximity measures.

Case Processing Summary

Cases		9
Sources		1
Objects		9
Proximities	Total Proximities	36[a]
	Missing Proximities	0
	Active Proximities[b]	36

a. Sum of all strictly lower-triangular proximities.

b. Active proximities include all non-missing proximities.

The iteration history with the normalised raw stress values is shown in the following. The raw stress values are an indication of how well the original proximities are represented by the distances in the final multidimensional solution. From a starting configuration, PROXSCAL iteratively moves the data points so that there is continuous improvement in the fit between the original proximities and distances in the final solution. After ten iterations, the iteration history stopped because the stress convergence of .0001 had been reached.

Iteration History

Iteration	Normalized Raw Stress	Improvement
0	.17692[a]	
1	.00942	.16750
2	.00697	.00246
3	.00600	.00097
4	.00549	.00051
5	.00514	.00035
6	.00489	.00025
7	.00470	.00019
8	.00455	.00014
9	.00444	.00011
10	.00436	.00009[b]

a. Stress of initial configuration: simplex start.

b. The iteration process has stopped because Improvement has become less than the convergence criterion.

There are several stress measures and measures of fit that indicate how well the original proximities are represented as distances in a multidimensional space. The most commonly used measure of fit is stress-I or Kruskal's stress. It is this value that needs to be minimised, because a lower stress value indicates a better fit between the original proximities and the derived distances. As a rule of thumb, when Kruskal's stress is less than 0.10, the fit is considered excellent, and anything over 0.10 is becoming less acceptable. Although an attempt is made to minimise stress values, high measures of the dispersion accounted for and Tucker's coefficient of congruence (greater than .90) indicate a reasonably good fit of the original proximities to the derived distances. In the working example, Kruskal's stress and Tucker's coefficient of congruence indicate that there is a good fit between the original proximity measures and derived distances.

Stress and Fit Measures

Normalized Raw Stress	.00436
Stress-I	.06600[a]
Stress-II	.18327[a]
S-Stress	.01119[b]
Dispersion Accounted For (D.A.F.)	.99564
Tucker's Coefficient of Congruence	.99782

PROXSCAL minimizes Normalized Raw Stress.

a. Optimal scaling factor = 1.004.

b. Optimal scaling factor = .997.

The coordinates of each of the nine data points (towns) for a two-dimensional solution are illustrated in the 'Final Coordinates' output below. These are the coordinates that IBM SPSS uses to plot the common space.

Final Coordinates

	Dimension	
	1	2
Perth	.016	-.803
Adelaide	-.416	-.269
Melbourne	-.623	.018
Hobart	-.767	.149
Sydney	-.208	.326
Brisbane	.164	.419
Darwin	.639	.035
Cairns	.532	.611
Broome	.663	-.486

Although stress and other goodness of fit measures may be used to provide an indication of how well the final configuration fits the original proximities data, one of the most important criteria is the interpretability of the final solution. The common space, illustrated in the chart, is certainly interpretable.

Object Points

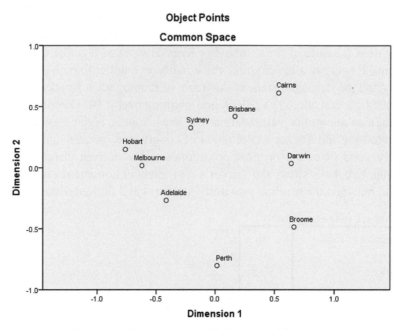

Further evidence of the reasonably high level of fit between the original proximities and derived distances is also shown in the Shepard diagram that follows, which plots the original but transformed proximities against the derived distances. As the fit improves, this relationship should increasingly approximate a straight-line relationship with minimal dispersion.

Residuals Plot

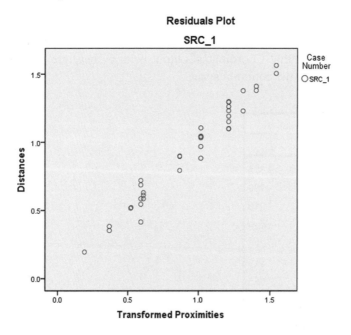

CHAPTER 22

Working with output

This chapter provides an overview of how to work with output within the IBM SPSS program.

Editing output in the SPSS Viewer

The **SPSS Viewer** or **Output Navigator** window, as it has been referred to in previous versions, provides a table of contents of all your output in a session. You can use this outline to navigate through your output and control the output display. Most actions undertaken in this pane have a corresponding effect on the contents pane. The outline pane is useful if you want to browse your results, to show or hide particular tables and charts, to change the display or ordering of results by moving particular items or to move between the outline pane and other applications.

To start working with some output, we first need to access some data. When the IBM SPSS program is installed, it comes with particular data sets. For the purpose of this chapter, we will use one of the data sets available within the program.

 To access the data and obtain some output

1   Double-click on the IBM SPSS program icon to begin your SPSS session.

2   The program will open to the **SPSS for Windows** dialogue box which will give you a number of choices, such as **Run the tutorial** and **Type in data**. Ensure the **Open an existing data source** radio button is selected.

3   You will notice a number of different files are listed. Click on the filename *Dugong assignment rev.sav*, then click on **OK**.

4   Click on the **Analyze** menu.

5   Click on **Descriptive Statistics** and then on **Frequencies** to open the **Frequencies** dialogue box.

6   Select the variable you require (i.e. *Where do you live [live]*) and click on the ⊡ button to move the variable into the **Variable(s):** box.

7   Click on the **Charts...** command pushbutton to open the **Frequencies: Charts** subdialogue box.

8   Click on the **Bar charts** radio button.

9   Click on **Continue** and then **OK**.

You should now be in the SPSS Viewer and the output of the procedure just run should be displayed.

Statistics

Where do you live

N	Valid	400
	Missing	0

Where do you live

		Frequency	Percent	Valid Percent	Cumulative Percent
Valid	Sunnydeck	61	15.3	15.3	15.3
	Dugong	296	74.0	74.0	89.3
	Sandstone	13	3.3	3.3	92.5
	Clearwater Bay	30	7.5	7.5	100.0
	Total	400	100.0	100.0	

The output results can now be browsed by expanding, collapsing, hiding and showing particular aspects of the output.

 To collapse and expand outline items

1   Click on the small yellow box to the left of the outline item you want to collapse (i.e. the small yellow box next to the **Frequencies** item). You will notice that a small red arrow has appeared to the left of **Frequencies**, and that all subitems beneath this output have been highlighted.

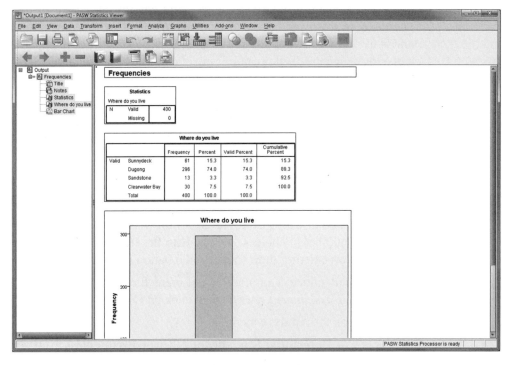

2   Select the **View** menu and click on **Collapse**. You will notice that the output in the contents pane has been collapsed and is no longer displayed.

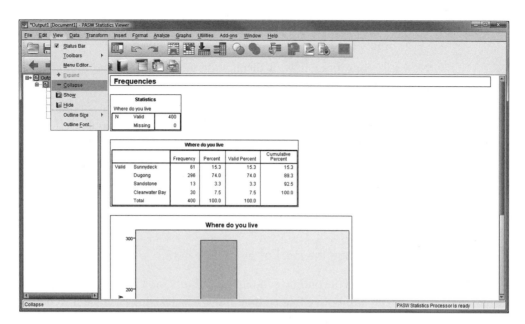

3 To expand the item, repeat the above procedure, but this time click on **Expand** not **Collapse**. The output is again displayed.

It is also possible to expand and collapse outline items without using the menu feature. This is as simple as clicking ⊞ / ⊟ located to the left of the outline item you wish to expand or collapse.

 To hide and show outline items

1 Click on the outline subitem titled *Statistics* within the **Frequencies** item. Again, you will notice that a small red arrow has appeared next to the *Statistics* subitem and that this arrow is also highlighting the corresponding statistics table in the contents pane. You will also notice that the symbol (a book) next to the *Statistics* subitem is open, indicating that the corresponding table is present in the contents pane.

2 Select the **View** menu and click on **Hide**. You will notice that the corresponding output in the contents pane has disappeared and is no longer displayed.

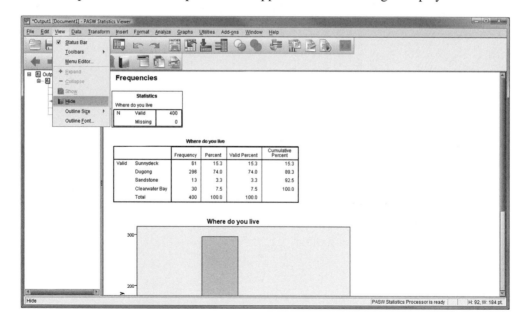

3 To show or display the output again, repeat the above procedure but click on **Show** not **Hide**. The output is again displayed.

Now it is your turn: show or display the output corresponding to *Notes* in the contents pane using this procedure.

As was the case with collapsing and expanding output, it is possible to hide and show output without using the menu system. This is done by double-clicking your mouse on the book icon that corresponds to each outline item. Remember, if the book icon is open, then the output is displayed; if the book is closed, then the output has been temporarily hidden from view. Alternatively, show and hide buttons are available on the toolbar.

It is also possible to change the level of an outline item in the outline pane; that is, to promote or demote an item.

To change the level of an outline item

1 Click on the outline subitem titled *Bar Chart* within the **Frequencies** item. Again, you will notice that a small red arrow has appeared next to this subitem and that this arrow is also highlighting the corresponding table in the contents pane. You will also notice that the book icon is open.

2 Select the **Edit** menu and click on **Outline** and then **Promote**. You will notice that the **Bar Chart** has now been promoted to an item of its own.

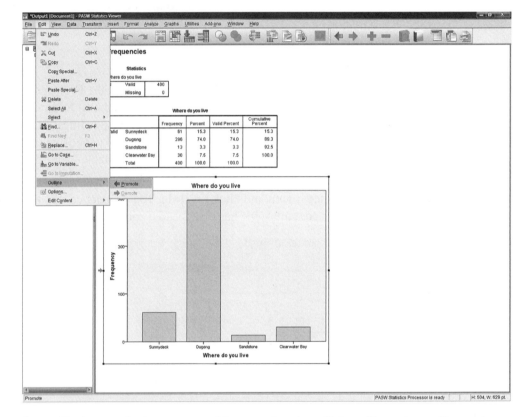

3 To demote the item, repeat this procedure but click on **Demote** not **Promote**.

Items can also be promoted and demoted by using the left arrow and right arrow keys on the SPSS Viewer toolbar.

▶ To move outline items in the SPSS Viewer

1   Click an item in the outline or contents pane to select it (i.e. *title*).

2   Use the mouse to click and drag the item to the bottom of the subitem listing.

3   Release the mouse button just above where you want to place the moved item. You will notice that the title has also moved in the contents pane.

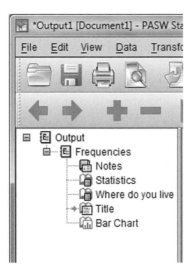

Items can also be cut, pasted or deleted in this manner using the **Edit** menu. To delete the *Notes* subitem, select it and then press the delete button.

▶ To change the size and font of items in the outline

1   Select the **View** menu and select **Outline Size**.

2   Click on **Medium**. You will notice that the font size in the outline pane has increased in size.

3   Select the **View** menu again and select **Outline Font**.

4   Select **Arial Narrow** from the list of fonts and click on **OK**.

You will notice that the font style has now changed.

To add a new title or text item to the outline contents pane

You may wish to add new titles or text items to your output that are not connected to particular tables or charts.

1   Click on the table, chart or object in the contents pane that will precede the title or text. This means that the new title will be inserted beneath the *item selected* in the contents pane.

2   Select the **Insert** menu and click on **New Title**.

3   Double-click on the new object/box that has been created in the contents pane.

4   Enter the text you want at this location (i.e. *Residential Location of Survey Respondents*).

5   Now with two titles, use the delete key to delete the old title *Frequencies*. New text and new headings can also be added in this manner using the **Insert** menu.

Modifying and improving charts for presentation

Now let us consider some chart outputs. Although the charts generated by IBM SPSS contain the requested information in a logical format, you may find that some changes are required for presentational purposes to improve the charts you have created. These may include inserting titles and subtitles; adding a 3-D effect to a bar chart; changing the intercluster spacing between bars on a bar chart; removing axis titles; altering the orientation of labels; enlarging scale axes and adding annotations such as average scores and other descriptive statistics.

Many of these functions can be achieved using the **Chart Editor** menu bar, which replaces the main menu bar when a Chart window is active. The **Chart Editor** menu bar contains six menu items: **File**, **Edit**, **View**, **Options**, **Elements** and **Help**.

Let us first generate some output with which to work.

1   Select the **Graphs** menu and click on **Legacy Dialogs** and then **Bar**.

2   Click on **Clustered**. Also ensure the **Summaries for groups of cases** radio button has been checked in the **Data in Chart Are** box.

3   Click on **Define**.

4   Select the variable which you require (i.e. *Where do you live [live]*) and click on the ⦿ button to move the variable into the **Category Axis:** box.

5   Select the variable by which you wish to define the above variable (i.e. *What is your gender [sex]*) and click on the ⦿ button to move the variable into the **Define clusters by:** box.

6   In the **Bars Represent** box, ensure that the **% of cases** radio button has been checked.

7   Click on **OK**.

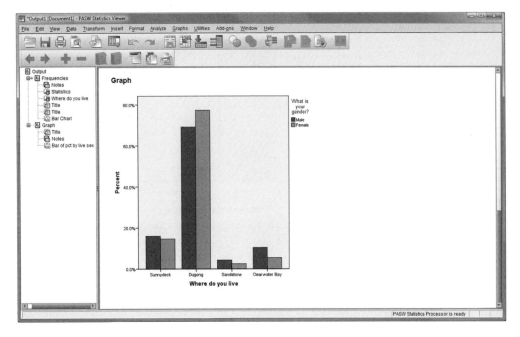

You should now be in the SPSS Viewer, where a bar graph of your results is displayed. Let us now open the Chart Editor to modify the chart and improve its presentation. This is achieved by double-clicking on the chart in the Viewer window to open the Chart Editor window. Also highlight the bars in the bar graph by clicking on the bar with your left mouse button. Now you are ready to modify the bar chart.

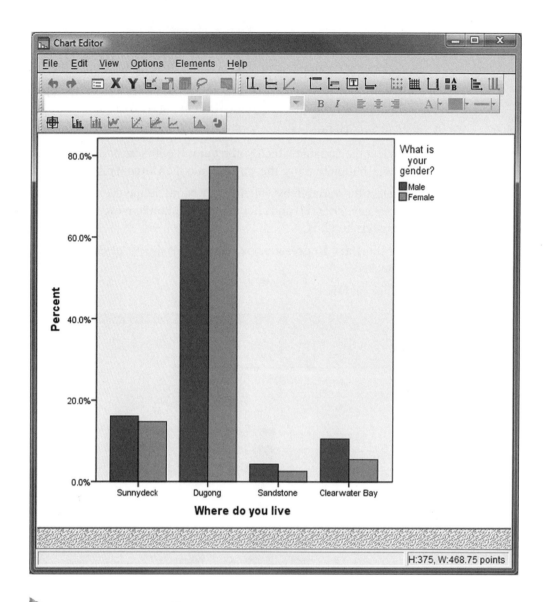

To create a 3-D effect

1   **Click on the bars on the bar chart**.

2   Click on the **Show Properties Window** tool located on the toolbar to open the **Properties** dialogue box. Alternatively, you may also double-click on any aspect of the chart to open the relevant **Properties** dialogue box.

3   Click on **Depth & Angle** tab and then click on the **3-D** radio button in the **Effect** box.

4 Click on **Apply** and on **Close**.

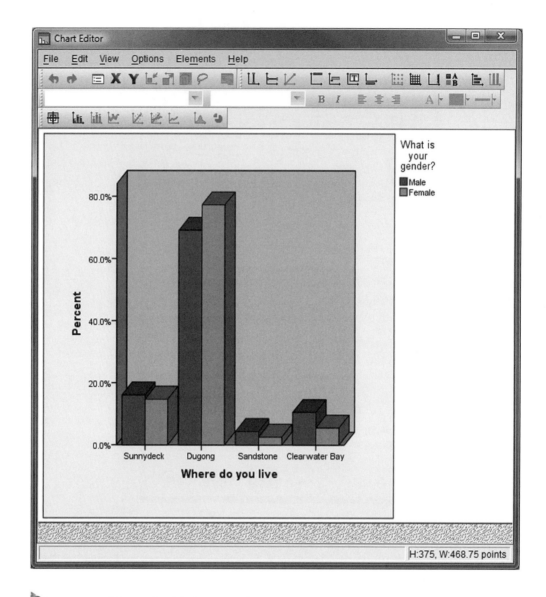

To modify and add chart attributes

Modifying and adding chart attributes is easy in the **Chart Editor** window. By double-clicking on any aspect of the chart, you can open the relevant **Properties** dialogue box to alter chart size, text, axis labels, number format, scale, fill, borders and so on. Take a few minutes to experiment with the chart currently in the editor. Always remember when modifying chart attributes to click on **Apply** to change the particular attribute and then to click on **Close** to close the dialogue box.

Right-clicking on any aspect of the chart opens a range of other options, such as adding chart elements (**annotations**, **textboxes**, **footnotes** and **titles**), **Hide Legend** and **Transpose Chart**. These functions are also available on the toolbar. Once again, have a go at using these functions yourself on the chart in the Chart Editor.

Another very useful tool within the chart editor is the **Data Label Mode**. If you click on this tool on the toolbar, and then click on a bar on the chart, the tool will attach the data value for that particular bar. Do the same for the other bars of the chart. To turn this function off, click on the **Data Label Mode** again.

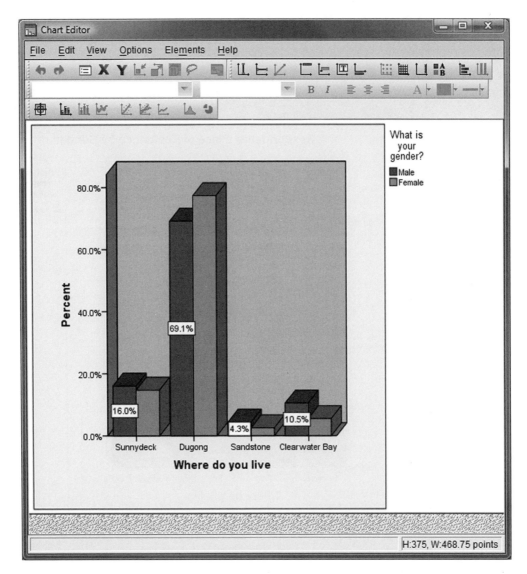

Now create a title for the chart by inserting a text box above the chart. Just click on the **Insert a Text Box** tool and a box will appear in the chart window; type in a chart title and place the title above the bar graph.

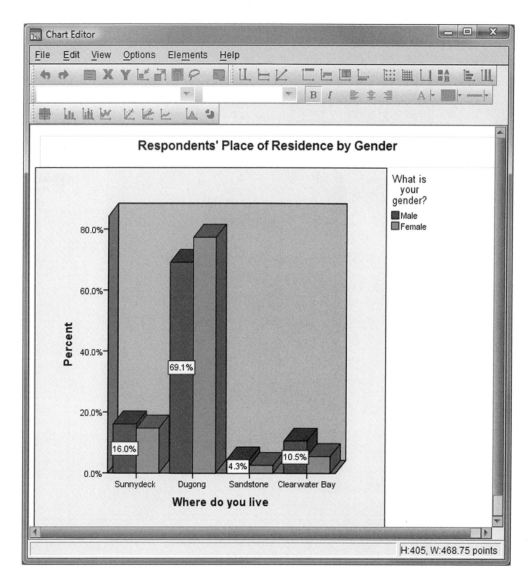

It really is very simple to make your charts look fabulous.

Now create a pie chart to modify.

 To create a pie chart

1   Select the **Graphs** menu. You will notice this can also be accessed from within the SPSS Viewer window as well as in the Data Editor window.

2   Click on **Legacy Dialogs** and then **Pie...** to open the **Pie Charts** dialogue box.

3   Ensure the **Summaries for groups of cases** radio button is checked and then click on the **Define** pushbutton.

4   Select the variable you require from the variable list (i.e. *Approval relating to the proposal [approval]*) and click on the ➡ button to move the variable into the **Define Slices by:** box. Also make sure that the **% of cases** radio button is selected.

5   Click on the **Options...** pushbutton and make sure that the **Display groups defined by missing values** check box is unchecked.

6   Click on **Continue** and then **OK**. This output has now been added to your Output Navigator/Viewer window, and your pie chart is displayed.

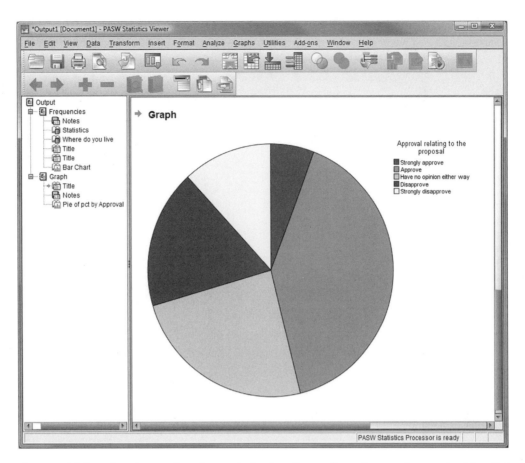

Try modifying the chart using the tools in the chart editor. Remember to double-click anywhere on the pie chart to activate the **Chart Editor** window — you will notice a few extra tools available to you, such as the Explode Slice tool. To make changes, just double-click on the aspect of the chart you are trying to modify or click your right mouse button to open the menu of tools available to you.

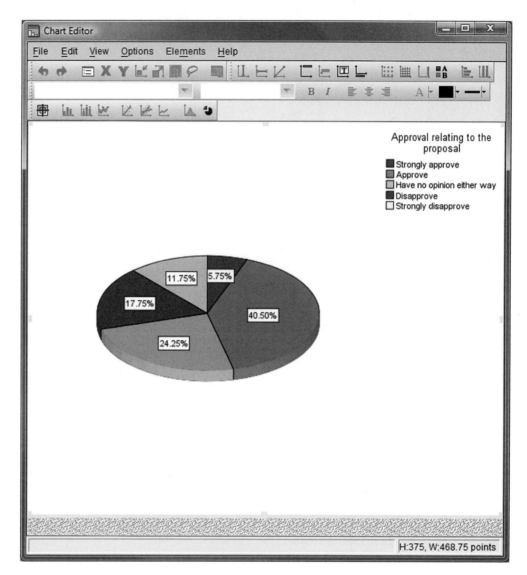

Now we are going to copy the chart and paste it into another application.

 To copy and paste a chart into another application

1   Ensure the Chart Editor window is active.

2   Select the **Edit** menu and click on **Copy Chart**. The chart has now been saved to the clipboard even though you cannot see it. You can view the chart in the clipboard viewer available in Windows if you wish.

3   Open a blank or existing file in a new application (for example, Microsoft Word).

4   Select the Edit menu in the new application and click on **Paste**.

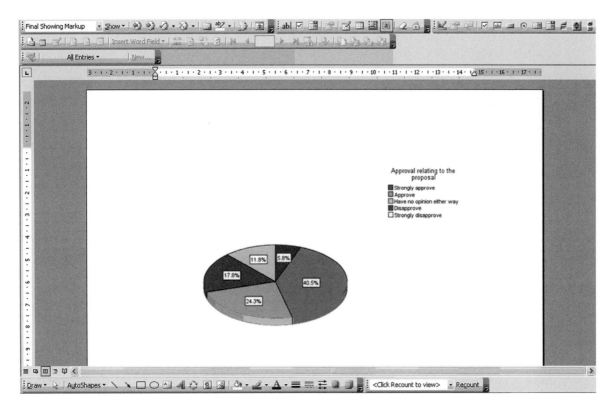

5   Save your Word file and return to IBM SPSS to finish the session.

Like earlier versions of SPSS, IBM SPSS version 18 has the capability to embed both pivot tables and charts interactively into other applications; that is, tables and charts can be copied and pasted into other applications.

Obviously, many other charts can be modified in SPSS, such as boxplots, scatterplots, histograms and line graphs. This section has provided you with a brief introduction to some of the basic procedures that can be undertaken to improve the presentation of bar graphs and pie charts in the Chart Editor window.

SECTION 2

Analysing data with **IBM SPSS**

Introduction and research questions

You have learned how to develop a data file and have worked through a range of analytical techniques. This section of the text allows you to extend this knowledge in doing analysis on a complete data set. Although not all the techniques that you have learned in section 1 (chapters 1 to 22) will be appropriate to apply to this data set, the file provided will give you an opportunity to interrogate the data set in several different ways through a range of research questions. This is obviously more in line with usual research practice.

The following section is comprehensive, comprising several research questions for you to work through using the full version of IBM SPSS version 18 software. Some of the research questions in this section cannot be answered using the student version of IBM SPSS 18 (which is an optional extra for a fee with this book) because the functions it has available are limited. A short-form list of the research questions in this section and associated short-form data set that are compatible with the student version of the software can be found on the website that accompanies this text.

Chapter 24 provides additional opportunities for students to work through research scenarios and homework exercises using the student version of the software.

When you open the data file, a list of all the variables in the data set can be found in the **Variable View** window in the SPSS Data Editor — this may help you visualise how the survey has been converted to an SPSS data file.

The following sections outline the context in which your research is based, describe the proposal or project under investigation and define your role in the research process.

Working example

The research context

The town of Dugong is situated in the far north of Queensland and has a population of 2400 residents, with many established families that have been living in the area for many years. Dugong is located on the tip of a peninsula and is approximately 5 km from the more established residential areas of Sunnydeck, Sandstone and Clearwater Bay. These areas have developed in more recent years, as residents from the south have migrated to the area for a more peaceful coastal lifestyle, away from the hustle and bustle of the larger regional centre: Ellington.

The town's major income centres around the commercial and recreational fishing industries, with many families owning small fishing licences. The coastline and reef is highly valued by local residents, who actively participate in a number of community and environmental groups. There is a strong sense of community among residents in the area.

The proposal

123 Developments is a development company specialising in the development of residential and tourism precincts. The company proposes to establish a residential and resort development on the Dugong Peninsula, spanning three kilometres of the coastline to the south. The area has been selected because of its natural beauty, proximity to the coast and pristine reef. The proposal, known as the 'Dugong Peninsula Sea Change Development', is being developed to meet the growing increase in population in the region and the desire by many Australians to change their pace of life.

The research project

You are currently working for a small consultancy practice that specialises in the area of community consultation. You have been approached by 123 Developments to ascertain community attitudes and perceptions in relation to the proposal and you have developed and implemented a survey instrument that attempts to measure the community's:

(a)   knowledge and awareness of the proposal

(b)   beliefs about the potential benefits and disadvantages of the proposal

(c)   support for the proposal.

It also includes:

(d)   questions related to the social and demographic characteristics of respondents.

Having administered the survey and entered your data, you are now ready to do some analysis. You are required to provide a report to your client on the key findings of the survey to help them better understand the attitudes of the community towards the proposal.

The next section, 'Research questions', outlines the questions that you will be required to work through to meet your client's (123 Developments) brief. The section that follows, 'Research findings', illustrates how you should have approached these research questions.

Consider each of the research questions that follow and do the appropriate preparatory and analytical procedures. If you are unsure, just have a go — good researchers learn to explore their data effectively, they become intimate with their data files; it is a bit like an expedition — sometimes when you begin you are really not sure which way you might go, but you have the necessary tools along the way to help you reach your destination.

We tend to think of research in the same way: it is a journey — using the tools and techniques available to us to reach a conclusion that attempts to further the current knowledge base.

The data can be found in *Dugong_takehome.sav* on the website that accompanies this title and are shown in the following figure.

If you are using a student version of the IBM SPSS software, a short-form list of the research questions in this section can be found in *Dugong_takehome.doc*, and the associated data can be found in *Dugong_takehome.sav*.

Dugong_takehome.sav [DataSet2] - PASW Statistics Data Editor

File Edit View Data Transform Analyze Graphs Utilities Add-ons Window Help

1 : Agecat

Visible: 144 of 144 Variables

	Id	Heard	Where	NrDugong	NrSunnyDeck	NrSandstone	NrClearwaters	Knowledge	Functioncentre	Sportreccentre	Shoppingcentre	Highriseapartments	Approvalprocess	Attract	Temporary	Permanent	Both	dontknowq6	Approval
1	.	2.00	2.00	.	.	.	.	2.00	.	.	.	.	.	.	.	.	.	.	5.0
2	2.00	1.00	2.00	.	.	.	.	2.00	.	.	.	.	.	.	.	.	.	.	3.0
3	3.00	2.00	2.00	.	.	.	.	2.00	.	.	.	.	.	.	.	.	.	.	1.0
4	4.00	2.00	2.00	.	.	.	.	2.00	.	.	.	.	.	.	.	.	.	.	2.0
5	5.00	1.00	2.00	.	.	.	.	2.00	.	.	.	.	.	.	.0	.0	.0	1.00	2.0
6	6.00	1.00	1.00	.0	1.00	.0	.0	1.00	1.00	.0	.0	.0	.0	.	.0	.0	.0	1.00	5.0
7	7.00	1.00	1.00	.0	.0	.0	1.00	1.00	1.00	.0	.0	.0	.0	.	.0	.0	.0	1.00	4.0
8	8.00	1.00	1.00	.0	.0	1.00	.0	2.00	.	.	.	.	.	1.00	.0	.0	1.00	.0	2.0
9	9.00	1.00	1.00	.0	.0	.0	1.00	2.00	.	.	.	.	.	2.00	.0	1.00	.0	.0	4.0
10	10.00	1.00	1.00	.0	.0	1.00	.0	1.00	1.00	.0	.0	.0	.0	2.00	.0	1.00	.0	.0	3.0
11	11.00	2.00	2.00	.	.	.	.	2.00	.	.	.	.	.	.	.	.	.	.	2.0
12	12.00	2.00	2.00	.	.	.	.	2.00	.	.	.	.	.	.	.	.	.	.	2.0
13	13.00	2.00	2.00	.	.	.	.	2.00	.	.	.	.	.	.	.	.	.	.	2.0
14	14.00	1.00	2.00	.	.	.	.	2.00	.	.	.	.	.	.	.0	.0	.0	1.00	3.0
15	15.00	2.00	2.00	.	.	.	.	2.00	.	.	.	.	.	.	.	.	.	.	3.0
16	16.00	1.00	1.00	.0	1.00	.0	.0	2.00	.	.	.	.	.	2.00	.0	1.00	.0	.0	2.0
17	17.00	2.00	2.00	.	.	.	.	2.00	.	.	.	.	.	.	.	.	.	.	4.0
18	18.00	2.00	2.00	.	.	.	.	2.00	.	.	.	.	.	.	.	.	.	.	4.0
19	19.00	2.00	2.00	.	.	.	.	2.00	.	.	.	.	.	.	.	.	.	.	3.0
20	20.00	2.00	2.00	.	.	.	.	2.00	.	.	.	.	.	.	.	.	.	.	2.0
21	21.00	1.00	1.00	.0	1.00	.0	.0	2.00	.	.	.	.	.	2.00	.0	1.00	.0	.0	2.0
22	22.00	1.00	1.00	.0	1.00	.0	.0	2.00	.	.	.	.	.	.	.0	.0	.0	1.00	3.0
23	23.00	1.00	1.00	.0	1.00	.0	.0	1.00	1.00	.0	.0	.0	.0	.	.0	.0	.0	1.00	5.0

Data View Variable View

PASW Statistics Processor is ready

Research questions

Data preparation and screening

••

Before you begin analysis, you want to make sure that the data have been correctly entered and that, where relevant, the distribution of variables that are to be used in the analysis is normal. This may influence what type of techniques you may choose to use, that is, parametric or nonparametric techniques. You will also need to consider the types of variables that you have in your data file; that is, categorical, continuous variables, to determine what types of analysis may be most appropriate. You will also notice that while many of the items on the questionnaire are closed in nature (specified response categories), others have followed what we call a *free recall* format, in which respondents have been asked to identify responses. Remember later on that for these items, multiple response and multiple dichotomy analysis may be useful techniques to employ.

1   You understand that your research assistant, who entered the data for you, has had some problems with a couple of the variables in the data file, namely the variables *heard* and *where*. Before commencing any analysis of the data, you want to make sure that the data have been correctly entered for these particular variables and that no errors have occurred in data entry.

2   You remember that certain items on the sense of community subscales are negatively worded and, therefore, require recoding. A five-point Likert scale response format was used for each of the scales. Items that are negatively worded include *influence items 3, 5, 8, 9 and 10, emotional connection items 1, 3, 4 and 7 and community trust scale items 6 and 7*.

3   Before we begin some descriptive analysis, let us develop a new variable called *age*. As you may be aware, respondents are often sensitive about providing their age directly on surveys but will often be happy to provide the year in which they were born — crazy really! Using the variable *born* compute a new variable called *age* in your data file.

4   Now collapse the variable age into a categorical variable called *agecategory*, which consists of the following age groupings:

- *15–24 years*
- *25–34 years*
- *35–44 years*
- *45–54 years*
- *55–64 years*
- *65–74 years*
- *75–84 years*
- *85+ years*

5   You wish to determine the internal consistency of the trust scale before commencing analysis. How reliable is the scale?

6   Having determined the reliability of the scale, you wish to create a new composite variable for further analysis. You may have noticed that a variable called *Trustscore2* already exists in the data set. Please ignore this variable for now as it will be used later for further analysis.

7   Given that you were involved in the implementation of the survey, you are unsure whether the distribution of the composite trust indicator is normal. You are aware that the assumption of normality is a prerequisite for many inferential statistical techniques for which you may want to use this variable. Therefore, you want to determine whether this particular variable has a normal distribution. Check whether normality is present using a histogram, boxplot and skewness and kurtosis statistics.

8   You have included in the questionnaire a sense of community scale that comprises four subscales. The scale has recently received much debate in the literature in relation to the robustness of the underlying factor structure. The four subscales have been reported to measure the concept of 'sense of community' and include the elements of:

- *membership:* a feeling of belonging or sharing a strong sense of personal relatedness
- *emotional connection:* shared history, common places, time together and similar experiences
- *reinforcement:* shared values, success of working together to achieve collective goals or outcomes
- *influence:* ability to make a difference and feel significant.

You decide to explore the scale data to look at the underlying factor structure of the scale, and determine whether the set of variables are reflected in the four theoretically proposed subscales.

Social and demographic characteristics

In reporting your survey results, it is important to document the social and demographic characteristics of respondents. Questionnaire items that relate to social and demographic characteristics are located towards the end of the data file, and include variables such as *howlong, worked, anyoneelsework, sex, age, agecat*.

1   You want to obtain appropriate frequency distributions for all of the social and demographic variables in your data file. Remember, the distribution you use will depend upon the type of variable you are interested in assessing, that is, continuous (measured on ratio or interval scales) or categorical (measured on nominal or ordinal scales). Also, determine measures of central tendency and variability as appropriate.

2   Is data transformation required for any variable?

Knowledge and awareness of the proposal

You are particularly interested in the results associated with respondents' knowledge and awareness of the proposal and whether this differs by particular social and demographic characteristics. Using the appropriate procedures, you are required to answer the following research questions:

1   What proportion of respondents had heard about the proposed Dugong Peninsula Sea Change Development?

2   Did awareness of the proposal differ by geographic location (Dugong township versus the other locations)?

3   Generally, were older respondents more aware of the proposal than younger respondents?

4   How many respondents knew where the proposed development was to be located?

5   Where did most respondents believe that the proposed development was to be located?

6   How many respondents knew something about the nature of the proposed development and what could they identify or what did they know?

7   Did respondents know what type of clientele the development may attract?

Evaluation and impact assessment

1   What was the degree of *approval* among respondents in relation to the proposed development?

2   Were respondents in the Dugong township more likely to disapprove of the proposal?

3   Is the respondent's knowledge of the proposal related to how they evaluate the proposal (their degree of approval)?

4   What were the perceived *benefits* of the proposed development?

5   What were the perceived *costs* of the proposed development?

6   In the survey you have included a trust scale, because previous project experience has highlighted that perceived trust is a determinant of community perception in relation to development projects. You have also observed that females tend to be more trusting of proponents than males, so you wish to test this hypothesis.

7   You also are interested in investigating whether degree of trust differs by geographic location and whether less trust is exhibited by respondents in the Dugong township as opposed to the smaller hamlets located to the south.

8   Given your interest in the issue of trust you also want to determine what contribution variables such as age and knowledge make to the perception of trust in the proposal.

9   Finally, because your community consultation program is now almost complete, you want to determine whether some of the information provision and information acquisition mechanisms that you have employed have been beneficial. You recontact respondents involved in the first survey and ask them to recomplete the trust scale. Having entered these additional data, you now want to determine whether your intervention has been successful and whether there has been any change in the trust indicator.

Research findings

Data preparation and screening

1   You understand that your research assistant, who entered the data for you, has had some problems with a couple of the variables in the data file, namely the variables *heard* and *where*. Before commencing any analysis of the data, you want to make sure that the data have been correctly entered for these particular variables and that no errors have occurred in data entry.

Do you know where the proposal is located?

		Frequency	Percent	Valid Percent	Cumulative Percent
Valid	Yes	123	30.8	30.8	30.8
	No	276	69.0	69.0	99.8
	12.00	1	.3	.3	100.0
	Total	400	100.0	100.0	

As you will see from your output, an error in data entry has occurred for the variable *where*. An incorrect value of 12 has been entered by mistake. You must now find this value in the data file and correct it to the value that it should be: the value of 2. You can use the **Find** option in the **Edit** menu to help you to find the value quickly and easily and make the change.

Find and Replace - Data View

Column: Id

Find: 12

☑ Replace

Replace with: 2

Show Options >>

| Find Next | Replace | Replace All | Close | Help |

---

2 You remember that certain items on the sense of community subscales are negatively worded and consequently require recoding. A five-point Likert scale response format was used for each of the scales. Items that are negatively worded include *influence items 3, 5, 8, 9* and *10, emotional connection items 1, 3, 4* and *7* and *community trust scale items 6* and *7*.

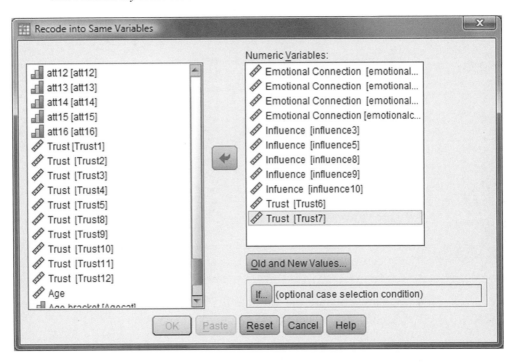

3 Before we begin some descriptive analysis, let us develop a new variable called *age*. Using the variable *born*, compute a new variable called *age* in your data file.

You will notice that a new variable *age* has been added to your data file.

		att16	Trust1	Trust2	Trust3	Trust4	Trust5	Trust6	Trust7	Trust8	Trust9	Trust10	Trust11	Trust12	Age
1	4	4	2.00	3.00	2.00	1.00	1.00	4.00	2.00	1.00	3.00	2.00	2.00	3.00	
2	4	4	1.00	2.00	3.00	2.00									24.00
3	4	4	1.00	4.00	4.00	2.00	3.00	3.00	2.00	2.00	3.00	3.00	4.00	3.00	42.00
4	4	4	2.00	4.00	3.00	2.00	2.00	5.00	4.00	1.00	4.00	4.00	3.00	4.00	40.00
5	2	4	3.00	4.00	3.00	3.00	3.00	3.00	3.00	3.00	2.00	2.00	3.00	3.00	47.00
6	5	5	1.00	1.00	1.00	4.00	1.00	5.00	2.00	3.00	3.00	2.00	1.00	4.00	57.00
7	5	5	1.00	1.00	1.00	1.00	1.00	2.00	2.00	1.00	1.00	1.00	1.00	4.00	50.00
8	4	4	4.00	4.00	4.00	4.00	4.00	3.00	2.00	3.00	4.00	4.00	4.00	3.00	52.00
9	5	5	3.00	4.00	3.00	4.00	4.00	2.00	4.00	4.00	4.00	4.00	4.00	3.00	52.00
10	4	5	2.00	3.00	2.00	2.00	2.00	3.00	4.00	2.00	3.00	3.00	2.00	3.00	45.00
11	3	3	3.00	4.00	3.00	3.00	3.00	3.00	3.00	4.00	4.00	3.00	3.00	3.00	18.00
12	3	4	2.00	3.00	2.00	2.00	1.00	2.00	3.00	2.00	2.00	2.00	2.00	3.00	25.00
13	5	5	1.00	1.00	2.00	1.00	2.00	4.00	2.00	2.00	2.00	2.00	2.00	3.00	77.00
14	5	5	3.00	3.00	3.00	3.00	3.00	3.00	3.00	3.00	3.00	3.00	3.00	3.00	49.00
15	5	5	3.00	3.00	3.00	3.00	3.00	3.00	3.00	3.00	3.00	3.00	3.00	3.00	
16	4	5	1.00	2.00	3.00	3.00	3.00	3.00	5.00	1.00	4.00	3.00	3.00	4.00	39.00
17	5	5	2.00	4.00	3.00	3.00	3.00	3.00	4.00	4.00	4.00	3.00	3.00	4.00	87.00
18	3	5	2.00	4.00	3.00	3.00	3.00	3.00	3.00	3.00	3.00	3.00	3.00	4.00	66.00
19	5	5	2.00	4.00	3.00	3.00	3.00	3.00	3.00	1.00	4.00	1.00	3.00	4.00	32.00
20	3	3	3.00	3.00	2.00	2.00	3.00	3.00	3.00	2.00	4.00	3.00	3.00	4.00	61.00
21	2	2	3.00	3.00	3.00	3.00	3.00	3.00	3.00	2.00	4.00	3.00	3.00	3.00	38.00
22	4	4	1.00	1.00	4.00	4.00	4.00	5.00	5.00	4.00	4.00	4.00	4.00	4.00	56.00
23	5	5	3.00	1.00	4.00	3.00	3.00	4.00	5.00	2.00	4.00	4.00	3.00	4.00	65.00
24	2	1	1.00	4.00	1.00	2.00	3.00	3.00	4.00	1.00	4.00	3.00	4.00	4.00	41.00

4   Now collapse the variable *age* into a categorical variable called *agecat*, which consists of the following age groupings:

- *15–24 years*
- *25–34 years*
- *35–44 years*
- *45–54 years*
- *55–64 years*
- *65–74 years*
- *75–84 years*
- *85+ years*

Now that you have created this variable, you will need to define the labels in the data file; remember to use the **Variable View** window.

5   You wish to determine the internal consistency of the trust scale before commencing analysis. How reliable is the scale?

Reliability Statistics

Cronbach's Alpha	Cronbach's Alpha Based on Standardized Items	N of Items
.820	.818	12

Item-Total Statistics

	Scale Mean if Item Deleted	Scale Variance if Item Deleted	Corrected Item-Total Correlation	Squared Multiple Correlation	Cronbach's Alpha if Item Deleted
Trust 1	30.5425	26.000	.489	.433	.805
Trust 2	29.5359	27.921	.193	.343	.837
Trust 3	29.9346	25.154	.670	.534	.790
Trust 4	29.9673	24.203	.742	.696	.782
Trust 5	29.9739	24.578	.754	.709	.782
Trust 6	29.1307	29.549	.137	.186	.830
Trust 7	29.1634	27.769	.301	.278	.821
Trust 8	30.2614	25.668	.517	.443	.803
Trust 9	29.3399	26.344	.454	.378	.808
Trust 10	29.7778	24.950	.707	.587	.787
Trust 11	29.8301	25.103	.735	.644	.786
Trust 12	29.2876	30.430	.036	.150	.834

The Cronbach's alpha coefficient for the trust scale is .82. While the removal of a few of the items (items *2*, *6*, *7* and *12*) may improve the reliability of the scale fractionally, given that the alpha is so high, you make the decision to retain all 12 items in the scale.

6   Having determined the reliability of the scale and deciding to retain all the items of the scale, a composite trust score variable can be developed and named *Trustscore1*. Remember that a composite trust score variable already exists in the data set called *Trustscore2*, which will be used later for further analysis.

7   Given that you were involved in the implementation of the survey, you are unsure whether the distribution of the composite trust indicator is normal. You are aware that the assumption of normality is a prerequisite for many inferential statistical techniques for which you may want to use this variable. Therefore, you want to determine whether this particular variable has a normal distribution. Check to see whether normality is present using a histogram, boxplot and skewness and kurtosis statistics.

Descriptives

			Statistic	Std. Error
Trustscore1	Mean		32.4314	.45010
	95% Confidence Interval for Mean	Lower Bound	31.5421	
		Upper Bound	33.3206	
	5% Trimmed Mean		32.3660	
	Median		32.0000	
	Variance		30.997	
	Std. Deviation		5.56749	
	Minimum		17.00	
	Maximum		46.00	
	Range		29.00	
	Interquartile Range		8.00	
	Skewness		.215	.196
	Kurtosis		-.272	.390

Histogram

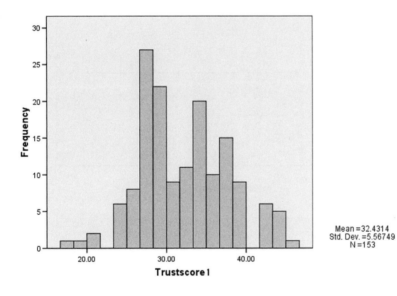

Mean = 32.4314
Std. Dev. = 5.56749
N = 153

Normal Q-Q Plot of Trustscore1

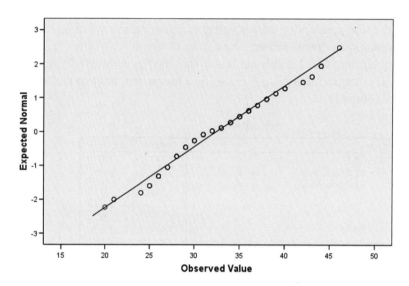

Detrended Normal Q-Q Plot of Trustscore1

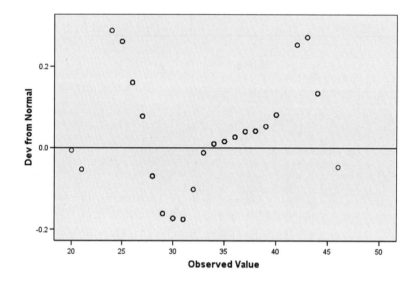

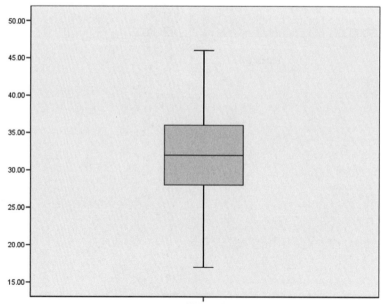

You can see from the histogram, plots and statistics that the distribution is relatively normal.

8   You have included in the questionnaire a sense of community scale, that comprises four subscales. The scale has recently received much debate in the literature in relation to the robustness of the underlying factor structure. The four subscales have been reported to measure the concept of 'sense of community' and include the elements of membership, emotional connection, reinforcement and influence.

You decide to explore the scale data to look at the underlying factor structure of the scale and determine whether the set of variables are reflected in the four theoretically proposed subscales.

KMO and Bartlett's Test

Kaiser-Meyer-Olkin Measure of Sampling Adequacy.		.877
Bartlett's Test of Sphericity	Approx. Chi-Square	6141.844
	df	595
	Sig.	.000

You can see that the Bartlett test of sphericity is significant and that the Kaiser–Meyer–Olkin measure of sampling adequacy is far greater than .6 with a value of .877.

In reviewing this table, you would expect four factors to be extracted as they have eigenvalues greater than 1. If four factors were extracted, then approximately 43 per cent of the variance would be explained. The scree plot that follows graphically displays the eigenvalues for each factor and suggests that two factors are prominent.

Scree Plot

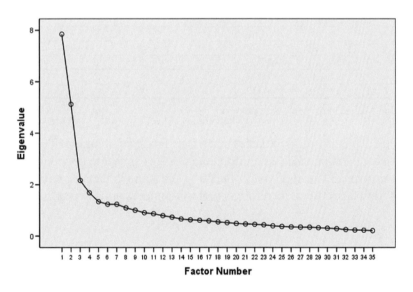

Total Variance Explained

Factor	Initial Eigenvalues			Extraction Sums of Squared Loadings			Rotation Sums of Squared Loadings		
	Total	% of Variance	Cumulative %	Total	% of Variance	Cumulative %	Total	% of Variance	Cumulative %
1	7.658	21.879	21.879	7.218	20.624	20.624	4.384	12.525	12.525
2	5.227	14.935	36.814	4.775	13.643	34.266	3.452	9.862	22.387
3	2.186	6.245	43.059	1.732	4.948	39.215	2.764	7.896	30.283
4	1.691	4.831	47.889	1.269	3.626	42.840	2.681	7.659	37.942
5	1.303	3.723	51.612	.840	2.399	45.239	1.190	3.399	41.341
6	1.248	3.566	55.178	.772	2.207	47.446	1.164	3.325	44.665
7	1.202	3.435	58.613	.687	1.962	49.408	1.070	3.056	47.721
8	1.148	3.279	61.892	.632	1.806	51.214	1.010	2.885	50.606
9	1.016	2.903	64.796	.554	1.583	52.797	.767	2.191	52.797
10	.909	2.596	67.392						
11	.851	2.431	69.823						
12	.828	2.365	72.188						
13	.739	2.113	74.301						
14	.664	1.898	76.199						
15	.635	1.815	78.013						
16	.610	1.742	79.755						
17	.583	1.665	81.420						
18	.531	1.516	82.937						
19	.516	1.474	84.410						
20	.492	1.407	85.817						
21	.464	1.325	87.142						
22	.443	1.265	88.407						
23	.425	1.214	89.620						
24	.392	1.121	90.742						
25	.381	1.088	91.829						
26	.364	1.041	92.870						
27	.344	.983	93.853						
28	.339	.969	94.823						
29	.312	.890	95.713						
30	.304	.870	96.583						
31	.269	.769	97.352						
32	.255	.730	98.081						
33	.233	.665	98.746						
34	.227	.648	99.394						
35	.212	.606	100.000						

Extraction Method: Principal Axis Factoring.

The rotated factor matrix indicates that a four-factor solution is evident in the data. Items comprising the influence and reinforcement scales appear to be grouping relatively well, however items of the emotional connection and some influence items seem to be loading on different factors and, therefore, simple structure is not apparent.

Rotated Factor Matrix[a]

	Factor								
	1	2	3	4	5	6	7	8	9
Membership	.726								
Membership	.699								
Influence	.658								.396
Influence	.588								
Membership	.577								
Membership	.551								
Membership	.526								
Emotional Connection	.501		.311						
Influence	.466	−.405							
Emotional Connection	.434								
Influence		.697							
Influence		.687							
Influence		.683							
Influence		.603				.520			
Influence		.588							−.364
Emotional Connection		.584					.433		
Emotional Connection		.494					.448		
Emotional Connection			.715						−.320
Influence	.391		.668						
Emotional Connection			.629						
Influence	.485		.563						
Membership	.409		.557						
Reinforcement				.765					
Reinforcement				.667					
Reinforcement				.659					
Reinforcement			.301	.646					
Reinforcement				.597					
Membership					.591				
Membership	.373				.569				
Reinforcement						.536			
Reinforcement						.406			
Emotional Connection							.534		
Emotional Connection							.347		
Reinforcement								.635	
Reinforcement								.587	

Extraction Method: Principal Axis Factoring.
Rotation Method: Varimax with Kaiser Normalization.
[a]Rotation converged in 8 iterations.

Given the nature of the concept under investigation, it is also likely that the factors extracted may be highly correlated. Therefore, a different rotation such as an oblique rotation (direct oblimin) may have been more appropriate to use. Why not have a look at the factor transformation on your output and see whether this is actually so?

In relation to the research question, conceptually, there is some truth in the factor structure as proposed in the literature but further examination of the internal consistency of items comprising the proposed factors may be beneficial to see whether the items that are grouping do actually produce a reliable scale. Alternatively, you may need to go back to the scale itself and consider the items and how they are loading.

Social and demographic characteristics

1 You want to obtain appropriate frequency distributions for all of the social and demographic variables in your data file. Remember, the distribution you use will depend upon the type of variable you are interested in assessing, that is, continuous (measured on ratio or interval scales) or categorical (measured on nominal or ordinal scales). Also, determine measures of central tendency and variability as appropriate.

Where do you live

		Frequency	Percent	Valid Percent	Cumulative Percent
Valid	Sunnydeck	61	15.3	15.3	15.3
	Dugong	296	74.0	74.0	89.3
	Sandstone	13	3.3	3.3	92.5
	Clearwater Bay	30	7.5	7.5	100.0
	Total	400	100.0	100.0	

Do you work in the fishing industry?

		Frequency	Percent	Valid Percent	Cumulative Percent
Valid	No	310	77.5	78.7	78.7
	Currently work in fishing industry	49	12.3	12.4	91.1
	Have worked in fishing industry in the past	35	8.8	8.9	100.0
	Total	394	98.5	100.0	
Missing	System	6	1.5		
Total		400	100.0		

Has anyone else in your household worked in the fishing industry?

		Frequency	Percent	Valid Percent	Cumulative Percent
Valid	Yes	108	27.0	27.3	27.3
	No	287	71.8	72.7	100.0
	Total	395	98.8	100.0	
Missing	System	5	1.2		
Total		400	100.0		

What is your gender?

		Frequency	Percent	Valid Percent	Cumulative Percent
Valid	Male	162	40.5	40.5	40.5
	Female	238	59.5	59.5	100.0
	Total	400	100.0	100.0	

Age categories

		Frequency	Percent	Valid Percent	Cumulative Percent
Valid	15-24 yrs	26	6.5	6.7	6.7
	25-34 yrs	57	14.3	14.7	21.4
	35-44 yrs	94	23.5	24.3	45.7
	45-54 yrs	67	16.8	17.3	63.0
	55-64 yrs	53	13.3	13.7	76.7
	65-74 yrs	51	12.8	13.2	89.9
	75-84 yrs	30	7.5	7.8	97.7
	85+ yrs	9	2.3	2.3	100.0
	Total	387	96.8	100.0	
Missing	System	13	3.3		
Total		400	100.0		

Where do you live

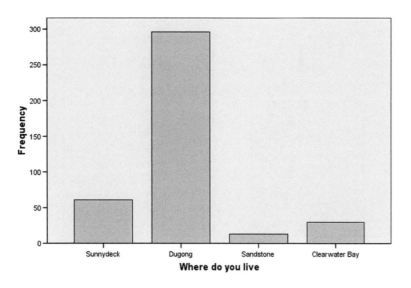

Do you work in the fishing industry?

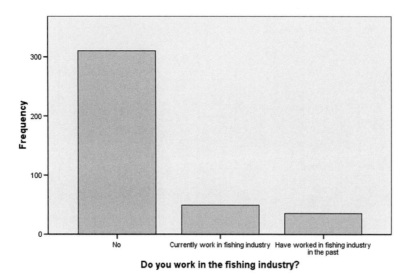

Has anyone else in your household worked in the fishing industry?

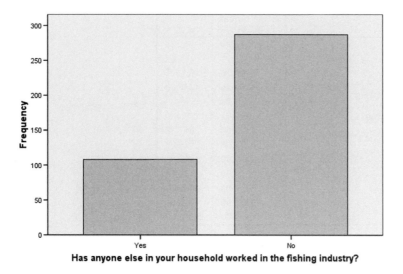

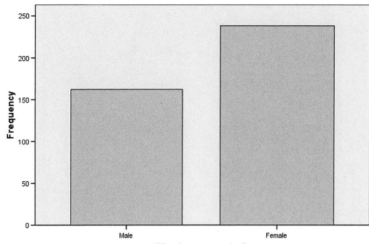

What is your gender?

Age bracket

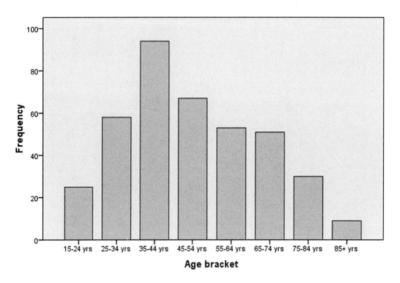

Statistics

		How long have you lived at your current address?	Age
N	Valid	399	388
	Missing	1	12
Mean		17.0526	49.1237
Median		11.0000	47.0000
Mode		1.00	42.00
Std. Deviation		16.52422	17.48680
Variance		273.050	305.788
Range		79.00	75.00
Minimum		1.00	13.00
Maximum		80.00	88.00
Percentiles	25	4.0000	36.0000
	50	11.0000	47.0000
	75	24.0000	63.0000

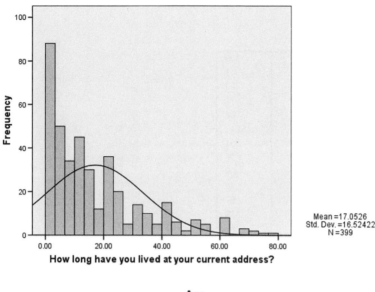

How long have you lived at your current address?

Mean =17.0526
Std. Dev. =16.52422
N =399

Age

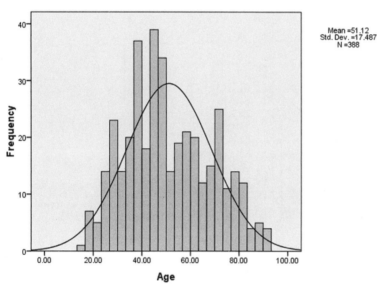

Mean =51.12
Std. Dev. =17.487
N =388

So what do the frequencies of the categorical and continuous variables tell us?

- A large proportion of the sample live in the township of Dugong (74 per cent).
- Only 12 per cent of the sample work in the fishing industry (less than we had thought!) and only 27 per cent know of someone else in their household who works in the industry.
- Of the sample, 40 per cent are male, with 60 per cent female.
- Of the sample, 63 per cent are aged 54 years or under.
- Average age is 51 years.
- On average, respondents have lived at their current address for 17 years, with a range of length of residence from one to 80 years.

2   Is data transformation required for any variable?

Given that the variable for 'how long have you lived at your current address' is significantly positively skewed, we could undertake a transformation. We would most likely have picked this up if we had screened all our variables right at the beginning, as you would have if this was your data set. Let us have a go at transforming the variable to see whether it makes any difference.

Statistics

Inhow

N	Valid	399
	Missing	1
Mean		2.2863
Median		2.3979
Mode		.00
Std. Deviation		1.16248
Variance		1.351
Range		4.38
Minimum		.00
Maximum		4.38
Percentiles	25	1.3863
	50	2.3979
	75	3.1781

Histogram

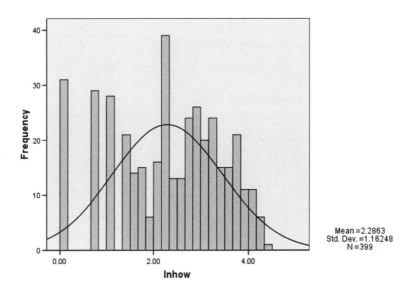

Mean =2.2863
Std. Dev. =1.16248
N =399

Normal Q-Q Plot of Inhow

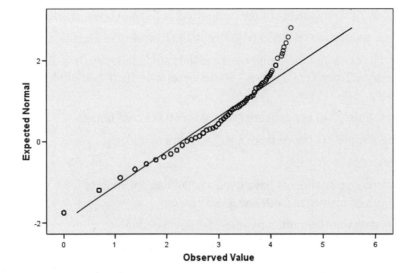

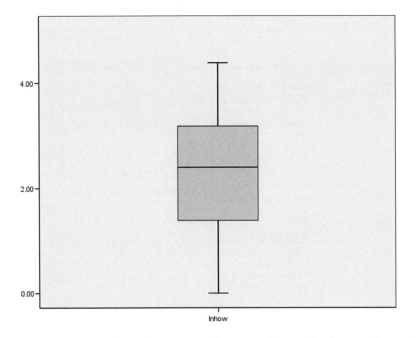

As you can see from the output, the natural logarithmic transformation of the variable *howlong* has changed the distribution and it is now relatively normal. Remember, if you were reporting on these results, you would need to mention that you had performed a transformation on the data.

Knowledge and awareness of the proposal
••

1   What proportion of respondents had heard about the proposed Dugong Peninsula Sea Change Development?

Have you heard of the proposal?

		Frequency	Percent	Valid Percent	Cumulative Percent
Valid	Yes	189	47.3	47.3	47.3
	No	211	52.8	52.8	100.0
	Total	400	100.0	100.0	

From the frequency analysis it was apparent that just fewer than half the respondents (47 per cent) had heard about the proposed Dugong Peninsula Sea Change Development.

2   Did awareness of the proposal differ by geographic location (Dugong township versus the other locations)?

Have you heard of the proposal? * Where do you live Crosstabulation

			Where do you live				Total
			Sunnydeck	Dugong	Sandstone	Clearwater Bay	
Have you heard of the proposal?	Yes	Count	38	127	6	18	189
		Expected Count	28.8	139.9	6.1	14.2	189.0
		% within Have you heard of the proposal?	20.1%	67.2%	3.2%	9.5%	100.0%
		% within Where do you live	62.3%	42.9%	46.2%	60.0%	47.3%
		% of Total	9.5%	31.8%	1.5%	4.5%	47.3%
	No	Count	23	169	7	12	211
		Expected Count	32.2	156.1	6.9	15.8	211.0
		% within Have you heard of the proposal?	10.9%	80.1%	3.3%	5.7%	100.0%
		% within Where do you live	37.7%	57.1%	53.8%	40.0%	52.8%
		% of Total	5.8%	42.3%	1.8%	3.0%	52.8%
Total		Count	61	296	13	30	400
		Expected Count	61.0	296.0	13.0	30.0	400.0
		% within Have you heard of the proposal?	15.3%	74.0%	3.3%	7.5%	100.0%
		% within Where do you live	100.0%	100.0%	100.0%	100.0%	100.0%
		% of Total	15.3%	74.0%	3.3%	7.5%	100.0%

Chi-Square Tests

	Value	df	Asymp. Sig. (2-sided)
Pearson Chi-Square	9.744[a]	3	.021
Likelihood Ratio	9.781	3	.021
Linear-by-Linear Association	.058	1	.810
N of Valid Cases	400		

a. 0 cells (.0%) have expected count less than 5. The minimum expected count is 6.14.

Yes, we can say that awareness of the proposal did differ across locations, $\chi^2(3, N = 400)$ = 9.74, p < .05, with greater awareness of the proposal among respondents in the outlying locations of Sunnydeck and Clearwater Bay than among respondents in Dugong.

3 Generally, were older respondents more aware of the proposal than younger respondents?

Have you heard of the proposal? * Age bracket Crosstabulation

			Age bracket								Total
			15-24 yrs	25-34 yrs	35-44 yrs	45-54 yrs	55-64 yrs	65-74 yrs	75-84 yrs	85+ yrs	
Have you heard of the proposal?	Yes	Count	11	21	49	37	29	29	10	0	186
		Expected Count	12.0	27.9	45.2	32.2	25.5	24.5	14.4	4.3	186.0
		% within Have you heard of the proposal?	5.9%	11.3%	26.3%	19.9%	15.6%	15.6%	5.4%	.0%	100.0%
		% within Age bracket	44.0%	36.2%	52.1%	55.2%	54.7%	56.9%	33.3%	.0%	48.1%
		% of Total	2.8%	5.4%	12.7%	9.6%	7.5%	7.5%	2.6%	.0%	48.1%
	No	Count	14	37	45	30	24	22	20	9	201
		Expected Count	13.0	30.1	48.8	34.8	27.5	26.5	15.6	4.7	201.0
		% within Have you heard of the proposal?	7.0%	18.4%	22.4%	14.9%	11.9%	10.9%	10.0%	4.5%	100.0%
		% within Age bracket	56.0%	63.8%	47.9%	44.8%	45.3%	43.1%	66.7%	100.0%	51.9%
		% of Total	3.6%	9.6%	11.6%	7.8%	6.2%	5.7%	5.2%	2.3%	51.9%
Total		Count	25	58	94	67	53	51	30	9	387
		Expected Count	25.0	58.0	94.0	67.0	53.0	51.0	30.0	9.0	387.0
		% within Have you heard of the proposal?	6.5%	15.0%	24.3%	17.3%	13.7%	13.2%	7.8%	2.3%	100.0%
		% within Age bracket	100.0%	100.0%	100.0%	100.0%	100.0%	100.0%	100.0%	100.0%	100.0%
		% of Total	6.5%	15.0%	24.3%	17.3%	13.7%	13.2%	7.8%	2.3%	100.0%

Chi-Square Tests

	Value	df	Asymp. Sig. (2-sided)
Pearson Chi-Square	18.888[a]	7	.009
Likelihood Ratio	22.465	7	.002
Linear-by-Linear Association	.084	1	.772
N of Valid Cases	387		

a. 2 cells (12.5%) have expected count less than 5. The minimum expected count is 4.33.

In conclusion, we can say that respondents aged 35 years and above seemed to be more aware of the proposal than those aged between 15 and 34 years. In particular, many respondents in the 25–34 age group were not aware of the proposal, in relation to the other age group categories, $\chi^2(7, N = 387) = 18.8$, p < .05.

4   How many respondents who were aware of the proposal knew where the proposed development was to be located?

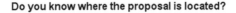

Do you know where the proposal is located?

		Frequency	Percent	Valid Percent	Cumulative Percent
Valid	Yes	123	65.1	65.1	65.1
	No	66	34.9	34.9	100.0
	Total	189	100.0	100.0	

Do you know where the proposal is located?

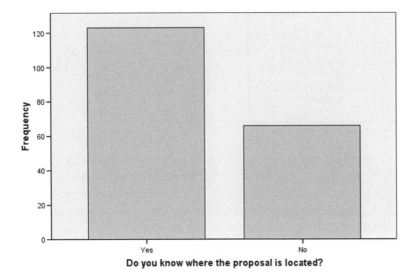

Do you know where the proposal is located?

Of those respondents who were aware of the proposal, 65 per cent knew where it was proposed to be located.

Did you get it right? To arrive at this result, you would have had to have selected only those respondents who had *heard* of the proposal using the **Select Cases: If** tool, and then performed a frequency distribution on the variable *where*; otherwise, your result would have been quite different. If you are unsure, go back to the 'Data selection' section in chapter 3.

5   Where did most respondents believe that the proposed development was to be located?

$Wherelocated Frequencies

		Responses		Percent of Cases
		N	Percent	
Where to be located ᵃ	Located near Dugong Peninsula	1	.8%	.8%
	Located near Sunnydeck	95	75.4%	77.2%
	Located near Sandstone dunes	3	2.4%	2.4%
	Located near Clearwaters Bay	27	21.4%	22.0%
Total		126	100.0%	102.4%

a. Dichotomy group tabulated at value 1.

Of those who were aware of the proposal, 75 per cent believed that it would be located near Sunnydeck, with a further 21 per cent believing it to be near Clearwater Bay.

Surprisingly, only 0.8 per cent of respondents identified that the proposal would be near Dugong. Given that result, I think some more consultation is required for this project!

This one was a little more complicated: first, you would have needed to set up a multiple response set for the variables *4, 5, 6* and *7* in your data file, as dichotomous variables. You then needed to do what you did for the previous question; that is, select only those respondents who had heard of the proposal using the **Select Cases: If** tool and then perform a frequency analysis on the multiple response set developed.

6   How many respondents knew something about the nature of the proposed development and what could they identify or what did they know about it?

$Whatknow Frequencies

		Responses		Percent of Cases
		N	Percent	
What do you know about the development[a]	Function Centre	80	90.9%	97.6%
	Sport and Recreation Centre	3	3.4%	3.7%
	Shopping Centre development	2	2.3%	2.4%
	High rise apartment development	2	2.3%	2.4%
	Approval process underway	1	1.1%	1.2%
Total		88	100.0%	107.3%

a. Dichotomy group tabulated at value 1.

Of the 82 respondents who had heard of the proposal and indicated they knew something about it, 90 per cent believed it involved the development of a function centre, and only 2 per cent outlined that they thought it involved development of high-rise apartments. This finding again illustrates that respondents on the whole are quite unaware of what the proposal involves and the aspects of the development.

This was another tricky one: you should have set up a multiple response set for the variables 9 to 13 in your data file. You then needed to do what you did for the previous question but this time you needed to select respondents who had *heard* about the proposal and had some knowledge of it, using the **Select Cases: If** tool. Then, as previously, perform a frequency analysis on the multiple response set that you created.

7   Did respondents know what type of clientele the development may attract?

$Clientele Frequencies

		Responses		Percent of Cases
		N	Percent	
Who will development attract?[a]	Temporary residents	2	3.6%	3.6%
	Mix of temporary and permanent residents	54	96.4%	96.4%
Total		56	100.0%	100.0%

a. Dichotomy group tabulated at value 1.

Of those respondents who said they knew what type of clientele the development would attract (56 respondents), 96 per cent believed that it would most likely be a mix of temporary and permanent residents.

Well, if you made it through that lot of tricky questions, then you are really doing well — you have started to truly interrogate your data.

Handy hint
* Always remember to turn your select cases option off; otherwise, your cases will remain filtered for further analysis.

Evaluation and impact assessment

1 What was the degree of *approval* among respondents in relation to the proposed development?

Approval relating to the proposal

		Frequency	Percent	Valid Percent	Cumulative Percent
Valid	Strongly approve	23	5.8	5.8	5.8
	Approve	162	40.5	40.5	46.3
	Have no opinion either way	97	24.3	24.3	70.5
	Disapprove	71	17.8	17.8	88.3
	Strongly disapprove	47	11.8	11.8	100.0
	Total	400	100.0	100.0	

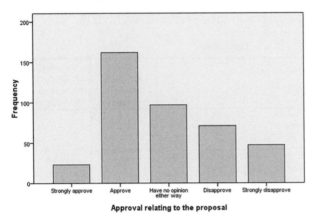

Approval relating to the proposal

As the frequency analysis indicates, approximately 46 per cent of respondents either approve or strongly approve of the proposal, 30 per cent disapprove or strongly disapprove and a further 24 per cent have no opinion either way.

2 Were respondents in the Dugong township more likely to disapprove of the proposal?

Live in or outside Dugong * Approval relating to the proposal Crosstabulation

			Approval relating to the proposal					Total
			Strongly approve	Approve	Have no opinion either way	Disapprove	Strongly disapprove	
Live in or outside Dugong	Live in Dugong	Count	16	121	81	50	28	296
		Expected Count	17.0	119.9	71.8	52.5	34.8	296.0
		% within Live in or outside Dugong	5.4%	40.9%	27.4%	16.9%	9.5%	100.0%
		% within Approval relating to the proposal	69.6%	74.7%	83.5%	70.4%	59.6%	74.0%
		% of Total	4.0%	30.3%	20.3%	12.5%	7.0%	74.0%
	Live outside Dugong	Count	7	41	16	21	19	104
		Expected Count	6.0	42.1	25.2	18.5	12.2	104.0
		% within Live in or outside Dugong	6.7%	39.4%	15.4%	20.2%	18.3%	100.0%
		% within Approval relating to the proposal	30.4%	25.3%	16.5%	29.6%	40.4%	26.0%
		% of Total	1.8%	10.3%	4.0%	5.3%	4.8%	26.0%
Total		Count	23	162	97	71	47	400
		Expected Count	23.0	162.0	97.0	71.0	47.0	400.0
		% within Live in or outside Dugong	5.8%	40.5%	24.3%	17.8%	11.8%	100.0%
		% within Approval relating to the proposal	100.0%	100.0%	100.0%	100.0%	100.0%	100.0%
		% of Total	5.8%	40.5%	24.3%	17.8%	11.8%	100.0%

Chi-Square Tests

	Value	df	Asymp. Sig. (2-sided)
Pearson Chi-Square	10.386[a]	4	.034
Likelihood Ratio	10.371	4	.035
Linear-by-Linear Association	2.350	1	.125
N of Valid Cases	400		

a. 0 cells (.0%) have expected count less than 5. The minimum expected count is 5.98.

Respondents in Dugong itself would more likely have an opinion on the proposal generally and were specifically more likely to approve or have no opinion than those respondents located in other towns, $\chi^2(4, N = 400) = 10.386$, p < .05.

For this analysis, we recoded our variable *live* into a new variable, *liveDugong*, which categorised respondents according to whether they lived in Dugong or in other towns.

3 Is the respondents' perceived level of knowledge of the proposal related to how they evaluate the proposal (their degree of approval)?

Correlations

			Approval relating to the proposal	Perceived level of knowledge of development
Spearman's rho	Approval relating to the proposal	Correlation Coefficient	1.000	-.029
		Sig. (2-tailed)	.	.570
		N	400	388
	Perceived level of knowledge of development	Correlation Coefficient	-.029	1.000
		Sig. (2-tailed)	.570	.
		N	388	388

Given that the variables *approval* and *perknowledge* are measured on ordinal scales, we undertook a Spearman's rank-order correlation. Results of the analysis indicate that no relationship between respondents' perceived knowledge and how they evaluate the proposal.

4 What were the perceived *benefits* of the proposed development?

$PropBenefit Frequencies

		Responses		Percent of Cases
		N	Percent	
Benefits of the proposal[a]	Don't know what benefits there may be	37	5.7%	9.4%
	There are no benefits of the proposal	54	8.3%	13.7%
	Ensures economic sustainability of the Peninsula	9	1.4%	2.3%
	Encourages tourism in the area	21	3.2%	5.3%
	Puts the area on the map	1	.2%	.3%
	Provision of community infrastructure	63	9.7%	16.0%
	Supports the local economy	170	26.2%	43.3%
	Provides employment	295	45.4%	75.1%
Total		650	100.0%	165.4%

a. Dichotomy group tabulated at value 1.

The most frequently identified benefits of the proposal raised by respondents included local employment (45 per cent) and support for the local economy (26 per cent). To obtain this result, you should set up a multiple response set for the variables *20* to *27* in your data file, then perform a frequency analysis on the multiple response set that you created.

5   What were the perceived costs of the proposed development?

$PropCosts Frequencies

		Responses		Percent of Cases
		N	Percent	
Costs associated with proposal[a]	Don't know	62	3.9%	15.8%
	No costs/disadvantages	44	2.8%	11.2%
	Environmental impacts	32	2.0%	8.1%
	Change in people's lifestyle	39	2.5%	9.9%
	Reduced access to the coast	48	3.0%	12.2%
	Reduced access to the sand dunes	44	2.8%	11.2%
	Reduction in property values	40	2.5%	10.2%
	Issues of road safety	22	1.4%	5.6%
	Dust during construction of the development	236	14.9%	60.1%
	Noise during construction of the development	123	7.8%	31.3%
	Impact on the local fishing industry	121	7.6%	30.8%
	An increase in road traffic	64	4.0%	16.3%
	People will leave the area	24	1.5%	6.1%
	Change in sense of community	55	3.5%	14.0%
	Increase in traffic noise	53	3.3%	13.5%
	Increase in noise from the precinct	71	4.5%	18.1%
	Change in how the area looks	53	3.3%	13.5%
	Change in visual impact of the coastline	52	3.3%	13.2%
	Difficulty in selling properties	40	2.5%	10.2%
	Impacts on native animals	69	4.4%	17.6%
	Impacts on native plants	65	4.1%	16.5%
	Pollution in the ocean	90	5.7%	22.9%
	Impact on Aboriginal middens/sites	10	.6%	2.5%
	A loss of generational history	67	4.2%	17.0%
	Erosion of coastline	55	3.5%	14.0%
	Loss of existing homes	5	.3%	1.3%
Total		1584	100.0%	403.1%

[a] Dichotomy group tabulated at value 1.

The most frequently identified costs of the proposal raised by respondents largely related to the construction phase of the development, that is, dust (15 per cent) and noise (8 per cent) generated during construction. Other perceived costs included the impact on the local fishing industry (8 per cent) and concerns relating to ocean pollution.

Once again, to achieve this result, you would set up a multiple response set for the variables *29* to *54* in your data file, then perform a frequency analysis on the multiple response set that you created.

It would also probably be a good idea to collapse some of the costs identified by the community into higher-order themes, for example, access to the coast and sand dunes could be one response theme, road traffic and safety issues could also be combined. Have a go at recoding these variables into higher-order variables and then run the analysis again.

6   In the survey you have included a trust scale because previous project experience has highlighted that perceived trust is a determinant of community perception in relation to development projects. You have also observed that females tend to be more trusting of proponents than males, so you wish to test this hypothesis.

Group Statistics

	What is your gender?	N	Mean	Std. Deviation	Std. Error Mean
Trustscore1	Male	55	31.7636	5.23154	.70542
	Female	98	32.8061	5.73946	.57977

Independent Samples Test

		Levene's Test for Equality of Variances		t-test for Equality of Means					95% Confidence Interval of the Difference	
		F	Sig.	t	df	Sig. (2-tailed)	Mean Difference	Std. Error Difference	Lower	Upper
Trustscore1	Equal variances assumed	.196	.658	-1.112	151	.268	-1.04249	.93729	-2.89437	.80940
	Equal variances not assumed			-1.142	120.886	.256	-1.04249	.91310	-2.85023	.76526

You have undertaken an independent-groups t-test distinguishing between gender on the trust score. Given that the Levene's test has a probability greater than .05, you can assume that the population variances are relatively equal. However, no significant difference is apparent, indicating that there is no difference in perceived trust in the proposal between males and females.

7   You are also interested in investigating whether degree of trust differs by geographic location and whether less trust is exhibited by respondents in the Dugong township as opposed to the other smaller hamlets located to the south.

Descriptives

Trustscore1

	N	Mean	Std. Deviation	Std. Error	95% Confidence Interval for Mean		Minimum	Maximum
					Lower Bound	Upper Bound		
Sunnydeck	18	31.3333	6.54397	1.54243	28.0791	34.5876	17.00	44.00
Dugong	117	32.6838	5.31045	.49095	31.7114	33.6562	20.00	46.00
Sandstone	5	38.2000	6.94262	3.10483	29.5796	46.8204	28.00	44.00
Clearwater Bay	13	29.4615	4.17563	1.15811	26.9382	31.9848	25.00	40.00
Total	153	32.4314	5.56749	.45010	31.5421	33.3206	17.00	46.00

Test of Homogeneity of Variances

Trustscore1

Levene Statistic	df1	df2	Sig.
1.467	3	149	.226

ANOVA

Trustscore1

	Sum of Squares	df	Mean Square	F	Sig.
Between Groups	310.199	3	103.400	3.500	.017
Within Groups	4401.330	149	29.539		
Total	4711.529	152			

Multiple Comparisons

Trustscore1
Tukey HSD

(I) Where do you live	(J) Where do you live	Mean Difference (I-J)	Std. Error	Sig.	95% Confidence Interval	
					Lower Bound	Upper Bound
Sunnydeck	Dugong	-1.35043	1.37606	.760	-4.9258	2.2249
	Sandstone	-6.86667	2.74752	.064	-14.0055	.2721
	Clearwater Bay	1.87179	1.97821	.780	-3.2681	7.0117
Dugong	Sunnydeck	1.35043	1.37606	.760	-2.2249	4.9258
	Sandstone	-5.51624	2.48199	.122	-11.9651	.9326
	Clearwater Bay	3.22222	1.58893	.182	-.9062	7.3507
Sandstone	Sunnydeck	6.86667	2.74752	.064	-.2721	14.0055
	Dugong	5.51624	2.48199	.122	-.9326	11.9651
	Clearwater Bay	8.73846*	2.86008	.014	1.3072	16.1697
Clearwater Bay	Sunnydeck	-1.87179	1.97821	.780	-7.0117	3.2681
	Dugong	-3.22222	1.58893	.182	-7.3507	.9062
	Sandstone	-8.73846*	2.86008	.014	-16.1697	-1.3072

*. The mean difference is significant at the 0.05 level.

Trustscore1

Tukey HSD

Where do you live	N	Subset for alpha = 0.05	
		1	2
Clearwater Bay	13	29.4615	
Sunnydeck	18	31.3333	
Dugong	117	32.6838	32.6838
Sandstone	5		38.2000
Sig.		.479	.071

Means for groups in homogeneous subsets are displayed.

The results of the one-way ANOVA reveal that differences are evident in trust scores across geographic locations, $F(3,149) = 3.5$, $p < .05$. A review of the Tukey post-hoc tests reveals that the difference lies between the hamlets of Clearwater Bay and Sandstone, with respondents in Clearwater Bay having greater trust in the proposal than respondents in Sandstone.

8   Given your interest in the issue of trust you also want to determine what contribution variables such as age and knowledge make to the perception of trust in the proposal.

Model Summary[b]

Model	R	R Square	Adjusted R Square	Std. Error of the Estimate
1	.106[a]	.011	-.003	5.58982

a. Predictors: (Constant), Perceived level of knowledge of development, Age

b. Dependent Variable: Trustscore

Normal P-P Plot of Regression Standardized Residual

Dependent Variable: Trustscore1

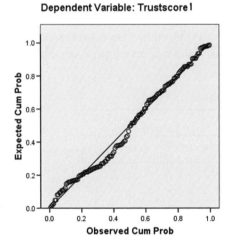

Scatterplot

Dependent Variable: Trustscore1

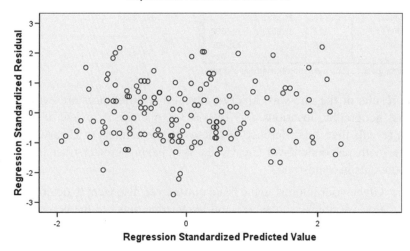

Despite the assumption of linearity having been made, as illustrated in the normal P–P plot of regression standardised residual, and the distribution of the trust score being relatively normal (refer to the Scatterdot), disappointingly neither of the independent variables — age or knowledge — significantly explains any variance in perceived trust in the proposal.

9   Finally, because your community consultation program is now almost complete, you want to determine whether or not some of the information provision and information acquisition mechanisms that you have employed have been beneficial. You recontact respondents involved in the first survey and ask them to recomplete the trust scale. Having entered these additional data, you now want to determine whether your intervention has been successful and whether there has been any change in the trust indicator over time — essentially, has your program made a difference?

Paired Samples Statistics

		Mean	N	Std. Deviation	Std. Error Mean
Pair 1	Trustscore2	27.2549	153	5.81913	.47045
	Trustscore1	32.4314	153	5.56749	.45010

Paired Samples Correlations

		N	Correlation	Sig.
Pair 1	Trustscore2 & Trustscore1	153	.973	.000

Paired Samples Test

		Paired Differences							
					95% Confidence Interval of the Difference				
		Mean	Std. Deviation	Std. Error Mean	Lower	Upper	t	df	Sig. (2-tailed)
Pair 1	Trustscore2 - Trustscore1	-5.17647	1.35781	.10977	-5.39335	-4.95959	-47.156	152	.000

Finally, we have some positive results. As can be seen from the output, a significant difference exists between trust scores before and after the consultation program. An examination of the means for *trustscore* (32.4) and *trustscore2* (27.2) indicates that after the consultation program, trust in the proposal has significantly increased — should be good for business!

Additional analyses

We have come to the end of our research questions, but plenty of variables remain in the data file, so you are encouraged to explore these data further with the various techniques that you have learned in Section 1 and the practice you have gained in this section of the book. The use of surveys is very common in the social sciences, so it should have been useful to work through a complete research example that uses this type of approach.

Practising analytical techniques

This chapter provides an opportunity for students to apply their knowledge of analytical techniques to new data sets that have been specifically tailored to the student version of the IBM SPSS software. A range of research scenarios and homework exercises with varying degrees of complexity are presented in this chapter, allowing students to practise what they have learned from using the text and their course of study.

A key feature of this latest edition of the text is that each homework exercise has been developed to mimic an actual social science research scenario and data collection methodology. Survey instruments and the data collected by social scientists in the field have been adapted for each homework exercise, affording students the opportunity to experience how SPSS's analytical techniques are used as part of applied social science research.

The student version of the SPSS software has limited functions and capabilities and, as such, not all of the techniques addressed in section one of the text will be covered in this section.

The answers to the research questions posed within this section have also not been included, so that students can attempt analysis without assistance, and tutors and lecturers can use the exercises as homework tasks or assignments.

This chapter comprises two main sections:

- **Section 1: Short homework exercises:** four short homework exercises in response to simple research scenarios using small data sets that can be found on the website that accompanies this title.

- **Section 2: Research scenario suitable for student version of SPSS software:** ten extended homework exercises in response to a comprehensive research scenario with a larger data set that can be found on the website that accompanies this title. This section enables students to apply their knowledge as would be required in applied research practice.

Section 1: Short homework exercises

The four homework exercises presented in this section have associated data sets that can be accessed on the website that accompanies this title.

Homework exercise 1 — Socio-demographic trends of new residents

A City Council has recently undergone exponential growth in its local population. To better understand the changing nature of local communities falling under the Council's jurisdiction, you have been employed by the Council to evaluate the socio-demographic trends of new residents who have recently moved into the area. The Council will use outcomes of your research to guide the implementation of new community development policies.

As part of your research methodology, you administer a survey of socio-demographic trends to residents who have lived in the local area for six months or less. Key items in the survey included *age characteristics, marital status, current residential type and tenure, English proficiency, religion* and *need for assistance*. The data can be found in *Homework_exercise1.sav* on the website that accompanies this title. Survey questions have been clearly labelled in the **Variable View** of the data file.

In your report to the Council, you may need to address some of the following questions. Do not limit yourself to the questions listed below. You may also come up with other questions which you think might be of interest to the Council.

1   What are the general age characteristics of the new residents?

2   Do the new residents speak English well?

3   What proportion of the new residents require someone to help them with their daily activities (e.g. self care, body movement and communication)?

4   What are the top three reasons for the new residents' requirement for care and assistance? *Handy tip: Your survey respondents have provided more than one reason for their need for assistance. Therefore you will need to undertake a multiple response frequency analysis.*

5   Of the new residents, what proportion are renting their current place of residence? Are a significant proportion of the new residents dependent on Government/public housing?

To make your research findings more accessible to the Council, it would also be useful to present your data analysis outcomes in the form of graphical illustrations. Have a play around with SPSS's charting features to examine how you can best present your data analysis outcomes visually.

Homework exercise 2 — Reviewing an area's level of skills proficiency and educational attainment

A state education and training department is currently undertaking a review of its resource allocation across four different regions of the state. The department therefore needs to better understand the current level of educational attainment and job skills proficiency in each region. Regions with lower levels of educational attainment and skill sets might require greater educational and training resources.

You have been commissioned by the department to research the current status of educational attainment and skill levels across the different state regions of interest. As part of your research methodology, you administered surveys to a select group of respondents from each region. Key items in the survey included *school enrolment trends, highest level of education attained, current use of qualifications, employment trends* and *perceptions of existing challenges in gaining access to training and employment in the area*. The data can be found in *Homework_exercise2.sav* on the website that accompanies this title. Survey questions have been clearly labelled in the **Variable View** of the data file.

Key questions you might address include:

1   What is the most prevalent occupation type in each region, and does this differ across regions?

2   What are the top three perceptions of existing challenges in gaining access to training and employment in each region?

3   How do the different regions compare in terms of educational attainment and employment trends?

4   What advice would you provide to the State Department in regard to resource allocations for each region, based on outcomes of your analysis?

Handy tip: For greater ease of comparison, use the Split File functionality from the Data Menu, or Crosstabs from the Analyze and Descriptive menus to group your outputs by region.

Homework exercise 3 — Survey of business employees

The human resources department of a resource company would like to obtain a better understanding of the socio-demographic characteristics of its employees, to assist in the development of more attractive employment incentives.

An employee survey was administered across 70 of the company's employees. Your task is to analyse the data collected, and provide a report on key employee characteristics and socio-demographic trends. The data can be found in *Homework_exercise3.sav* on the website that accompanies this title. Survey questions have been clearly labelled in the **Variable View** of the data file.

Key trends which you might want to report include, but are not limited to:

1   What is the age distribution of the company's employees? *Handy tip: To obtain the age distribution, you will need to categorise the existing raw age data into distinct age categories by creating a new AgeCat variable and adding value labels for each age category in the **Variable View** window. Typical workforce age categories are 18–34 years, 35–54 years, and 55 years plus.*

2   What is the predominant length of employment for the company's employees?

3   Is there a correlation between the different workforce age groups and length of employment? *Handy tip: A correlation between two dichotomous or categorical variables is called a Phi Coefficient, available through the **Crosstabs** option from the **Analyze** and **Descriptive Statistics** menus.*

4   What is the most common education/training qualification among the company's employees?

5   Is the company characterised by a greater proportion of male or female workers?

Do not forget: to make the data more accessible to your audience, always try to present your data analysis outcomes in the form of graphs and charts.

Homework exercise 4 — Evaluating community perceptions towards a mining company's local community contributions

MineCo has two major mining operations situated in close proximity to a large regional town centre. As part of the company's social responsibility and investment guidelines, it has in place a community contributions program which guides company contributions in support of the town's community activities and development.

To assess the effectiveness and viability of its community contributions program, MineCo has commissioned you to undertake a random telephone survey of households in the town to ascertain resident perceptions and recognition of MineCo's community contributions. Items on the survey include *community awareness* of the company's community contributions, as well as perceptions of *key community areas* MineCo should be focusing their investment efforts on. The data can be found in *Homework_exercise4.sav* on the website that accompanies this title. Survey questions have been clearly labelled in the **Variable View** of the data file.

Key discussion points in your report to MineCo should consider the questions:

1   Were most residents aware of MineCo's community contributions program? Do age and length of residence in the locality have a significant effect on the residents' recollection?

2   What are the top three organisations, events, or activities that local residents can recall being supported by MineCo?

3   What are the top three areas in which residents think the company should be focusing its community contributions? Are there any differences in perceptions across the different suburbs?

Section 2: Research scenario suitable for student version of SPSS software

This section of the text enables you to extend your knowledge of how to develop a data file and implement a range of analytical techniques, by providing an opportunity for you to work through a research scenario using a complete data set that is compatible with the student version of the SPSS software.

The answers to the research questions posed in this section have not been included, to encourage you to attempt the analysis without assistance, and to provide the opportunity for tutors and lecturers to use this section as a homework exercise or assignment.

The associated data set can be found on the website that accompanies this title and represents the outcomes of a questionnaire, comprised of a range of different types of test items, administered through a hypothetical random household survey.

When you open the data file, a list of all the variables in the data set can be found in the **Variable View** window in the SPSS Data Editor. Each variable has a description in the label column, which may help you to visualise how the survey has been converted to an SPSS data file.

The following sections outline the context in which your research is based, describe the research project and define your role in the research process.

Working example

The research context

Elix Resources has several mining operations situated around Western Australia, which is currently the centre of Australia's mining boom. These mining operations were strategically developed a number of years ago in rural areas with low population density so as to minimise the potential negative impacts resulting from operational activity.

In recent years, Western Australia has experienced significant population growth and development. As a result, the company's mining operations are now located in areas with medium- to high-density populations. This means that the company now has more near neighbours surrounding its operations, and therefore potentially more complaints!

One of the communities affected by Elix's larger operations is Kentsworth, a thriving and expanding community supported by a strong industry presence.

The research project

Elix Resources has commissioned you to undertake a random telephone survey of households in the Kentsworth area as part of a community consultation program that will inform the company's new social responsibility and investment guidelines. The survey has been designed to measure community attitudes towards mining and community concerns related to Elix's mining operations in the area. The survey also includes questions related to the social and demographic characteristics of respondents.

The questionnaire comprises different types of test items:

- Closed questions or *forced-choice items*. Respondents respond using predetermined response categories

- Open questions or *free recall items*. Respondents identify responses themselves. Multiple response and multiple dichotomy analysis may be useful techniques to employ for these items.

- Economic Contribution scale[1] measuring perceptions of how much the company contributes to Kentsworth's local economy. This comprises six contribution areas across which respondents can rate company contributions.

- Trust scale[2] measuring trust in the company. This comprises eleven attitude statements to which respondents must agree or disagree, using a five-point Likert scale.

  – Individual items (attitude statements) that comprise the scale form a composite trust score.

  – It should be noted that items 3 and 11 on the scale are negatively worded.

- Reputation Rating scale.[3] Respondents rate company reputation from 1 to 10, with 1 representing a very poor reputation and 10 representing an excellent reputation.

Negatively worded items are designed to detect participant response bias, or tendency to respond in the same way (i.e. always agree) to every attitude statement that comprises the attitude scale. Negatively worded items are phrased in a way that requires the participant to respond in the opposite way to the other items.

Having administered the survey and entered your data, you are now ready to do some analysis. You are required to provide a report to your client on the key findings of the survey to help them better understand community attitudes towards the company and their operations in the locality.

The data can be found in *Research_scenario_student_version.sav* on the website that accompanies this title. Missing data have been entered as 99 in the data set.

The research questions

1   One of Elix Resources' goals is to ensure that its mining operations do not create significant harm to the environment within which it operates. Therefore, to obtain a better understanding of Kentsworth residents' perceptions of the company's environmental performance, one of the survey questions required survey respondents to indicate how satisfied they were with the company's approach to environmental management.

    (a) What percent of survey respondents were not at all satisfied with the company's approach to environmental management? Please generate a suitable graph to illustrate the response to this variable.

2   In its efforts to engage the Kentsworth community, it is worthwhile for Elix Resources to obtain community suggestions and views on ways it could improve its environmental management strategies. Therefore, one of the survey questions specifically asked respondents to record these suggestions. The data from this question was recorded as a free-recall multiple response in the variables: *Improve_env1* and *Improve_env2*.

---

1 © Sheridan Coakes Consulting
2 © Sheridan Coakes Consulting
3 © Sheridan Coakes Consulting

(a) What were the three most frequently suggested ways in which respondents felt that the company could improve its environmental management? *Hint: a good way to present this would be to generate a graph which shows response frequencies for the different responses.*

3   One of the benefits of living in close proximity to a large-scale mining operation is the flow-on economic effects resulting from the operation's activities in the area. Therefore, the company is interested in finding out whether Kentsworth residents perceive its presence to be economically beneficial to their community. One of the survey questions required survey respondents to rate, on the Economic Contribution scale which ranges from 1 to 5 (with 1 being 'very little' and 5 being 'a lot'), how much they considered that the company contributed to different areas of the town's economy (e.g. local employment, support and sponsorship of community services, and local businesses).

(a) What were the three areas where the community perceived the company to be contributing the most?

4   You will remember that items 3 and 11 on the Trust scale (variables *Trust3* and *Trust11*) are negatively worded and, therefore, require recoding. You need to determine the internal consistency of the Trust scale before commencing analysis. Once you are certain that the scale is reliable you compute the composite Trust score for each participant. Call this new variable *trust_score*.

(a) How reliable is the scale?

(b) Is the *trust_score* variable normally distributed? Please demonstrate.

(c) What is the mean Trust score for the Kentsworth community? Is this good news for the company?

5   One of the questions in the survey asked respondents to indicate how far they lived from the company's mining operations. The responses to this item have been recorded in the variable *Distance*. As respondents living closer to mining operations are more likely to experience immediate impacts such as noise and dust, you are interested in assessing whether these respondents are likely to have lower trust levels in the company compared to those who live farther away.

(a) What is the most appropriate statistical test to assess this?

(b) Outline the assumptions that must be met and whether they have been violated.

(c) What conclusions can you draw from this analysis?

6   The company would also like to know if their sponsorship of community organisations, events and activities has had any impact on community attitudes towards the company. The survey asked respondents to indicate whether they could recall company sponsorship. Responses to this question have been recorded in the variable *Recall_spon*. You decide to assess whether those respondents who could recall sponsorships demonstrate higher levels of trust.

(a) What is the most appropriate statistical test to assess this?

(b) Outline the assumptions that must be met and whether they have been violated.

(c) What conclusions can you draw from this analysis?

7   You would like to know if there is a relationship between the respondents' length of residence in the area and their level of trust in the company. You have a feeling that newer residents in the areas will have less trust in the company. The respondents' length of residence has been recorded in the variable *Length_residence*. You decide to compare mean trust levels for three different residential groups:

- those who have lived in the area for less than 5 years
- those who have lived in the area 6–10 years
- those who have lived in the area for more than 10 years.

Hint: remember to create a new categorical variable that represents the identified length of residence categories.

8   Elix Resources is also interested in finding out what Kentsworth residents perceive of its reputation status. Therefore, one of the survey items required survey respondents to rate, on a reputation scale of one to ten, their perceptions of the company's reputation. The respondents' reputation ratings have been recorded in the variable *Reputation_rat*.

(a) Obtain an overall distribution of reputation ratings to determine the average reputation score for the company.

(b) Were those respondents who could recall Elix Resources sponsorships in their local community (*Recall_spon*) more likely to give the company higher reputation ratings?

9   You have also collected socio-demographic data as part of the survey (age and gender). You are interested in assessing the socio-demographic characteristics of your sample to ensure that it is representative.

(a) Generate and present appropriate graphs for the socio-demographic variables in the data set. Remember, the distribution you use will depend upon the type of variable you are interested in assessing, that is, continuous (measured on ratio or interval scales) or categorical (measured on nominal or ordinal scales).

(b) Determine measures of central tendency and variability as appropriate.

(c) Is data transformation required for any variable? If so please perform the transformation.

10   Your final report to Elix Resources will include recommendations regarding areas for enhanced company financial contribution. To inform these recommendations, you have asked an open-ended question about the respondents' preferred areas for company contribution in the areas of education (coded as the variables *Education1*, *Education2*, *Education3*), youth (coded as the variables *Youth1*, *Youth2*, *Youth3*), and environment (coded as the variables *Environment1*, *Environment2*, *Environment3*).

(a) For each of the areas (education, youth, environment), in what areas would you recommend that the company contribute its investment budget?

(b) Based on the outcomes of all of your analysis, is there anything else that you would recommend to the company? Please outline.

SECTION 3

Further **practice**

CHAPTER 25

Extra practice

To ensure that you are kept busy, in this section we have included all the practice examples from previous versions of the text for you to work through. A list of all these examples is provided below and data files corresponding to the examples are located on the website that accompanies this title.

Practice 20b   Factors influencing purchase of a used car

Practice 21   Tourist perceptions of similarity among distance between nine cities

Please note that there is no practice example for chapter 1.

Given the number of pages required to include the output for all of these examples, it has not been provided. Each of the practice examples is outlined in detail in the following pages. By now, you should be really well versed in the IBM SPSS system, and so your own output should flow freely!

Practice example 2: Preparation of data files

You have surveyed individuals within your local community to determine their attitude towards the opening of a new school. You have collected data on the variables in the following table.

id	gender	length of residence	number of children	would you use the school?
1	Female	2	2	Yes
2	Male	3	1	No
3	Male	6	2	Yes
4	Male	5	4	No
5	Female	8	3	Yes
6	Female	9	2	Yes
7	Female	11	2	Yes
8	Male	3	0	Yes
9	Male	5	2	Yes
10	Female	12	3	Yes
11	Male	10	1	No
12	Female	8	1	Yes
13	Female	9	4	Yes
14	Male	9	2	Yes
15	Male	3	0	No
16	Female	1	3	Yes
17	Male	0.5	1	Yes
18	Female	4	2	Yes
19	Male	3	1	?
20	Female	2	1	Yes

Given these data, your task is to create a data file in IBM SPSS. Remember, you must define each variable, allocating appropriate variable and value labels. Other definitions are optional. Data must then be entered and saved in a data file.

Practice example 3: Data screening and transformation

The following scale measured how adolescents feel about their future. Data from 100 year 11 students was collected. The scale comprised six items:

1   I feel optimistic about my future.

2   I believe that every cloud has a silver lining.

3   I doubt that I can achieve what I want to in life.

4   I have what it takes to create a bright future.

5   If anything bad can happen, it will.

6   I deserve to have good things come my way.

The response format for these items was:

       1 = strongly agree

       2 = agree

       3 = neutral

       4 = disagree

       5 = strongly disagree.

Given the data in Prac3.sav, your tasks are to:

1   Check for incorrect data entry.

2   Recode negatively worded items.

3   Recode missing values using mean substitution.

4   Compute a total hope score.

5   Screen for normality for the composite variable.

6   Attempt an appropriate transformation on the composite variable and compare the output of this transformation with the distribution of the original variable.

7   Select a random sample of 50 cases from the data set and obtain the mean hope score for this subset.

Practice example 4: Descriptive statistics

Sales in $1000s by 20 junior and senior salespeople working in a whitegoods shop were recorded at the end of a week. Given the data in Prac4.sav, your task is to obtain a frequency table and the appropriate chart and descriptive statistics for each variable in the data file.

Practice example 5: Correlation

Medical researchers believe that there is a relationship between smoking and lung damage. Data were collected from smokers who have had their lung function assessed and their average daily cigarette consumption recorded. Lung function was assessed so that higher scores represent greater health. Therefore, a negative relationship between the variables was expected.

The researchers also believe that the relationship between these variables may be influenced by the number of years for which the person has been a smoker. Given the data in Prac5.sav, your tasks are to:

1   Check your data for violations of assumptions.

2   Conduct the appropriate analysis to determine whether cigarette consumption is related to lung capacity.

3   ·Determine whether the above relationship remains significant, having controlled for the length of the smoking habit.

Practice example 6: t-tests

You have been asked to determine whether hypnosis improves memory. Forty men and women are given five minutes to attempt to memorise a list of unrelated words. They are then asked to recall as many as they can. The next week they are asked to memorise a similar list of words and then to recall as many as possible while under hypnosis. You performed a study last year with another sample, so you have access to descriptive statistics from a similar group of adults. The mean words recalled in the earlier study, without hypnosis, was 34.6. Given the data in Prac6.sav, your tasks are to:

1   Determine whether the participants in the present study are comparable with those in the earlier study in terms of recall in a normal state.

2   Determine whether there was any change in recall as a result of hypnosis for the entire sample.

3   Determine whether men and women recall equal numbers of words when under hypnosis.

Practice example 7: One-way between-groups ANOVA with post-hoc comparisons

A biologist wished to examine the nutrient value of six different food supplements. One hundred and fifty-four rats of the same species were randomly assigned to one of six groups. Each group had a different supplement added to its food, and the rats' weight gain over the ensuing six months was recorded in grams. Given the data in Prac7.sav, your tasks are to:

1   Test the underlying assumptions of analysis of variance (ANOVA).

2   Determine whether there are significant differences in weight gain across the food supplements.

3   Locate the source of these differences using post-hoc analysis.

Practice example 8: One-way between-groups ANOVA with planned comparisons

The previous practice example examined the effect of food supplements on weight gain in rats. One hundred and fifty-four rats were randomly assigned to receive one of six food supplements, and their weight gain over six months was recorded. Given the data in Prac8.sav, your tasks are to:

1   Test the underlying assumptions of ANOVA.

2   Determine whether there are significant differences in weight gain across the six food supplements.

3   Test the hypothesis that supplement B is associated with a significantly higher weight gain than that associated with the other five supplements.

Practice example 9: Two-way between-groups ANOVA

A researcher is interested in determining the effect of density of traffic (light, medium or peak) and type of intersection (lights or roundabouts) on the number of accidents. Given the data in Prac9.sav, your tasks are to:

1   Check for violations of assumptions.

2   Determine whether traffic density influences the number of accidents.

3   Determine whether type of intersection influences the number of accidents.

4   Determine whether the influence of traffic density on the number of accidents depends on the type of intersection.

Practice example 10: One-way repeated-measures ANOVA

A real estate agent wished to determine whether the number of house sales in ten different suburbs changed significantly over the four quarters of the year. She asked her representatives in these ten suburbs to record the number of houses sold in each quarter. Given the data in Prac10.sav, your tasks are to:

1   Check your data for violations of assumptions.

2   Determine whether differences in the number of house sales exist across the four quarters.

Practice example 11: Two-way repeated-measures ANOVA

A graphic designer wished to determine which combination of colours and backgrounds produces the most aesthetically pleasing display. Five participants were exposed to two different types of background (hatched and spotted) and lettering of four different colours (red, blue, green and yellow). Participants were requested to rate the pleasing nature of these displays on a 20-point scale (1 = least pleasing to 20 = most pleasing). Given the data in Prac11.sav, your tasks are to:

1   Check the data for violations of assumptions.

2   Determine whether background influences the participants' ratings.

3   Determine whether colour of lettering influences the participants' ratings.

4   Determine whether the influence of background on rating depends on letter colouring.

Practice example 12: Trend analysis

Researchers wished to examine the effect of caffeine on the performance of a simple motor task. Sixty participants performed under one of three caffeine consumption conditions (0, 150 and 300 mL) and were required to perform a sequential finger-tapping task. The number of errors made was recorded. Given the data in Prac12.sav, your tasks are to:

1   Check for violations of assumptions.

2   Determine whether caffeine consumption significantly influences ability to perform the task accurately (i.e. the number of errors made).

3   Determine whether this trend is linear.

Practice example 13: Mixed/split plot design (SPANOVA)

In designing a new concert hall, an architect wished to determine whether the size of the auditorium and the choice of soundproofing material influenced the quality of the acoustics. Two sizes of auditorium were investigated (small and large), with four different types of soundproofing material. Ten different conductors were randomly assigned to the different sized auditoriums. These conductors listened to four orchestral performances under different soundproofing conditions. Conductors were asked to rate the quality of sound using a 20-point rating scale (1 = poor sound to 20 = excellent sound). Given the data in Prac13.sav, your tasks are to:

1   Check the data for violation of assumptions.

2   Determine whether auditorium size influences sound quality.

3   Determine whether soundproofing material influences sound quality.

4   Determine whether the influence of auditorium size on sound quality depends on soundproofing material.

Practice example 14: One-way analysis of covariance (ANCOVA)

Ninety-six male and female second-year psychology students participated in a peer-tutoring program designed to reduce computer anxiety. Of these students, 47 volunteered to act as peer tutors in first-year research methods computing workshops, while 49 preferred not to be tutors. Computer anxiety for all potential tutors was measured before the beginning of the course and then on completion. Given the data in Prac14.sav, your tasks are to:

1   Determine whether the reduction in computer anxiety is the same for males and females.

2   Determine whether the reduction in computer anxiety is the same for those who acted as tutors and those who did not.

Practice example 15: Reliability analysis

A researcher wished to determine the reliability of four independent personality scales, namely, hope, optimism, locus of control and self-esteem. The hope and optimism scales consisted of eight items each, the locus of control scale consisted of nine items and the self-esteem scale consisted of ten items. A five-point Likert scale response format was used for each of these scales. Items 1, 3, 4 and 7 of the optimism scale and items 3, 5, 8, 9 and 10 of the self-esteem scale were negatively worded. Three hundred and sixty-three people responded to each of the four scales, but not all scales were fully completed. Given the data in Prac15.sav, your tasks are to:

1   Determine the Cronbach's alpha coefficient for each scale.

2   Make recommendations about the inclusion or exclusion of items.

Practice example 16: Factor analysis

A researcher wished to determine the factor structure of four independent personality scales: hope, optimism, locus of control and self-esteem. The hope and optimism scales consisted of eight items each, the locus of control scale consisted of nine items and the self-esteem scale consisted of ten items. A five-point Likert scale response format was used for each of these scales. Items 1, 3, 4 and 7 of the optimism scale and items 3, 5, 8, 9 and 10 of the self-esteem scale were negatively worded. Three hundred and sixty-three people responded to each of the four scales but not all scales were completed fully. Given the data in Prac16.sav, your tasks are to:

1   Determine the factor structure of each of the four scales independently.

2   Make recommendations regarding the inclusion and exclusion of items from each scale.

Given the size of the output, please note that the syntax below has been displayed for the hope scale only.

Practice example 17: Regression

In a study concerning the relationship between the volume of wood provided by a forest area and various characteristics of the area, an experimental forest containing mixed softwood trees was divided into plots, of which 25 were selected at random. Measurements were made on each of the plots at the beginning of the study: initial wood volume, number of trees, average age of trees and average volume of trees. Five years later, at the end of the study, the final wood volume was measured. Given the data in Prac17.sav, your tasks are to:

1   Assess the data for violation of assumptions.

2   Test the hypothesis indicated by previous forestry research that initial wood volume is the best predictor of final wood volume, followed by the number of trees in the plot.

Practice example 18: MANOVA

Three hundred and sixty-four male and female subjects completed a personality inventory comprising a self-esteem, optimism and hope scale. The researcher is aware that these subscales are highly correlated. Given the data in Prac18.sav, your tasks are to:

1   Check for violations of assumptions.

2   Determine whether gender differences exist across the combination of scales.

Practice examples 19a–19g: Nonparametric tests

You will remember that nonparametric tests, or distribution-free tests, do not rely on parameter estimation or assumptions about parameters or the shape of distributions. Assuming that these assumptions cannot be met, perform the appropriate nonparametric test for each of the practice examples below.

Practice example 19a: Chi-square test for goodness of fit

A coffee company is about to launch a range of speciality coffee bags and would like to know whether some varieties are likely to sell better than others. Four of its new varieties are placed on a supermarket shelf for one week. The number of boxes sold for each variety are: 20 Mocha Kenya, 40 Colombian, 30 Lebanese and ten Swiss. Given the data in Prac19a.sav, your task is to:

1   Determine whether the distribution of sales suggests that some varieties of coffee bags are more popular than others.

Practice example 19b: Chi-square test for relatedness or independence

A researcher was interested in determining whether drinking preference was gender related. Given the data in Prac19b.sav, your task is to:

1   Determine whether drinking preference is gender related, that is, whether most men prefer to drink beer rather than wine.

Practice example 19c: Mann–Whitney U test (Wilcoxon rank sum W test)

A psychologist is interested in the relationship between personality types and religious affiliation. Fifteen Baptist and 15 Anglican churchgoers were randomly selected from their respective communities and asked to complete a personality questionnaire measuring introversion–extroversion on a scale from 0 to 100: the higher the score on the scale, the more extroverted the individual. Given the data in Prac19c.sav, your task is to:

1   Determine whether personality types differ significantly across the two religions.

Practice example 19d: Wilcoxon signed-rank test

A human-factors specialist working for an airline company wishes to examine the effect of temperature on performance. The performances of a random sample of 15 pilots were recorded following participation in an air simulation task, in cockpits of differing temperatures (20 degrees Celsius and 35 degrees Celsius). Given the data in Prac19d.sav, your task is to:

1   Determine whether temperature influences pilot performance.

Practice example 19e: Kruskal–Wallis test

A physical education teacher observes that many sporting injuries result from ball sports such as football, basketball and rugby. He records the number of injuries sustained by 45 boys actively involved in one of the three sports over a month. Given the data in Prac19e.sav, your task is to:

1   Determine whether the number of injuries sustained differs according to the type of sport played.

Practice example 19f: Friedman test

A veterinarian wishing to start a new dog-breeding business wants to determine which of four breeds of small dog is more companionable: the silky terrier, Jack Russell, Bichon Frise or pug. He randomly samples 20 people who regularly attend his clinic and asks them to complete a perceived companionability scale — the higher the score, the more companionable the breed of dog. Given the data in Prac19f.sav, your task is to:

1   Determine whether certain breeds of small dog are more companionable than others.

Practice example 19g: Spearman's rank-order correlation

A truck manufacturer notices that a truck's fuel consumption depends on the load it is carrying. He keeps a log of diesel consumption and load for 20 trucks over a six-month period. Given the data in Prac19g.sav, your tasks are to:

1   Plot the relationship between the two variables.

2   Determine whether there is a relationship between load and diesel consumption.

Practice examples 20a and 20b: Multiple response analysis and multiple dichotomy analysis

Practice example 20a

A counselling psychologist was interested in determining why people marry. The maximum number of reasons given by any one person was three. These reasons were coded as follows:

01 Love	05 Security
02 Company	06 To have children
03 Money	07 Familiarity
04 Sex	

Given the data in Prac20a.sav, your tasks are to:

1   Determine the most frequently quoted reason for marriage.

2   Determine the most frequently quoted reason for marriage given by men.

Practice example 20b

A random sample of drivers was asked to indicate factors that influenced their decision when purchasing a used car. The following criteria were specified:

01 Year of manufacture

02 Mileage

03 State of the interior

04 State of the chassis

05 State of the duco

06 Other

Given the data in Prac20b.sav, your task is to:

1   Determine the most influential criterion on vehicle purchase.

Practice example 21: Multidimensional scaling

In the chapter, three tourists judged the distances between nine towns in Australia. Their judgements were averaged and their average scores were used to develop a single matrix of proximities representing their judgements of the distances between towns.

In this practice example, the three tourists are asked to use a five-point scale to make a judgement of the similarity between each of the nine towns. A score of 1 would indicate the pair of towns were very similar and a score of 5 would indicate they were very dissimilar. They are instructed they can base their judgement on any criteria they like.

In this example, we shall derive solutions in not only two dimensions but two to five dimensions. The data for the practice example are given in Prac22.sav.

In doing the analysis, in the **Multidimensional Scaling: Plots** subdialogue box, make sure that you have entered 2 for **Minimum dimensions** and 2 for **Maximum dimensions**. Run the analysis using the same configuration as you did before and record the value of Stress I.

Repeat the process for three through to five dimensions and record the Stress I values for each dimensional solution.

Appendix

TABLE 1 *t* CRITICAL VALUES

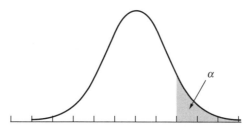

Degrees of freedom	Upper tail probability (α)								
	0.15	0.10	0.05	0.025	0.015	0.01	0.005	0.001	0.0005
1	1.963	3.078	6.314	12.706	21.205	31.821	63.657	318.309	1273.155
2	1.386	1.886	2.920	4.303	5.643	6.965	9.925	22.327	44.703
3	1.250	1.638	2.353	3.182	3.896	4.541	5.841	10.215	16.326
4	1.190	1.533	2.132	2.776	3.298	3.747	4.604	7.173	10.305
5	1.156	1.476	2.015	2.571	3.003	3.365	4.032	5.893	7.976
6	1.134	1.440	1.943	2.447	2.829	3.143	3.707	5.208	6.788
7	1.119	1.415	1.895	2.365	2.715	2.998	3.499	4.785	6.082
8	1.108	1.397	1.860	2.306	2.634	2.896	3.355	4.501	5.617
9	1.100	1.383	1.833	2.262	2.574	2.821	3.250	4.297	5.291
10	1.093	1.372	1.812	2.228	2.527	2.764	3.169	4.144	5.049
11	1.088	1.363	1.796	2.201	2.491	2.718	3.106	4.025	4.863
12	1.083	1.356	1.782	2.179	2.461	2.681	3.055	3.930	4.717
13	1.079	1.350	1.771	2.160	2.436	2.650	3.012	3.852	4.597
14	1.076	1.345	1.761	2.145	2.415	2.625	2.977	3.787	4.499
15	1.074	1.341	1.753	2.131	2.397	2.602	2.947	3.733	4.417
16	1.071	1.337	1.746	2.120	2.382	2.583	2.921	3.686	4.346
17	1.069	1.333	1.740	2.110	2.368	2.567	2.898	3.646	4.286
18	1.067	1.330	1.734	2.101	2.356	2.552	2.878	3.611	4.233
19	1.066	1.328	1.729	2.093	2.346	2.539	2.861	3.579	4.187
20	1.064	1.325	1.725	2.086	2.336	2.528	2.845	3.552	4.146
21	1.063	1.323	1.721	2.080	2.328	2.518	2.831	3.527	4.109
22	1.061	1.321	1.717	2.074	2.320	2.508	2.819	3.505	4.077
23	1.060	1.319	1.714	2.069	2.313	2.500	2.807	3.485	4.047
24	1.059	1.318	1.711	2.064	2.307	2.492	2.797	3.467	4.021
25	1.058	1.316	1.708	2.060	2.301	2.485	2.787	3.450	3.997
26	1.058	1.315	1.706	2.056	2.296	2.479	2.779	3.435	3.974
27	1.057	1.314	1.703	2.052	2.291	2.473	2.771	3.421	3.954
28	1.056	1.313	1.701	2.048	2.286	2.467	2.763	3.408	3.935
29	1.055	1.311	1.699	2.045	2.282	2.462	2.756	3.396	3.918
30	1.055	1.310	1.697	2.042	2.278	2.457	2.750	3.385	3.902
40	1.050	1.303	1.684	2.021	2.250	2.423	2.704	3.307	3.788
50	1.047	1.299	1.676	2.009	2.234	2.403	2.678	3.261	3.723
60	1.045	1.296	1.671	2.000	2.223	2.390	2.660	3.232	3.681
120	1.041	1.289	1.658	1.980	2.196	2.358	2.617	3.160	3.578
Z critical value	1.036	1.282	1.645	1.960	2.170	2.326	2.576	3.090	3.290
Level of significance for a one-tailed test	0.15	0.10	0.05	0.025	0.015	0.01	0.005	0.001	0.0005
Level of significance for a two-tailed test	0.30	0.20	0.10	0.05	0.03	0.02	0.01	0.002	0.001

TABLE 2 CHI-SQUARE DISTRIBUTION TABLE

The entries in this table give the critical value of χ^2 for the specified number of degrees of freedom and areas in the right tail.

Degrees of freedom	Upper tail areas											
	0.995	0.99	0.975	0.95	0.9	0.75	0.25	0.1	0.05	0.025	0.01	0.005
1	0.000	0.000	0.001	0.004	0.016	0.102	1.323	2.706	3.841	5.024	6.635	7.879
2	0.010	0.020	0.051	0.103	0.211	0.575	2.773	4.605	5.991	7.378	9.210	10.597
3	0.072	0.115	0.216	0.352	0.584	1.213	4.108	6.251	7.815	9.348	11.345	12.838
4	0.207	0.297	0.484	0.711	1.064	1.923	5.385	7.779	9.488	11.143	13.277	14.860
5	0.412	0.554	0.831	1.145	1.610	2.675	6.626	9.236	11.070	12.832	15.086	16.750
6	0.676	0.872	1.237	1.635	2.204	3.455	7.841	10.645	12.592	14.449	16.812	18.548
7	0.989	1.239	1.690	2.167	2.833	4.255	9.037	12.017	14.067	16.013	18.475	20.278
8	1.344	1.647	2.180	2.733	3.490	5.071	10.219	13.362	15.507	17.535	20.090	21.955
9	1.735	2.088	2.700	3.325	4.168	5.899	11.389	14.684	16.919	19.023	21.666	23.589
10	2.156	2.558	3.247	3.940	4.865	6.737	12.549	15.987	18.307	20.483	23.209	25.188
11	2.603	3.053	3.816	4.575	5.578	7.584	13.701	17.275	19.675	21.920	24.725	26.757
12	3.074	3.571	4.404	5.226	6.304	8.438	14.845	18.549	21.026	23.337	26.217	28.300
13	3.565	4.107	5.009	5.892	7.041	9.299	15.984	19.812	22.362	24.736	27.688	29.819
14	4.075	4.660	5.629	6.571	7.790	10.165	17.117	21.064	23.685	26.119	29.141	31.319
15	4.601	5.229	6.262	7.261	8.547	11.037	18.245	22.307	24.996	27.488	30.578	32.801
16	5.142	5.812	6.908	7.962	9.312	11.912	19.369	23.542	26.296	28.845	32.000	34.267
17	5.697	6.408	7.564	8.672	10.085	12.792	20.489	24.769	27.587	30.191	33.409	35.718
18	6.265	7.015	8.231	9.390	10.865	13.675	21.605	25.989	28.869	31.526	34.805	37.156
19	6.844	7.633	8.907	10.117	11.651	14.562	22.718	27.204	30.144	32.852	36.191	38.582
20	7.434	8.260	9.591	10.851	12.443	15.452	23.828	28.412	31.410	34.170	37.566	39.997
21	8.034	8.897	10.283	11.591	13.240	16.344	24.935	29.615	32.671	35.479	38.932	41.401
22	8.643	9.542	10.982	12.338	14.041	17.240	26.039	30.813	33.924	36.781	40.289	42.796
23	9.260	10.196	11.689	13.091	14.848	18.137	27.141	32.007	35.172	38.076	41.638	44.181
24	9.886	10.856	12.401	13.848	15.659	19.037	28.241	33.196	36.415	39.364	42.980	45.558
25	10.520	11.524	13.120	14.611	16.473	19.939	29.339	34.382	37.652	40.646	44.314	46.928
26	11.160	12.198	13.844	15.379	17.292	20.843	30.435	35.563	38.885	41.923	45.642	48.290
27	11.808	12.878	14.573	16.151	18.114	21.749	31.528	36.741	40.113	43.195	46.963	49.645
28	12.461	13.565	15.308	16.928	18.939	22.657	32.620	37.916	41.337	44.461	48.278	50.994
29	13.121	14.256	16.047	17.708	19.768	23.567	33.711	39.087	42.557	45.722	49.588	52.335
30	13.787	14.953	16.791	18.493	20.599	24.478	34.800	40.256	43.773	46.979	50.892	53.672
31	14.458	15.655	17.539	19.281	21.434	25.390	35.887	41.422	44.985	48.232	52.191	55.002
32	15.134	16.362	18.291	20.072	22.271	26.304	36.973	42.585	46.194	49.480	53.486	56.328
33	15.815	17.073	19.047	20.867	23.110	27.219	38.058	43.745	47.400	50.725	54.775	57.648
34	16.501	17.789	19.806	21.664	23.952	28.136	39.141	44.903	48.602	51.966	56.061	58.964
35	17.192	18.509	20.569	22.465	24.797	29.054	40.223	46.059	49.802	53.203	57.342	60.275
40	20.707	22.164	24.433	26.509	29.051	33.660	45.616	51.805	55.758	59.342	63.691	66.766
60	35.534	37.485	40.482	43.188	46.459	52.294	66.981	74.397	79.082	83.298	88.379	91.952
120	83.852	86.923	91.573	95.705	100.624	109.220	130.055	140.233	146.567	152.211	158.950	163.648

TABLE 3 THE *F* DISTRIBUTION TABLE

a. Area in the right tail under the *F* distribution curve = .01

Degrees of freedom — denominator	— Degrees of freedom — numerator																
	1	2	3	4	5	6	7	8	9	10	11	12	13	14	15	16	17
1	4052.185	4999.340	5403.534	5624.257	5763.955	5858.950	5928.334	5980.954	6022.397	6055.925	6083.399	6106.682	6125.774	6143.004	6156.974	6170.012	6181.188
2	98.502	99.000	99.164	99.251	99.302	99.331	99.357	99.375	99.390	99.397	99.408	99.419	99.422	99.426	99.433	99.437	99.441
3	34.116	30.816	29.457	28.710	28.237	27.911	27.671	27.489	27.345	27.228	27.132	27.052	26.983	26.924	26.872	26.826	26.786
4	21.198	18.000	16.694	15.977	15.522	15.207	14.976	14.799	14.659	14.546	14.452	14.374	14.306	14.249	14.198	14.154	14.114
5	16.258	13.274	12.060	11.392	10.967	10.672	10.456	10.289	10.158	10.051	9.963	9.888	9.825	9.770	9.722	9.680	9.643
6	13.745	10.925	9.780	9.148	8.746	8.466	8.260	8.102	7.976	7.874	7.790	7.718	7.657	7.605	7.559	7.519	7.483
7	12.246	9.547	8.451	7.847	7.460	7.191	6.993	6.840	6.719	6.620	6.538	6.469	6.410	6.359	6.314	6.275	6.240
8	11.259	8.649	7.591	7.006	6.632	6.371	6.178	6.029	5.911	5.814	5.734	5.667	5.609	5.559	5.515	5.477	5.442
9	10.562	8.022	6.992	6.422	6.057	5.802	5.613	5.467	5.351	5.257	5.178	5.111	5.055	5.005	4.962	4.924	4.890
10	10.044	7.559	6.552	5.994	5.636	5.386	5.200	5.057	4.942	4.849	4.772	4.706	4.650	4.601	4.558	4.520	4.487
11	9.646	7.206	6.217	5.668	5.316	5.069	4.886	4.744	4.632	4.539	4.462	4.397	4.342	4.293	4.251	4.213	4.180
12	9.330	6.927	5.953	5.412	5.064	4.821	4.640	4.499	4.388	4.296	4.220	4.155	4.100	4.052	4.010	3.972	3.939
13	9.074	6.701	5.739	5.205	4.862	4.620	4.441	4.302	4.191	4.100	4.025	3.960	3.905	3.857	3.815	3.778	3.745
14	8.862	6.515	5.564	5.035	4.695	4.456	4.278	4.140	4.030	3.939	3.864	3.800	3.745	3.698	3.656	3.619	3.586
15	8.683	6.359	5.417	4.893	4.556	4.318	4.142	4.004	3.895	3.805	3.730	3.666	3.612	3.564	3.522	3.485	3.452
16	8.531	6.226	5.292	4.773	4.437	4.202	4.026	3.890	3.780	3.691	3.616	3.553	3.498	3.451	3.409	3.372	3.339
17	8.400	6.112	5.185	4.669	4.336	4.101	3.927	3.791	3.682	3.593	3.518	3.455	3.401	3.353	3.312	3.275	3.242
18	8.285	6.013	5.092	4.579	4.248	4.015	3.841	3.705	3.597	3.508	3.434	3.371	3.316	3.269	3.227	3.190	3.158
19	8.185	5.926	5.010	4.500	4.171	3.939	3.765	3.631	3.523	3.434	3.360	3.297	3.242	3.195	3.153	3.116	3.084
20	8.096	5.849	4.938	4.431	4.103	3.871	3.699	3.564	3.457	3.368	3.294	3.231	3.177	3.130	3.088	3.051	3.018
21	8.017	5.780	4.874	4.369	4.042	3.812	3.640	3.506	3.398	3.310	3.236	3.173	3.119	3.072	3.030	2.993	2.960
22	7.945	5.719	4.817	4.313	3.988	3.758	3.587	3.453	3.346	3.258	3.184	3.121	3.067	3.019	2.978	2.941	2.908
23	7.881	5.664	4.765	4.264	3.939	3.710	3.539	3.406	3.299	3.211	3.137	3.074	3.020	2.973	2.931	2.894	2.861
24	7.823	5.614	4.718	4.218	3.895	3.667	3.496	3.363	3.256	3.168	3.094	3.032	2.977	2.930	2.889	2.852	2.819
25	7.770	5.568	4.675	4.177	3.855	3.627	3.457	3.324	3.217	3.129	3.056	2.993	2.939	2.892	2.850	2.813	2.780
26	7.721	5.526	4.637	4.140	3.818	3.591	3.421	3.288	3.182	3.094	3.021	2.958	2.904	2.857	2.815	2.778	2.745
27	7.677	5.488	4.601	4.106	3.785	3.558	3.388	3.256	3.149	3.062	2.988	2.926	2.872	2.824	2.783	2.746	2.713
28	7.636	5.453	4.568	4.074	3.754	3.528	3.358	3.226	3.120	3.032	2.959	2.896	2.842	2.795	2.753	2.716	2.683
29	7.598	5.420	4.538	4.045	3.725	3.499	3.330	3.198	3.092	3.005	2.931	2.868	2.814	2.767	2.726	2.689	2.656
30	7.562	5.390	4.510	4.018	3.699	3.473	3.305	3.173	3.067	2.979	2.906	2.843	2.789	2.742	2.700	2.663	2.630
40	7.314	5.178	4.313	3.828	3.514	3.291	3.124	2.993	2.888	2.801	2.727	2.665	2.611	2.563	2.522	2.484	2.451
60	7.077	4.977	4.126	3.649	3.339	3.119	2.953	2.823	2.718	2.632	2.559	2.496	2.442	2.394	2.352	2.315	2.281
120	6.851	4.787	3.949	3.480	3.174	2.956	2.792	2.663	2.559	2.472	2.399	2.336	2.282	2.234	2.191	2.154	2.119

(continued)

TABLE 3 *(continued)*

a. Area in the right tail under the F distribution curve = .01

Degrees of freedom — denominator	\multicolumn{16}{c}{Degrees of freedom — numerator}															
	18	19	20	21	22	23	24	25	26	27	28	29	30	40	60	120
1	6191.432	6200.746	6208.662	6216.113	6223.097	6228.685	6234.273	6239.861	6244.518	6249.174	6252.900	6257.091	6260.350	6286.427	6312.970	6339.513
2	99.444	99.448	99.448	99.451	99.455	99.455	99.455	99.459	99.462	99.462	99.462	99.462	99.466	99.477	99.484	99.491
3	26.751	26.719	26.690	26.664	26.639	26.617	26.597	26.579	26.562	26.546	26.531	26.517	26.504	26.411	26.316	26.221
4	14.079	14.048	14.019	13.994	13.970	13.949	13.929	13.911	13.894	13.878	13.864	13.850	13.838	13.745	13.652	13.558
5	9.609	9.580	9.553	9.528	9.506	9.485	9.466	9.449	9.433	9.418	9.404	9.391	9.379	9.291	9.202	9.112
6	7.451	7.422	7.396	7.372	7.351	7.331	7.313	7.296	7.281	7.266	7.253	7.240	7.229	7.143	7.057	6.969
7	6.209	6.181	6.155	6.132	6.111	6.092	6.074	6.058	6.043	6.029	6.016	6.003	5.992	5.908	5.824	5.737
8	5.412	5.384	5.359	5.336	5.316	5.297	5.279	5.263	5.248	5.234	5.221	5.209	5.198	5.116	5.032	4.946
9	4.860	4.833	4.808	4.786	4.765	4.746	4.729	4.713	4.698	4.684	4.672	4.660	4.649	4.567	4.483	4.398
10	4.457	4.430	4.405	4.383	4.363	4.344	4.327	4.311	4.296	4.283	4.270	4.258	4.247	4.165	4.082	3.996
11	4.150	4.123	4.099	4.077	4.057	4.038	4.021	4.005	3.990	3.977	3.964	3.952	3.941	3.860	3.776	3.690
12	3.910	3.883	3.858	3.836	3.816	3.798	3.780	3.765	3.750	3.736	3.724	3.712	3.701	3.619	3.535	3.449
13	3.716	3.689	3.665	3.643	3.622	3.604	3.587	3.571	3.556	3.543	3.530	3.518	3.507	3.425	3.341	3.255
14	3.556	3.529	3.505	3.483	3.463	3.444	3.427	3.412	3.397	3.383	3.371	3.359	3.348	3.266	3.181	3.094
15	3.423	3.396	3.372	3.350	3.330	3.311	3.294	3.278	3.264	3.250	3.237	3.225	3.214	3.132	3.047	2.959
16	3.310	3.283	3.259	3.237	3.216	3.198	3.181	3.165	3.150	3.137	3.124	3.112	3.101	3.018	2.933	2.845
17	3.212	3.186	3.162	3.139	3.119	3.101	3.083	3.068	3.053	3.039	3.026	3.014	3.003	2.920	2.835	2.746
18	3.128	3.101	3.077	3.055	3.035	3.016	2.999	2.983	2.968	2.955	2.942	2.930	2.919	2.835	2.749	2.660
19	3.054	3.027	3.003	2.981	2.961	2.942	2.925	2.909	2.894	2.880	2.868	2.855	2.844	2.761	2.674	2.584
20	2.989	2.962	2.938	2.916	2.895	2.877	2.859	2.843	2.829	2.815	2.802	2.790	2.778	2.695	2.608	2.517
21	2.931	2.904	2.880	2.857	2.837	2.818	2.801	2.785	2.770	2.756	2.743	2.731	2.720	2.636	2.548	2.457
22	2.879	2.852	2.827	2.805	2.785	2.766	2.749	2.733	2.718	2.704	2.691	2.679	2.667	2.583	2.495	2.403
23	2.832	2.805	2.780	2.758	2.738	2.719	2.702	2.686	2.671	2.657	2.644	2.632	2.620	2.536	2.447	2.354
24	2.789	2.762	2.738	2.716	2.695	2.676	2.659	2.643	2.628	2.614	2.601	2.589	2.577	2.492	2.403	2.310
25	2.751	2.724	2.699	2.677	2.657	2.638	2.620	2.604	2.589	2.575	2.562	2.550	2.538	2.453	2.364	2.270
26	2.715	2.688	2.664	2.642	2.621	2.602	2.585	2.569	2.554	2.540	2.526	2.514	2.503	2.417	2.327	2.233
27	2.683	2.656	2.632	2.609	2.589	2.570	2.552	2.536	2.521	2.507	2.494	2.481	2.470	2.384	2.294	2.198
28	2.653	2.626	2.602	2.579	2.559	2.540	2.522	2.506	2.491	2.477	2.464	2.451	2.440	2.354	2.263	2.167
29	2.626	2.599	2.574	2.552	2.531	2.512	2.495	2.478	2.463	2.449	2.436	2.423	2.412	2.325	2.234	2.138
30	2.600	2.573	2.549	2.526	2.506	2.487	2.469	2.453	2.437	2.423	2.410	2.398	2.386	2.299	2.208	2.111
40	2.421	2.394	2.369	2.346	2.325	2.306	2.288	2.271	2.256	2.241	2.228	2.215	2.203	2.114	2.019	1.917
60	2.251	2.223	2.198	2.175	2.153	2.134	2.115	2.098	2.083	2.068	2.054	2.041	2.028	1.936	1.836	1.726
120	2.089	2.060	2.035	2.011	1.989	1.969	1.950	1.932	1.916	1.901	1.886	1.873	1.860	1.763	1.656	1.533

b. Area in the right tail under the F distribution curve = .05

Degrees of freedom – denominator	Degrees of freedom – numerator																
	1	2	3	4	5	6	7	8	9	10	11	12	13	14	15	16	17
1	161.446	199.499	215.707	224.583	230.160	233.988	236.767	238.884	240.543	241.882	242.981	243.905	244.690	245.363	245.949	246.466	246.917
2	18.513	19.000	19.164	19.247	19.296	19.329	19.353	19.371	19.385	19.396	19.405	19.412	19.419	19.424	19.429	19.433	19.437
3	10.128	9.552	9.277	9.117	9.013	8.941	8.887	8.845	8.812	8.785	8.763	8.745	8.729	8.715	8.703	8.692	8.683
4	7.709	6.944	6.591	6.388	6.256	6.163	6.094	6.041	5.999	5.964	5.936	5.912	5.891	5.873	5.858	5.844	5.832
5	6.608	5.786	5.409	5.192	5.050	4.950	4.876	4.818	4.772	4.735	4.704	4.678	4.655	4.636	4.619	4.604	4.590
6	5.987	5.143	4.757	4.534	4.387	4.284	4.207	4.147	4.099	4.060	4.027	4.000	3.976	3.956	3.938	3.922	3.908
7	5.591	4.737	4.347	4.120	3.972	3.866	3.787	3.726	3.677	3.637	3.603	3.575	3.550	3.529	3.511	3.494	3.480
8	5.318	4.459	4.066	3.838	3.688	3.581	3.500	3.438	3.388	3.347	3.313	3.284	3.259	3.237	3.218	3.202	3.187
9	5.117	4.256	3.863	3.633	3.482	3.374	3.293	3.230	3.179	3.137	3.102	3.073	3.048	3.025	3.006	2.989	2.974
10	4.965	4.103	3.708	3.478	3.326	3.217	3.135	3.072	3.020	2.978	2.943	2.913	2.887	2.865	2.845	2.828	2.812
11	4.844	3.982	3.587	3.357	3.204	3.095	3.012	2.948	2.896	2.854	2.818	2.788	2.761	2.739	2.719	2.701	2.685
12	4.747	3.885	3.490	3.259	3.106	2.996	2.913	2.849	2.796	2.753	2.717	2.687	2.660	2.637	2.617	2.599	2.583
13	4.667	3.806	3.411	3.179	3.025	2.915	2.832	2.767	2.714	2.671	2.635	2.604	2.577	2.554	2.533	2.515	2.499
14	4.600	3.739	3.344	3.112	2.958	2.848	2.764	2.699	2.646	2.602	2.565	2.534	2.507	2.484	2.463	2.445	2.428
15	4.543	3.682	3.287	3.056	2.901	2.790	2.707	2.641	2.588	2.544	2.507	2.475	2.448	2.424	2.403	2.385	2.368
16	4.494	3.634	3.239	3.007	2.852	2.741	2.657	2.591	2.538	2.494	2.456	2.425	2.397	2.373	2.352	2.333	2.317
17	4.451	3.592	3.197	2.965	2.810	2.699	2.614	2.548	2.494	2.450	2.413	2.381	2.353	2.329	2.308	2.289	2.272
18	4.414	3.555	3.160	2.928	2.773	2.661	2.577	2.510	2.456	2.412	2.374	2.342	2.314	2.290	2.269	2.250	2.233
19	4.381	3.522	3.127	2.895	2.740	2.628	2.544	2.477	2.423	2.378	2.340	2.308	2.280	2.256	2.234	2.215	2.198
20	4.351	3.493	3.098	2.866	2.711	2.599	2.514	2.447	2.393	2.348	2.310	2.278	2.250	2.225	2.203	2.184	2.167
21	4.325	3.467	3.072	2.840	2.685	2.573	2.488	2.420	2.366	2.321	2.283	2.250	2.222	2.197	2.176	2.156	2.139
22	4.301	3.443	3.049	2.817	2.661	2.549	2.464	2.397	2.342	2.297	2.259	2.226	2.198	2.173	2.151	2.131	2.114
23	4.279	3.422	3.028	2.796	2.640	2.528	2.442	2.375	2.320	2.275	2.236	2.204	2.175	2.150	2.128	2.109	2.091
24	4.260	3.403	3.009	2.776	2.621	2.508	2.423	2.355	2.300	2.255	2.216	2.183	2.155	2.130	2.108	2.088	2.070
25	4.242	3.385	2.991	2.759	2.603	2.490	2.405	2.337	2.282	2.236	2.198	2.165	2.136	2.111	2.089	2.069	2.051
26	4.225	3.369	2.975	2.743	2.587	2.474	2.388	2.321	2.265	2.220	2.181	2.148	2.119	2.094	2.072	2.052	2.034
27	4.210	3.354	2.960	2.728	2.572	2.459	2.373	2.305	2.250	2.204	2.166	2.132	2.103	2.078	2.056	2.036	2.018
28	4.196	3.340	2.947	2.714	2.558	2.445	2.359	2.291	2.236	2.190	2.151	2.118	2.089	2.064	2.041	2.021	2.003
29	4.183	3.328	2.934	2.701	2.545	2.432	2.346	2.278	2.223	2.177	2.138	2.104	2.075	2.050	2.027	2.007	1.989
30	4.171	3.316	2.922	2.690	2.534	2.421	2.334	2.266	2.211	2.165	2.126	2.092	2.063	2.037	2.015	1.995	1.976
40	4.085	3.232	2.839	2.606	2.449	2.336	2.249	2.180	2.124	2.077	2.038	2.003	1.974	1.948	1.924	1.904	1.885
60	4.001	3.150	2.758	2.525	2.368	2.254	2.167	2.097	2.040	1.993	1.952	1.917	1.887	1.860	1.836	1.815	1.796
120	3.920	3.072	2.680	2.447	2.290	2.175	2.087	2.016	1.959	1.910	1.869	1.834	1.803	1.775	1.750	1.728	1.709

(continued)

Degrees of freedom – denominator	Degrees of freedom – numerator															
	18	19	20	21	22	23	24	25	26	27	28	29	30	40	60	120
1	247.324	247.688	248.016	248.307	248.579	248.823	249.052	249.260	249.453	249.631	249.798	249.951	250.096	251.144	252.196	253.254
2	19.440	19.443	19.446	19.448	19.450	19.452	19.454	19.456	19.457	19.459	19.460	19.461	19.463	19.471	19.479	19.487
3	8.675	8.667	8.660	8.654	8.648	8.643	8.638	8.634	8.630	8.626	8.623	8.620	8.617	8.594	8.572	8.549
4	5.821	5.811	5.803	5.795	5.787	5.781	5.774	5.769	5.763	5.759	5.754	5.750	5.746	5.717	5.688	5.658
5	4.579	4.568	4.558	4.549	4.541	4.534	4.527	4.521	4.515	4.510	4.505	4.500	4.496	4.464	4.431	4.398
6	3.896	3.884	3.874	3.865	3.856	3.849	3.841	3.835	3.829	3.823	3.818	3.813	3.808	3.774	3.740	3.705
7	3.467	3.455	3.445	3.435	3.426	3.418	3.410	3.404	3.397	3.391	3.386	3.381	3.376	3.340	3.304	3.267
8	3.173	3.161	3.150	3.140	3.131	3.123	3.115	3.108	3.102	3.095	3.090	3.084	3.079	3.043	3.005	2.967
9	2.960	2.948	2.936	2.926	2.917	2.908	2.900	2.893	2.886	2.880	2.874	2.869	2.864	2.826	2.787	2.748
10	2.798	2.785	2.774	2.764	2.754	2.745	2.737	2.730	2.723	2.716	2.710	2.705	2.700	2.661	2.621	2.580
11	2.671	2.658	2.646	2.636	2.626	2.617	2.609	2.601	2.594	2.588	2.582	2.576	2.570	2.531	2.490	2.448
12	2.568	2.555	2.544	2.533	2.523	2.514	2.505	2.498	2.491	2.484	2.478	2.472	2.466	2.426	2.384	2.341
13	2.484	2.471	2.459	2.448	2.438	2.429	2.420	2.412	2.405	2.398	2.392	2.386	2.380	2.339	2.297	2.252
14	2.413	2.400	2.388	2.377	2.367	2.357	2.349	2.341	2.333	2.326	2.320	2.314	2.308	2.266	2.223	2.178
15	2.353	2.340	2.328	2.316	2.306	2.297	2.288	2.280	2.272	2.265	2.259	2.253	2.247	2.204	2.160	2.114
16	2.302	2.288	2.276	2.264	2.254	2.244	2.235	2.227	2.220	2.212	2.206	2.200	2.194	2.151	2.106	2.059
17	2.257	2.243	2.230	2.219	2.208	2.199	2.190	2.181	2.174	2.167	2.160	2.154	2.148	2.104	2.058	2.011
18	2.217	2.203	2.191	2.179	2.168	2.159	2.150	2.141	2.134	2.126	2.119	2.113	2.107	2.063	2.017	1.968
19	2.182	2.168	2.155	2.144	2.133	2.123	2.114	2.106	2.098	2.090	2.084	2.077	2.071	2.026	1.980	1.930
20	2.151	2.137	2.124	2.112	2.102	2.092	2.082	2.074	2.066	2.059	2.052	2.045	2.039	1.994	1.946	1.896
21	2.123	2.109	2.096	2.084	2.073	2.063	2.054	2.045	2.037	2.030	2.023	2.016	2.010	1.965	1.916	1.866
22	2.098	2.084	2.071	2.059	2.048	2.038	2.028	2.020	2.012	2.004	1.997	1.990	1.984	1.938	1.889	1.838
23	2.075	2.061	2.048	2.036	2.025	2.014	2.005	1.996	1.988	1.981	1.973	1.967	1.961	1.914	1.865	1.813
24	2.054	2.040	2.027	2.015	2.003	1.993	1.984	1.975	1.967	1.959	1.952	1.945	1.939	1.892	1.842	1.790
25	2.035	2.021	2.007	1.995	1.984	1.974	1.964	1.955	1.947	1.939	1.932	1.926	1.919	1.872	1.822	1.768
26	2.018	2.003	1.990	1.978	1.966	1.956	1.946	1.938	1.929	1.921	1.914	1.907	1.901	1.853	1.803	1.749
27	2.002	1.987	1.974	1.961	1.950	1.940	1.930	1.921	1.913	1.905	1.898	1.891	1.884	1.836	1.785	1.731
28	1.987	1.972	1.959	1.946	1.935	1.924	1.915	1.906	1.897	1.889	1.882	1.875	1.869	1.820	1.769	1.714
29	1.973	1.958	1.945	1.932	1.921	1.910	1.901	1.891	1.883	1.875	1.868	1.861	1.854	1.806	1.754	1.698
30	1.960	1.945	1.932	1.919	1.908	1.897	1.887	1.878	1.870	1.862	1.854	1.847	1.841	1.792	1.740	1.683
40	1.868	1.853	1.839	1.826	1.814	1.803	1.793	1.783	1.775	1.766	1.759	1.751	1.744	1.693	1.637	1.577
60	1.778	1.763	1.748	1.735	1.722	1.711	1.700	1.690	1.681	1.672	1.664	1.656	1.649	1.594	1.534	1.467
120	1.690	1.674	1.659	1.645	1.632	1.620	1.608	1.598	1.588	1.579	1.570	1.562	1.554	1.495	1.429	1.352

Index